Theories of Income Distribution

Recent Economic Thought Series

Warren J. Samuels, Editor
Michigan State University
East Lansing, Michigan, U.S.A.

Other titles in the series:
Feiwel, G.R., *Samuelson and Neoclassical Economics*
Wade, L.L., *Political Economy: Modern Views*
Zimbalist, A., *Comparative Economic Systems: Recent Views*
Darity, W., *Labor Economics: Modern Views*
Jarsulic, M., *Money and Macro Policy*
Samuelson, L., *Microeconomic Theory*
Bromley, D., *Natural Resource Economics: Policy Problems and Contemporary Analysis*
Mirowski, P., *The Reconstruction of Economic Theory*
Field, A.J., *The Future of Economic History*
Lowry, S.T., *Pre-Classical Economic Thought*
Officer, L.H., *International Economics*

This series is devoted to works that present divergent views on the development, prospects, and tensions within some important research areas of international economic thought. Among the fields covered are macromonetary policy, public finance, labor and political economy. The emphasis of the series is on providing a critical, constructive view of each of these fields, as well as a forum through which leading scholars of international reputation may voice their perspectives on important related issues. Each volume in the series will be self-contained; together these volumes will provide dramatic evidence of the variety of economic thought within the scholarly community.

Theories of Income Distribution

edited by
Athanasios Asimakopulos
Department of Economics
McGill University

Kluwer Academic Publishers
Boston/Dordrecht/Lancaster

Distributors

for the United States and Canada: Kluwer Academic Publishers, 101 Philip Drive, Assinippi Park, Norwell, MA 02061, USA

for the UK and Ireland: Kluwer Academic Publishers, MTP Press Limited, Falcon House, Queen Square, Lancaster LA1 1RN, UK

for all other countries: Kluwer Academic Publishers Group, Distribution Centre, P.O. Box 322, 3300 AH Dordrecht, The Netherlands

Library of Congress Cataloging-in-Publication Data

Theories of income distribution.
  (Recent economic thought series)
  Bibliography: p.
  Includes index.
  1. Income distribution.   I. Asimakopulos, A.,
1930–   . II. Series.
HB523.T44 1987   339.2   87–3248
ISBN 0–89838–232–7

Copyright © 1988 by Kluwer Academic Publishers

Printed in the United States of America

Contents

Contributing Authors

Athanasios Asimakopulos
Department of Economics
McGill University
855 Sherbrooke St. West
Montreal, Quebec, Canada, H3A 2T7

Allan J. Braff
HCR 68, Box 36
Cushing, Maine 04563

Camilo Dagum
Department of Economics
Faculty of Social Sciences
University of Ottawa
Ottawa, Ontario, Canada, K1N 6N5

Michael C. Howard
Department of Economics
University of Waterloo
Waterloo, Ontario, Canada, N2L 3G1

David P. Levine
Department of Economics
University of Denver
University Park
Denver, Colorado 80208−0180

Alessandro Roncaglia
Department of Economics
University of Rome
Via Nomentana, 41
00161 Rome, Italy

Robin Rowley
Department of Economics
McGill University
855 Sherbrooke St. West
Montreal, Quebec, Canada, H3A 2T7

J.C. Weldon
Department of Economics
McGill University
855 Sherbrooke St. West
Montreal, Quebec, Canada, H3A 2T7

John K. Whitaker
Department of Economics
University of Virginia
Rouss Hall
Charlottesville, Virginia 22901

Preface

This book brings together the work of scholars who have written for it independent essays in their areas of particular expertise in the general field of income distribution. The first eight chapters provide a review of the major theories of income distribution, while the final two are concerned with problems of empirical estimates and inferences. One of these chapters presents estimates of factor shares in national income in the United States, the United Kingdom and Canada, while the other examines how relationships between the size distribution of income and economic development are being investigated.

A convenient way of conveying an understanding of how economic theorists have dealt with the distribution of income is to examine separately each major approach to this subject. Each contributor was thus assigned a particular approach, or a major theorist. No attempt was made to avoid the apparent duplication that occurs when the same references are examined by different contributors. The reader gains by seeing how the same material can be treated by those looking at it from different perspectives. A chapter each has been devoted to Marx and Marshall. The choice of the former for such treatment needs no comment, but perhaps something should be said for singling out the latter. Alfred Marshall was firmly in the neo-classical school, but he saw himself as carrying on the classical tradition, and he wanted to balance demand and marginal productivity influences with the classical emphasis on the importance of factor supply. This, and the relatively little attention paid to Marshall's theory of distribution in the literature, led to the decision to give him separate treatment. Professor Whitaker's masterly essay on the distribution theory of Marshall's *Principles of Economics* admirably fills this gap in the literature.

It is with sorrow and a deep sense of loss that I report the death of Professor Weldon at the end of February 1987. He completed the final draft of his chapter on the classical theory of distribution during the summer of 1986, just before his fatal illness made sustained work impossible.

I gratefully acknowledge the assistance of my wife, Marika, in helping me to edit this volume. She has shared the proofreading chores, and she took responsibility for the index. The editing of this volume was completed while I was on a sabbatical leave that was financed in part by the Social Sciences and Humanities Research Council.

Theories of Income Distribution

1 INTRODUCTION

Athanasios Asimakopulos

Economists have devoted considerable attention to the distribution of income, to how total output is divided among those who are involved in its production. The explanation of the main forces determining the distribution of income is of interest in itself, but this distribution may also affect how the economy will evolve over time. Different theories of distribution reflect differences in the ways the economies being considered are visualized, and in the analytical tools and approaches utilized. With the welfare of particular groups being intimately related to the income they obtain, it should not be surprising that value judgments about the shares particular groups could "in justice" claim, could affect the nature of the economic analysis, and the terminology, employed. An examination of different theories of income distribution can help the reader to better understand their different institutional settings, and their relative strengths and weaknesses. The following seven chapters present the major approaches to the

This chapter was written while I was on sabbatical leave that was financed in part by a Social Sciences and Humanities Research Council Leave Fellowship.

1

theory of income distribution. The final two chapters look at empirical estimates of income distribution, and consider attempts to show how the size distribution of income is affected by the different stages of economic development.

Each of the following chapters is a self-contained essay that is complete in its own right, but each benefits by being read in conjunction with the others because of the comparisons and contrasts between different theories. This introductory chapter is designed to provide an overview of the rest of this book by indicating some of the features that keep appearing, in various forms, in these theories of distribution.[1] In particular, the relative importance they give to institutional and social arrangements, the types of equilibrium assumed, their treatment of time, and the scope for residual incomes will be examined.

Institutional and Social Arrangements

The early systematic treatises on economic matters — Adam Smith's *Wealth of Nations* is a prime example — developed a theory of income distribution that is called "classical," and that often serves as a point of reference for other approaches to this subject. Weldon's presentation of classical theory emphasizes its concern with reality and its use of abstractions derived from this reality. "It was invariably theory founded on social relationships, on the economics of a connected community, theory not merely formal but institutional" [Weldon, ch. 2, p. 18]. He considers that the institutional setting of the theory reflects reasonably well the reality surrounding the classical theorists. There was also a traditional economy that was a source of labor for industrial capitalism, as well as a state that, among other things, arranged transfer payments. It was the industrialized sector, which included commercial agriculture, that had the potential for growth, a potential due to the "surplus" produced by this sector. It was argued that production resulted in output greater than that required to replace the material inputs used, to make good the depreciation of capital equipment, and to provide the necessary subsistence for the workers during the period of production. These economists were interested in developing policies that would foster growth in this surplus, and in determining the "laws" by which it would be distributed. Ricardo, in the Preface to his *Principles of Political Economy and Taxation*, even gave pride of place to the latter: "To determine the laws which regulate this distribution, is the principal problem in Political Economy."

The capitalists, who own fixed and circulating capital, have the central role in this theory. They organize and control production, they rent land, hire labor, and advance wages prior to the completion of production and sale of goods. It is the capitalists who make the decisions to invest in capital equipment and who bear the risks that this equipment may not be profitably employed throughout its period of useful life. The return to capitalists is, in the nature of things, a residual since they must pay wages to the labor hired and rent to the landlords, and recover the cost of material inputs and depreciation from the value (net of taxes imposed by the state) of goods sold, before profit (including interest) can be calculated. Although actual profits are residuals, competition among capitalists who are continually striving to obtain the highest returns for their energy and capital would tend to equate (again in the absence of artificial barriers) expected rates of profit in different lines of activity. If the step (and it is a *big* step) is then taken to assume that actual rates of profit approximate these expected rates, then these rates are important constituents of the "natural" prices of commodities. Classical writers saw competition as tending to enforce these natural prices.

An important difference between the classical and neo-classical approaches, as emphasized by both Braff and Whitaker, is the shift in the latter to a model where capital and labor are on an equal footing as contributors to production. The institutional features of the model are thus altered in a significant way, since the neo-classical theory can be viewed as having labor hire capital, just as much as it has capital hire labor. For example, Wicksell, in considering the optimal choice of technique, gives equal emphasis to a situation where workers with no capital can obtain loans to finance production [Wicksell, 1954, p. 120], and to one where entrepreneur-capitalists hire workers [p. 123]. The theory of distribution tends to be treated in this approach as a subset of the general problem of pricing. The independent or exogenous elements are tastes, technology, and factor supplies, and the assumptions of utility and profit maximization lead to equilibrium values for the prices of the factors of production as well as for products. This concentration on static equilibrium values is another contrast with a classical theory that was concerned with economies experiencing secular growth. Whitaker notes Marshall's attempt to keep a substantial part of his classical heritage, and in particular his recognition that distributional questions should be treated in a setting of secular growth, but in his later writings static equilibrium predominated. The theory of distribution that receives most emphasis in Marshall's *Principles* is the one dealing with long-period stationary equilibrium. In the modern-day Walrasian general equilibrium theory examined by Howard, the desire for precision and completeness has led to the disappearance of many of the institutional features that earlier theories had incorporated to keep in touch with reality. This very abstract theory focuses on equilibrium prices and quantities in a perfectly competitive market system where forward markets for all commodities and for all future time periods exist. These equilibrium values, whose existence, uniqueness, and stability are examined, are determined by the exogenously specified elements in the model. These are the state of preferences and technology, and the institutions that foster the making and enforcement of voluntary contracts.

The explicit recognition of interdependence of economic variables predates, of course, the elaboration of a theory of general equilibrium. Weldon emphasizes that classical analysis was *general*, that it recognized the interdependence of the values of its variables and that it dealt with the economic system as a whole. A pervasive role was given to competition — competition that Weldon sees as acting by way of *arbitrage* that tends to enforce a law of one price. This term is interpreted broadly to cover not only the simultaneous buying and selling of commodities to take advantage of differences in the price of the same commodity at different locations (an activity that tends to eliminate these differences) but also to cover the increased production of goods that can be sold at prices that provide higher than normal rates of return on capital (an activity that tends to eliminate differences in profit rates in different lines of activity). In the absence of monopolistic restrictions — restrictions that were not absent in the economic reality these economists saw around them — they argued that this arbitrage or competition tended to result in "natural" prices, prices that, once provision is made for the cost of material inputs and depreciation, are just sufficient to provide profits, rent, and wages at their natural levels. It is interesting to note Howard's use of the Arrow-Debreu theory of general equilibrium "to argue against the distribution theories emanating from the surplus tradition" [ch. 8, p. 189] in a situation where arbitrage does not eliminate the difference between the prices of a particular commodity in adjacent time periods. With the equilibrium prices for this commodity in the two time periods differing, then the maximum rate of profit that can be obtained by using this commodity and labor to produce it is not determined solely by the technical conditions of production that define the "surplus".

The post-Keynesian and neo-Ricardian theories of distribution make use of institutional arrangements that parallel those of classical theory. The social relations of capitalism are emphasized, and the distribution between wages and profits is very much affected in post-Keynesian theory by the rate of accumulation. Consideration is also given to the effects of oligopolistic markets and trade unions on the distribution of income. The class struggle that was emphasized by Marx reappears in the form of pressures on money-wage rates, pressures that might affect markups in oligopolistic industries according to Kalecki, and that also produce inflationary tendencies.

Residual Incomes in Theories of Distribution

One of the revealing ways in which the different theories of distribution can be compared is in terms of the scope allowed for residual payments, and the causal factors that give rise to them. In classical theory profit is the residual element, even when incomes are at their "natural" values and all the temporary disturbances that affect "market" values have been eliminated. Labor was assumed to be combined in fixed proportions with fixed and circulating capital, proportions that could be changed as technology and capital equipment changed. Substitution, even with given technology, was recognized in agricultural production where different amounts of labor and capital (with the amount of labor being used as an index measure for all the factors that are employed in fixed proportions with labor) could be used with a given amount of land. (The heterogeneity of labor — the different degrees of skills — was recognized and dealt with by assuming that relative wage rates reflected differences in skills.) Competition among capitalist-farmers would tend to bring about a situation where the rents paid for different types of land would reflect their differential fertility, with the marginal production of the combined labor-capital input being the same at the extensive and intensive margins. The rent payments would be equal to the marginal productivity of land, a value that depends on technology and the extent of cultivation.

The division of the marginal product between labor and capital is based on the notion of a "subsistence" wage that determines the labor share of the marginal product of the joint input. This subsistence wage tends to be enforced in Malthus' analysis by population pressure, while in Marx's analysis it is the existence, and maintenance, of a reserve army of unemployed that serves this purpose. Subsistence wages were seen as being socially and culturally determined, and thus they could increase over time in progressive economies as the experience of higher standards of living changed the accepted level of subsistence. But at any given time and place there was a tendency to bring about the subsistence wage as a result of competition for jobs, a tendency that could be temporarily suspended when the demand for labor was augmented by increased investment.

Given the subsistence wage, profit is then what remains from the return to the joint input. The amount of profit has a key role in classical theory because this income is the source of accumulation through its role both as a supplier of savings and as an incentive for investment. Profit, as an income category, includes both the returns to the enterpreneur-capitalists for their activities and interest on the value of capital employed. The rate for this interest payment would be determined, in Weldon's words, "from an interplay of supply and demand, as between those on the one side who wished to surrender present income for future income on the best terms possible, and those on the other side who saw investment opportunities by which future income could be acquired" [ch. 2, p. 35].

Marx's economic analysis, as both Weldon and Levine emphasize, lies within the classical tradition, but the latter points out the presence of conflicting elements in Marx's treatment of the relation between wages and profits. The distribution of income between wages and profits is treated by Marx as being logically prior to the determination of capital accumulation, either by allowing the wage bargain directly to determine real wages, or by taking the value of labor-power to be given. There is also to be discerned in Marx's writings a theory of distribution that treats the accumulation of capital as the independent variable and the wage as the dependent variable. "Distribution must accommodate the needs of accumulation. This theory, while in many ways the most interesting, is the least well developed by Marx" [ch. 3, p. 65]. There is a striking similarity between this approach and the post-Keynesian theories of Kaldor and Pasinetti. (One important difference should be mentioned. The latter assume full employment of labor, but for Marx and the other classical writers, as Weldon notes, this term did not have any meaning in a world where traditional and industrial economies coexisted.)

In these post-Keynesian theories the rate of accumulation takes the value required to result in both the full employment of labor and the normal utilization of productive capacity at prices consistent with long-period equilibrium for firms. The profit share and the rate of profit are then determined by the exogenously given rate of accumulation and the propensities to save. For Kaldor the relevant propensities to save are those attached to factor incomes, to wages, and to profits, while for Pasinetti it is the propensity to save of capitalists, those whose only source of income is profits, that is crucial. The wage share and the wage rate are residuals in this theory, and thus the relative positions accorded to wages and profits in classical theory are reversed. The wage share and the wage rate are determined as residuals, given the profit share and the rate of profit, by the technical conditions of production that determine output per unit of labor. (It should be noted that these results only hold if the wage rate determined in this way exceeds some minimum level. If it does not, then it is the margin between output per man and the minimum real wage acceptable under the circumstances that constrains investment, and profit becomes the residual.)

The neo-Ricardian approach, based on Sraffa's *Production of Commodities By Means of Commodities*, represents a return to the classical view of production as a circular process that results in a surplus, but the notion of a subsistence wage is scrapped, and workers are assumed to obtain a share in the surplus. One of the distributive variables (wage rate or rate of profits) is determined exogenously to the system depicting the conditions of production and market exchanges, while the other has the characteristics of a residual and is determined simultaneously with the prices of production of the commodities. Different values for the exogenously given distributive variable change the relative prices of the commodities as well as the value for the remaining distributive variable. The relation between the two distributive variables, in a given production system, is generally represented by a negatively sloped wage-profit curve. Although the most immediate interpretation of the wage-profit curve suggests that class conflict is a key factor affecting income distribution, Roncaglia notes that trade-union bargaining is over money-wage rates and this, by itself, does not determine real-wage rates. He then examines various attempts to show that the rate of profits can be assumed to be exogenously determined, either by the requirements for full employment and full capacity utilization (Pasinetti), or by reference to a causal relationship between interest and profit rates (Panico and Pivetti). Roncaglia does not find these attempts to obtain natural or equilibrium values to be satisfactory solutions to the problem of income distribution, and he suggests a change in the objectives of economic analysis in this area. Its role should be "...to deal with the factors affecting changes over time of wages and profits" [ch. 7, p. 175]. His sketch of the logical steps of this type of analysis, within the Sraffa tradition, begins with a given wage-profit frontier and a given point on that frontier that reflects the important influences on distribution of past history, conventions, and institutional factors. Money-wage bargaining is one of the institutional features of this analysis, and the resulting money-wage rates affect unit labor costs, product prices, and technology. The outcomes of the wage-bargaining process will itself be affected by technology, as well as by the current levels of unemployment and industrial activity. There will also be a "feedback" influence of income distribution on these factors with, for example, current profits influencing the expectations that help determine investment in subsequent periods. With this emphasis on change, and interacting influences, there is much less scope for a residual element to play a crucial role in income distribution.

The symmetry among all factors of production precludes any role in neo-classical theories of distribution for residual payments. Braff points out that it was important for neo-classical theorists to show that the sum of the payments to all elements of production, when these payments are based on their marginal products, just exhausts the value of total output. This "adding-up" problem is solved if the production function is homogeneous of degree one, and differentiable with respect to all its arguments taken separately. These arguments are the elements of production required to produce the particular output, and they must all be specified quantitatively, including the time and effort of the entrepreneur in organizing and directing production. In an equilibrium position for a perfectly competitive economy, the profit-maximizing action of enterpreneurs will lead them to pay each element of production at the rate determined by the value of its marginal product, and the sum of such payments must equal the value of the product for a production function that is homogeneous of degree one. There is no profit element, distinct from interest, in this equilibrium position, since the earnings of entrepreneurs are on the same footing as the earnings of labor, and interest is reflected in the payments for items of capital equipment.

The assumption of competitive long-period equilibrium that underlies this neo-classical theory of distribution is extremely powerful. The exhaustion of total product, when all factor payments are based on marginal productivity, can be inferred from this condition without any assumptions being made about the nature of the production function. Competition will force all firms to pay each element of production according to the value of its marginal product. These payments reflect the differences in efficiency of inputs that are otherwise in the same category. Payments according to this rule must, in a position of long-period equilibrium, just exhaust the value of total output because the existence of any "residual," whether positive or negative, is incompatible with long-period equilibrium. The condition that total cost is equal to total revenue can be represented by the equation $\sum_{i=1}^{n} v_i w_i = P_x x$, where v_i ($i = 1, 2, \ldots n$) is the amount of the ith element of production employed in a typical firm, w_i is the rate of pay for that element, x is the amount of output, and P_x is the price of that output. Profit maximization and competition will result in each element being paid at a rate equal to the value of its marginal product ($P_x MP v_i$), and in long-period equilibrium

the sum of payments determined in this way ($\sum_{i=1}^{n} v_i P_x MPv_i$) must be equal
to the value of output ($P_x x$). This is the same as the result obtained when
the production function is assumed to be homogeneous of degree one,
even though no such assumption has been made here.

There is no room in this approach for the broad factor payments of
classical theory, since the elements of production appearing in the production function must be specified in the physical units appropriate to the
technical relation between inputs and output, and there is generally a
very large number of such inputs. The classical categories of income
reappear with this approach, as Braff points out, as "analytical income
categories," with individual input prices being broken down to an opportunity or "wage" element, an "interest" return on the past investment
that helped create this input, and a "rent" element that is the difference
between its price and these "necessary" costs. The broad classical income
categories only reappear in neo-classical theory in the aggregate production function approach pioneered by J.B. Clark. This attempt to explain
factor payments, and in particular to justify profit as the productive
contribution of capital, in opposition to Marx's theory of exploitation, is
fatally flawed, even if it is taken to be only a parable. The value of capital
that appears in an aggregate production function cannot be determined
unless the rate of profit is known [Sraffa, 1960]. It can thus not be used as
an independent determinant of this rate.

The marginal productivity approach to the theory of distribution only
explains the demand for the elements of production, but their equilibrium
prices also depend on the conditions of supply for these elements. The
importance of these conditions of supply was emphasized, as Whitaker
points out, by Marshall, who saw himself as carrying on the classical
tradition, while modifying it in order to fill in gaps especially in the
treatment of demand, and to allow full scope for the principle of substitution [Shove, 1942]. The latter leads to the idea of balance at the margin,
to hiring inputs up to the point where their prices are equal to the values
of their net marginal products. The marginalist approach to distribution
thus had an important role in Marshall's writings, as Whitaker rightly
emphasizes, but the role given to the conditions of supply, especially in
the *Principles*, suggests an interpretation that allows for a residual payment in long-period equilibrium. There is Marshall's well-known statement that "[T]he doctrine that the earnings of a worker tend to be equal
to the net product of his work, has by itself no real meaning, since in
order to estimate net product, we have to take for granted all the
expenses of production of the commodity on which he works, other than

his own wages" [Marshall, 1920, p. 518]. These other "expenses of production" include, in long-period equilibrium, profit on the value of capital used by the worker at a rate equal to the "normal" rate of profit. This equilibrium rate of profit is the "supply price of business ability in command of capital." It is composed, according to Marshall, of three elements.

> The first is the supply price of capital; the second is the supply price of business ability and energy; and the third is the supply price of that organization by which the appropriate business ability and the requisite capital are brought together. We have called the price of the first of these three elements *interest*; we may call the price of the second taken by itself *net earnings of management*, and that of the second and third, taken together, *gross earnings of management* [1920, p. 313; italics in original].

In a situation of long-period equilibrium, the rate of interest is just sufficient to maintain the amount of capital appropriate for that equilibrium, and together with the gross earnings of management, it determines the equilibrium rate of profit. The payment to labor in this long-period equilibrium situation is a residual, the difference between the value of the joint product of labor and capital, and the necessary profit. This residual payment must be equal to the marginal net product of labor, but this value can only be determined after the deduction of capital expenses.

There is some similarity between this reading of Marshall's long-period equilibrium and the theories of distribution associated with Kaldor and Pasinetti. In all these cases, the rate of profit is determined by the requirements for long-period equilibrium with the wage, given technology, being a residual. There are also important differences. Marshall's long-period equilibrium is part of a static analysis [ch. 5, p. 123], while Kaldor and Pasinetti assume dynamic economies with a positive rate of accumulation. Marshall sees the ". . . interest on capital as the reward of the sacrifice involved in waiting for the enjoyment of material resources" [Marshall, 1920, p. 232]; it is a payment for a "real" cost, but no such association is made by Kaldor or Pasinetti.

Accumulation, Profits, Equilibrium, and Time

Most of the theories of distribution presented in this book are concerned with positions of long-period equilibrium where natural prices and incomes prevail. An important exception is Kalecki's theory which does not make use of long-period equilibrium, and that brings to the foreground the macroeconomic determination of profits.[2] There is also to be found in his writings an interesting suggestion of how to trace out the changes over time in the values of the economic variables of interest. The explicit recognition of the time sequence of the investment process allows Kalecki to incorporate the classical emphasis on the important role of profits in determining the rate of accumulation, along with his use of the rate of investment as an important determinant of profits.

Kalecki's analysis is, like that of Keynes in *The General Theory of Employment, Interest and Money*, anchored in a particular short period that has the characteristics of an interval of time in an historical sequence. The available capital equipment, technical knowledge, skills, and attitudes have been determined by decisions and events in earlier periods, with current short-term expectations determining the degree of utilization of this equipment in this period. Kalecki, like Keynes, implicitly assumes short-period equilibrium, so that entrepreneurial short-term expectations are borne out by events, with actual investment in the period being equal to planned investment, and with saving being in the desired relation to the level and distribution of income. In Kalecki's simple model of a closed economy, where workers do not save and there is no significant government economic activity, profits in the short period are shown to be determined by capitalists' expenditures in that short period. (The modifications required for an open economy with government economic activity and workers' saving, are discussed in chapter 6 of this book.) More emphasis is placed by Kalecki on the influence of investment on profits because the values for this variable are more volatile than the values for capitalists' consumption expenditures. He thus obtains one part of his double-sided relationship between profits and investment, with *current* investment expenditures as important determinants of *current* profits.

It is the time sequence of the investment process — the normal time lags between investment decisions and the resulting investment expenditures — that allows Kalecki to obtain a clear causal relation from current investment to current profits, without his denying the importance of profits as a determinant of investment decisions and thus, eventually, their significant impact on future investment. Recognition of this causal influence of *current* profits — through their effects on long-term expectations and the ability of firms to finance investment — on *future* investment is the second part of Kalecki's double-sided relation between profits and investment.

Kalecki's theory of the business cycle was based on the working out of this double-sided relationship, with the resulting fluctuations in investment, and output, following some initiating cause, being observed by linking a sequence of adjacent short periods. He also thought that it could be used to deal with changes in an economy over time. "I do not see why this approach should be abolished in the face of the problem of long-run growth. In fact, the long-run trend is but a slowly changing component of a chain of short-period situations; it has no independent entity, and the two basic relations mentioned above should be formulated in such a way as to yield the trend cum business-cycle phenomenon" [Kalecki, 1971, p. 165]. Kalecki was not satisfied with his various attempts to obtain a good functional expression for the second relation. He realized that it could not be too "mechanistic" and that it had to allow for the influence of past economic, social, and technological developments. "This, however, is no excuse for dropping this approach, which seems to me the only key to the realistic analysis of the dynamics of a capitalist economy" [p. 165]. Kalecki's double-sided relation illustrates the complex interconnection between accumulation and the distribution of income.

Kalecki's attempt to deal with the question of income distribution outside the special conditions of long-period equilibrium was combined with explicit recognition that oligopolistic pricing practices in manufacturing industries would also affect distribution. For example, the ability of firms to secure a higher markup, given the level of investment, would result in lower real wages. The effectiveness of the wage-bargaining activity of trade unions thus depends, in a significant way, on their ability to restrain markups. The writings on the "inflation barrier" referred to by Levine, and in chapter 6, share this concern with distribution in non-equilibrium situations. Roncaglia's suggestion that the major problem of distribution has to do with the factors leading to changes in distribution over time, rather than with the determination of equilibrium values, leads to an analysis that is not inconsistent with Kalecki's, even though factors are introduced, such as the influence of external competition and changes in the exchange rate, that Kalecki did not consider in detail. This need to try and grapple in a systematic way with real-world problems in a setting that does not assume equilibrium has also influenced recent work that comes out of the neo-classical tradition. Braff points to the increasing recognition of the importance of market imperfections, institutional processes, and new notions of equilibrium that allow for nonmarket clearing, that go some way toward the concerns and techniques used by those working with other approaches. For example, Malinvaud's [1977, 1980] attempt to reproduce Keynesian results, and to illuminate problems of stagflation, thrusts neo-classical theory into new areas, where there is an overlap with, among others, Kalecki.[3] This tendency to converge on the analysis of problems in a nonequilibrium setting is a helpful sign of progress in dealing with the question of income distribution in actual economies.

Notes

1. This overview can only touch briefly on some of the material presented in depth in the remaining chapters. The interpretations made of this material is the writer's, and the other contributors may not agree with the views expressed in this introductory chapter.

2. Kalecki [1966, p. ln] pointed out, in the Foreword to a collection of his early studies in the theory of the business cycle, that "[I]t is worth noticing that there is a certain affinity between these theories of mine and those of Rosa Luxemburg."

3. Asimakopulos [1983, pp. 29–30] notes that profits in Malinvaud's [1977] model are determined in the manner emphasized by Kalecki. In Malinvaud [1980, p. 10] there is also explicit recognition of the feedback effects on accumulation of the endogenous changes in distribution over the cycle.

References

Asimakopulos, A. (1983). The role of the short period. In J.A. Kregel (ed.), *Distribution, Effective Demand and International Economic Relations*. London: Macmillan, pp. 28–34.

Kalecki, Michal. (1966). *Studies in the Theory of Business Cycles: 1933–1939*. Oxford: Basil Blackwell.

—————. (1971). *Selected Essays on the Dynamics of the Capitalist Economy: 1933–1970*. Cambridge: Cambridge University Press.

Malinvaud, E. (1977). *The Theory of Unemployment Reconsidered*. Oxford: Basil Blackwell.

—————. (1980). *Profitability and Unemployment*. Cambridge: Cambridge University Press.

Marshall, A. (1920). *Principles of Economics*, 8th edition. London: Macmillan.

Shove, G.F. (1942). The place of Marshall's *Principles* in the development of economic theory. *Economic Journal* 52 (December): 294–329.

Sraffa, P. (1960). *Production of Commodities by Means of Commodities*. Cambridge: Cambridge University Press.

Wicksell, K. (1954). *Value, Capital and Rent*. London: Allen and Unwin.

2 THE CLASSICAL THEORY OF DISTRIBUTION

J.C. Weldon

Since [labour, capital, and land] may be separately appropriated, the industrial community may be considered as divided into landowners, capitalists, and productive labourers. Each of these classes, as such, obtains a share of the produce: no other person or class obtains anything except by concession from them.
— J.S. Mill [1871]

About the Stage Setting

Let me begin with a message that will be repeated. Classical theorists borrowed their stage setting from the durable institutions of their everyday experience. Industrial capitalism in primitive or developed form was *part* of their system but always lived in company with a large traditional

I am grateful to colleagues who set aside a seminar for an earlier version. They were generous in listening to the piece and debating its themes. A. Asimakopulos, S.H. Ingerman, and L. Soderstrom later provided useful (and usually used) written comments.

economy and with many arrangements for transfer payments. Not surprisingly, full employment of labor and involuntary unemployment were terms without meaning for the theory of a classical economy (as *a fortiori* was equilibrium or disequilibrium related to these terms). Full employment and partial employment of fixed capital,[1] however, were operational concepts that measured activity in the industrialized sector, and that at second hand determined the employment of complementary factors (the amounts of labor, of raw materials, even of land, that were technologically required for using fixed capital at given levels).

Fixed capital, then, was set in a technology where little freedom was allowed for one factor to be substituted for another. There was one important exception, for it was plain that many kinds of *land* would enter production and in many different proportions. For each kind of land, given fixed capital would be used with one amount of land rather than another, over a wide range of technical possibilities. If "marginalist" computations were in general not needed within classical distributive theory, here were two instances where they had to be considered. Fixed capital would be increased by accumulation and so would involve *investors* in marginalist computations. Each packet of land would be associated with more or less fixed capital, and so would involve the *capitalists* who organize production (the capitalist-entrepreneurs) in marginalist computations. Where the facts were marginalist, so after a fashion — not deliberately or self-consciously! — was the theory.

The stage setting will be used by strongly differentiated types, the productive laborers, the capitalists, the landowners of whom Mill has just spoken in the epigraph. There is a government, there is a state. Reality contains many composites of the pure types but is better approximated by those "pure types" than by homogenized consumers.

Scope of the Theory

For something like 200 years, the classical theory of distribution was the dominant account of its subject, widely accepted and easily recognized even in its long period of gestation. Its development began with description and casual abstraction, but then took the form of a deliberate search for connected ideas. The durability of that system has been proven not only by authority once enjoyed but by authority retained to the present day. Complementary and competitive arguments still pay their respects in both journals and textbooks. If the apparatus has long been regarded as *insufficient* for the analysis of advanced economies, it remains a foundation for the more elaborate statements such economies require, and continues to be a good first approximation for distributive theory in developing economies where facts and institutions have a classical form.

Names rather than dates give the better measure of these 200 years — say, the names of Sir William Petty and Gregory King at the beginning and of Karl Marx at the end. Petty's speculations, King's methodology, and the political *arithmetick* of both innovators described natural categories for reporting how surplus is produced and distributed, and then sought out statistics and explanations to connect the facts of production with the facts of distribution. Since Marx's view of technique was conservative, he rejected little of this inheritance but was content to elaborate: but it may be less expected that within the two centuries Turgot, Smith, Say, Ricardo, Rae, Malthus, J.S. Mill, all of these would make their strikingly varied contributions to political economy within the same framework about shares in depreciation and surplus that Petty and Marx employed.[2] Consequently one stresses the similarities and continuity in their analyses rather than the novelties.

Unity and relevance had their source in a mixture of good sense and fortunate circumstance. Good sense appeared early, in the careful and ingenious description of economic realities, in the posing of natural *questions* about surplus and the social classes to whom it was distributed, in the formulation of laws offering pragmatic *answers*, and so overall, in a prudent and admirable use of scientific method. Fortunate circumstance also appeared early, for the scanty store of facts happened to point to a stable future, happened to suggest *good* questions and answers; and such critical categories as "surplus" and "social classes" happened to have taken a shape that would be visibly real for many generations to come.

First Themes: Interdependence, Competition, Arbitrage

Those who contrast the post-classical (or neo-classical) economics born in the 1870s with classical theory often point to the supposed "first discovery" of general equilibrium as the sign most sharply distinguishing post-classical economics from classical political economy. In his presidential address to the American Economics Association, Paul Samuelson said, in a somewhat restrained tribute to Walras, that "there is but one grand concept of general equilibrium, and it was Walras who had the insight (and luck) to find it."[3] This may be the usual perception, but it seems historically mistaken and logically perverse. It confuses the microeconomic discoveries of the 1870s with an interdependence already well known at a macroeconomic level.

Post-classical writers, it is true, found methods of quantifying use-values that their predecessors had overlooked, and they accordingly found methods of incorporating specific, individual wants in their analysis, so that "demands" and "supplies" from consumers could be recorded against supplies and demands from producers. They found the virtues of argument in which marginal rather than average values were regularly used, and they developed all of this in that systematic and comprehensive framework the textbooks in too proprietary a way call "general equilibrium."

These accomplishments most unfortunately led to the nonsequitur that classical theorists had not understood that the variables of an economic system were interrelated and needed to be studied *en bloc*. The fact is that classical analysis invariably attended first or even exclusively to economic systems as a whole, as students of Ricardo or Marx are almost painfully aware. Classical analysis was judged vulnerable because it did not base interdependence upon the behavior of *individual* consumers and producers. What the microeconomics added may be debatable, but certainly classical distributive theory would have had no life at all without its emphasis on how shares in surplus are *simultaneously* determined. It was invariably theory founded on social relationships, on the economics of a connected community,[4] theory not merely formal but institutional.

Another preliminary is to express the pervasive role given competition in classical theory, competition that affects events by way of *arbitrage*. Arbitrage in various forms is applied everywhere to support a law of one price, and that law of one price then is invoked to explain economic process. Where two distinct prices for the moment live together an arbitrageur will buy at the low price and sell at the high, and will do so with diminishing marginal returns[5] that point to convergence on a single price. In this essential form marginalism thus long predates the work of the "marginalists."

Arbitrage was at its simplest when goods were bought for final use at the lowest prices in sight, so that "high" prices would become very rare. It had roundabout forms where speculators bought in order to sell, and still more roundabout forms where producers noticed that by purchasing "factors of production" they could transform the factors at a profit. It had even more roundabout forms where entrepreneurs saw they could combine production with trade in international markets to improve on production for domestic trade alone. It was "even more roundabout forms," incidentally, that distinguished the foreign trade of Ricardo from the undifferentiated trade of Smith.[6]

A final "preliminary" is to observe that classical *full employment*, where mentioned at all, was a quality of the use of fixed capital and not of labor.[7] Classical writers always had systems in mind where a primary

economy with factories and capitalistic farms shared the national economy with institutions of a traditional kind. Fixed capital in the primary
economy might or might not be operated at capacity. Whether underuse
was frequent or rare, persistent or self-erasing, was a hotly debated topic.
Wage-laborers, in any event, were employed at whatever level was suitable to the use made of fixed capital. Employment in, say, a Keynesian
sense *had* meaning; unemployment of labor did not, nor did full employment of labor (in any context!).

Surplus

What precisely in classical theory was it that would be distributed? A
community of persons had first to be identified and, then, processes of
production and exchange which generated a *surplus*, or a revenue, or a
net revenue, a net national product, or a national income — the one idea
has acquired many names. Just as it would be of interest who and what
had contributed to those processes, and what the various goods were that
appeared in the surplus, so it would be of interest what and why such
and such portions of the surplus were *distributed* to use and control by
particular persons and particular sectors of the community, not least by
the community as a society or state. It would then be of similar interest as
to what claims, if any, had to be made good from those processes before
a surplus could be counted.

From the beginning the concept had its foundation in a stylized model
of agriculture, in a model where crops set aside from the harvest of the
past would have generated similar but larger crops in the harvest of the
present. Within the community of this model the production of grain
would have been undertaken in a process that occupied a year. At the
end of the year a harvest had become available that allowed all depreciation to be made good, that offset the use of seed-grain, of fertilizer, of
stocks depleted to sustain workers, of tools and equipment reduced by
their employment in the year, that allowed all this to be made good but
still provided a surplus of grain itself, a material excess that would be
available for whatever purposes the community might decide.

Out of a given economic apparatus, then, the grain of last year becomes the larger total of grain this year, and does so without any impair-
ment of the apparatus: such was the original idea of surplus, such was the
idea in the agricultural examples of the physiocrats, such was the idea
(with "grain" become "labor power") in the examples from the factories
and heavy industry of Marx, such indeed is the core of the contemporary
conception. Its origin in so idealized an agriculture has made the idea a

fertile source of both political and theoretical debate, for on the one side as *surplus* is sought in real economies, questions arise that have only arbitrary answers, and on the other, as the idea is dissected it reveals other ideas that need definition if "net products" and the like are to be interesting.

Membership in real communities has no settled scope, either as to which inhabitants are members or which persons are inhabitants. Persons in real communities are heterogeneous from one to the other but also within their given life spans. The things that are grain in those communities can be chosen in many ways and will always be composed of physically distinct objects. Depreciation and the offsetting of depreciation will be represented in those physical and *inescapably* distinct objects, but not within some natural scheme of measurement; and the relationship of surplus to real institutions (folkways, markets, governments) depends on how those institutions function.

As to the interior of the idea, it is plain that even when surplus is merely described as a feature of *positive* economics, it is of negligible interest except as it points to good or bad fortune for persons and societies. However *surplus* is recorded, its connection to welfare is almost always the explanation of *why* it has been recorded. That connection, however, has to the present day proved elusive in its details: Smith's "toil and trouble"[8] homogenizes physical products but also appears as a shorthand for usefulness; Ricardo's exchange-values and riches[9] show that no single shorthand can be enough; Marx's use-values directly[10] link surplus to welfare but are fully described by a mere count of the various commodities a system has produced. "Usefulness" in marginal and measureable forms gives a hallmark to post-classical ideas, but leaves debate alive about the kind of measurability, about the relation of private to social welfare, about the meaning of welfare in the face of uncertainty, and about the logical problems of conflating expected satisfactions into present utility.

One adds a caution. Surplus is always to be measured completely and finally at *a point of time*, usually the here-and-now. Since it is fed by future prospects as well as by "present" events, its magnitude will be greatly affected by how uncertain the future appears.

Categories and Quantities, and the Claims of the State

Few students of economics have escaped Adam Smith's taxonomy of "price": "Wages, profit and rent are the three original sources of all revenue as well as of all exchangeable value." Smith then carefully amplifies his text: "The gross revenue of the inhabitants of a great country, comprehends the whole annual produce of their land and labor; the neat revenue [*i.e., Smith's "surplus"*] what remains free to them after deducting; first, their fixed; and secondly, their circulating capital; or what, without encroaching upon their capital, they can place in their stock for immediate consumption, or spend upon their subsistence, conveniences, and amusements."[11] Consume *all* neat revenue? No! "Whatever a person saves from his revenue he adds to his capital."[12] But then there are also the activities of the state: "...private revenue arises ultimately from...Rent, Profit and Wages. Every tax must finally be paid from some one or other of these three different sources of revenue, or from all of them indifferently."[13] Smith may or may not have selected the taxonomy most appropriate to his facts, but seems guiltless of confusing taxonomy with behavioral argument, and he describes succinctly much the same categories as *all* authorities of the classical tradition apply in their own descriptions of reality.

Why work with these categories and not some others? And if there are good reasons for choosing this classification of facts, can numbers to go with the facts be found, so that a classical economy can be described, so that its laws of operation can be explained, and so that good policy can be advocated and bad policy rejected? Petty had 100 years earlier responded to precisely these questions in his marvelous flood of pamphlets. He would be guided in social analysis by the scientific method, and accordingly would look only for facts conformable to number, weight, or measure. He would gather his facts in the first instance as they would plainly appear in the happenings of his own society. His little essay on the "Method of Enquiring into the State of any Country"[14] is a model of searching for the few facts within reach that could give orders of magnitude for most of the economic variables an infant capitalism would produce.

In its applied forms his scheme very largely anticipates (and no doubt partly generates) Smith's abstractions. On the one side there are commodities of various kinds measured by their natural prices, by private and public "spendings."[15] On the other side there is a distributive account of surplus received, in gross rather than net form, but in enduring classical categories (wage, rents proper, a composite of rents and profits attached to housing and stock, *and* the state's receipts of excise taxes). All of this is "ex-post," of course, but is the necessary preliminary to distributive theory.

Petty in philosophic terms is somewhere between sophisticated mercantilism and naive "free enterprise"; but in programmatic terms his concern about "surplus" is to see what the state can prudently take for its own use. One will extract two points that bear particularly on the continuity of classical distributive doctrine. Here at the beginning is the same view of unemployment that Malthus and Marx will share, that it represents the normal state of things, but it is extended by the opinion that the state might mobilize some of these idle resources to enhance growth. Somewhat later, here is a second notion pointing to radical intervention, that the state might do well to tax surplus in the hands of the profligate in order to subsidize saving and investment planned by the industrious. Out of the surplus, society as a collective takes some share!

Gregory King also investigated "surplus" chiefly to see what distributive claim the state might reasonably impose. He is a good deal more methodical than Petty was, and succeeds in giving a quite detailed review of (among others) the national account for the year of Glorious Revolution, 1688. Rents totaled some 13½ million pounds, wages some 30½ million, consumption expenditures, rather over 40½ million, and *net* investment, somewhat under 2 million. Particularly interesting is the extension King attempts from income to wealth. He makes no effort to endow wealth with an independent existence but simply "capitalizes" the income flow at a socially determined 6%.

Wages and Subsistence

Within the stylized model neither the participants nor an observer is to have any doubt that wages at a *subsistence* level are the reference for all further discussion. When a cycle of production and exchange has been completed, the community has its surplus in hand for allocation, either in respect of claims imposed by the old cycle or now arranged for the new. It is common ground among the classical theorists that those who are employed as laborers either receive nothing from that surplus, that is to say, receive subsistence wages, or experience wage rates at some higher or lower level that should be explained in terms of subsistence, by their relationship to subsistence.

There is no requirement (one repeats the basic point) that employment carry any implication of *full employment*. In general the system hires some definite number of persons as wage-laborers but gives no corresponding count of unemployment, of capable wage-laborers the system has not hired. True, in a system where employment is usually determined without regard to the total of would-be wage laborers, unemployment of a conventional kind will almost always exist and may well be widespread, but it appears in a community where markets have a limited sovereignty. An idle artisan or tenant farmer might or might not be reckoned as an unemployed wage laborer, but the reckoning would be arbitrary and would be unneeded in the theory.

Multiple meanings for *subsistence*, however, present a problem that the classical writers agree must be resolved. The idea[16] might refer to some kind of physiological minimum of necessaries that would just sustain life, but so severe a reading would rarely correspond to real events and would in any case still have multiple meanings (for how long was life sustained, with what capacities, in respect of the individual only or of the household or of the community). If so technocratic an interpretation were bound to be unsatisfactory, it might reasonably give way to interpretation in social terms, to a minimum computed as necessary for perpetuating the community, a minimum that might even prove independent of time or place.[17] Once that step in conceptualization had been taken, though, the reality had to be faced that a social minimum would inevitably vary with the society considered, would certainly be affected by *both* time and place. *Subsistence* is socially and culturally determined, is a minimum of necessaries, does allow the individual and the household enough to restore themselves, and varies accordingly with custom and culture (and not least, will be a secularly increasing "minimum" in a progressive economy).

So defined, subsistence in England of mid-Victorian years fixed a higher minimum than did subsistence of a half-century earlier (among other social changes one should remember legislation about factories and the working-day), or subsistence in the period of the Tudors (where comparison points to vast changes in productivity); and that same subsistence fixed a much higher minimum than did subsistence in contemporary Ireland or contemporary Russia. On the need for this flexible usage writers of the classical school were wholly agreed, however diverse the ways in which they then connected subsistence to wages.[18]

Plainly, though, while a flexible usage helped keep reality in sight, it would particularly benefit from tests that could decide in any given case whether it had been correctly applied. At least two such tests (they prove to be complementary) have been repeatedly proposed. Those who receive *subsistence* wages for their labor do not save, do not accumulate, do not invest. They are the stereotypes whose propensity to save out of wages is zero. On the other side of the market for labor, those who attempt to pay less than subsistence wages encounter easily visible difficulties. There will be legal obstacles, for the community will perceive a difference between private and public interest should living standards be debased. There will be obstacles in the market itself, for wage laborers can retreat to the secondary economy or can elect to take their chances with income (and charity) separated from wages. Set against less than subsistence wages, alternative sources of a livelihood leave wage laborers with little or nothing to lose. Finally, offers of wages at "less than subsistence" will often have illusory results even when they are nominally successful. The wage laborers that do respond and are recruited will come from a pool in which the less able must be disproportionately represented (rather as they might be segregated in the dual labor markets of contemporary theory, although here segregation is a risk to which all wage laborers are exposed).

So much for subsistence in its own right: the argument now urgently needs something that will supply relationships between subsistence and wages. As almost everywhere else in the classical system *competition* is invoked to explain the connection between economic magnitudes. Subsistence is a socially determined floor to the general level of wages. Wage laborers are numerous, those already employed and those who wish to be employed, and compete among themselves for whatever positions are offered.[19] At a first approximation the classical theorist expects a law of one price to hold wherever there is competition, and so expects that the indistinguishable wage laborers for whom employment exists at the subsistence rate will all receive competitively determined subsistence wages. Labor in any other category, since it has somehow found means of survival, will have received income from secondary economies within the community and from some mixture of public transfers and private charity engrafted upon the system, that is to say, from the classical precursors of the welfare state.

Certain minor but permanent improvements in the "first approximation" are immediately made, as in Turgot's "Reflections" or (derivatively) in "The Wealth of Nations."[20] Wage laborers of real communities are not paid equal wages. On the one hand occupations vary in the "toil and trouble" they demand and in the skills and accomplishments that will accompany toil and trouble, and real wage laborers are unequal in their suitability for particular tasks, heterogeneous just as the real occupations are. On the other hand, even where such diversities in jobs and workers could reasonably be regarded as negligible, the single marketplace of idealized competition may in reality be several marketplaces kept apart by law or privilege, by custom or policy.

To deal with heterogeneity the classical theorists converted real occupations, real skills, and real wage laborers into multiples of single, well-identified types. Smith's treatment "of wages. . .in the different Employments of Labor"[21] amounts in this respect to the notion that where competition has full play, observed differences in wages correspond precisely to equal differences in occupations. The denominators of nominally different wage rates could thus be adjusted to standard units by producing equality with the actual rate for some familiar occupation. Since the structure of wage rates varies, some *particular* structure needs to be given preference in this homogenization.

Where the theorists *are* explicit on this matter, their choice is usually to employ either the present structure or an average of structures from the recent past, as well as *any* structure that can be identified in fragments of raw data. At an applied level no other device seems ever to have had much weight. True, in abstract terms there have been variants. Malthus was attracted to standardized wage units as providing a measure of real costs, the only measure he could imagine that would be unchanging and universal.[22] Marx from time to time, though not consistently, wrote of differences in skills as so much invested capital.[23] The principal statement, though, is simpler than the variants and seems quite sufficient for the substance of the classical argument.

Where inequalities are attributed to institutions that impede competition, the texts are less easy to interpret. In relation to the idealized model of competition the earlier voices among the classical writers appear as analysts who are also advocates. A regime of "natural liberty"[24] is the reference for their arguments, is treated as already displacing those actual systems where monopoly abounds and markets are primitive, is praised for its power greatly to increase surplus, but determines actual distribution only in terms of tendencies and of present imperfections. Distribution that is theoretically possible under natural liberty is the distribution "natural liberty" would determine when calculated incomes have been adjusted (1) to reclaim the social waste that characterizes centralized and monopolistic economies, and (2) to discount the relative advantages in sharing a smaller surplus that possessors of monopoly power have enjoyed. Later writers (say, James Mill, Senior, Marx) argue as though the regime of "natural liberty" were already firmly in place throughout the primary, capitalistic economy, and so are less concerned about the imperfections that interfere with competitive markets. Capitalism, so such successor authors teach, is safely treated as competitive capitalism. It remains true, however, that throughout classical theory secondary, residual economies exist and influence the way regimes of natural liberty perform.

Given that there *is* a close relationship between subsistence wages and the earnings of the wage laborer, the central question is what form the relationship might take other than equality. It may be the most interesting question that classical theory presents. Certainly it is a question to which the theorists give sharply contrasting answers (although as their arguments unfold one finds that differences arise more from variety in perception rather than variety in logic).

For those who were most sanguine about the height wages might reach under natural liberty, the expected outcome was to be a growth in surplus so rapid that growth of population would be outdistanced, so rapid that consumption per head would rise, so rapid that subsistence itself would also rise, so rapid indeed that wages would increasingly surpass that advancing level of subsistence. Wage laborers would experience sizeable improvements in the package of *necessaries*, and would win a significant share of surplus from which they could then save and accumulate. It would have been true even of subsistence wages that the laborer could match saving at one period against dissaving at some other period. Now there would be net saving, continuous saving from wage laborers as a group.

As to the mechanics of this achievement, those who were its prophets echoed in the main Smith's famous and optimistic discussion of "the nature, Accumulation, and Employment of Stock."[25] Production takes time. Wage laborers who are hired in the process of production must be supported by the advance of commodities produced and stored at some earlier time. Such wages as they get will then be contingent upon how large that prior accumulation has been.[26] The employment of wage laborers is in one-to-one correspondence with the land and fixed capital already in place, and so has been technically determined; and the amount of circulating capital produced for that now-known total of employed laborers will have been determined by competition.

With waste reduced by competition, productivity and surplus will have been increased; "parsimony"[27] will have been given a larger base in surplus on which to function; and as this parsimony succeeds in reducing uncertainty and binding the future, it will continuously take a higher place in public preferences.[28] Malthus was to object that so uncritical a hymn to prudence would lead to absurdity if intentions to save were given no upper bound and led purposelessly only to further intentions to save. Among careful writers, however, the praise bestowed on parsimony was expressed in *relative* terms, praise for saving that would be decidedly higher than it had been in less progressive times but at a *best* rather than *maximum* rate.

Socialist writers had quite different expectations about the likely rela-

tionship between wages and subsistence. One may as well look directly to
Marx, for with so dominant a figure one can hardly say, "Take Marx, for
example."[29] For the author of *Capital* the central point was that competition would reduce employment because it would force labor-saving accumulation and labor-saving innovation upon the industrial capitalist,[30]
would do this especially when expansion was rapid but also when it was
slow. (Ricardo had conceded that here was a major question of fact:
". . . the substitution of machinery for human labour, is often very in-
jurious to the interests of the class of labourers."[31]) This technological
displacement of workers would occur, argues Marx, even if population
were stationary, even if there were no trace of assistance from Malthusian
forces to enlarge the "reserve army of the unemployed."[32]

Marx's bitter references to Malthus no doubt contain personal distaste
for a parson he saw as both plagiarist and apologist, but may at bottom
depend on the confusions Marx knows he cannot escape with readers who
will interchange Malthus' "subsistence" with his own. Population is increasing, and in some degree by its increase exacerbates the miseries of
the working class. But while that is *fact* for Marx, it is incidental fact and
demoralizing fact. Malthus' subsistence has no special connection to the
regime of natural liberty for it marks a tendency in all economic systems,
indeed in all societies whether human or not; and Malthus' subsistence (if
it is a problem or has a solution) cannot be improved upon by class
struggle or the dissolution of capitalism. Marx as a classical theorist is
concerned with the classical economy, the system dominated by a capitalistic sector; and Marx must separate his explanations from forces that are
not peculiar to capitalism. Malthus' subsistence operates in relation to
generations,[33] but Marx's, in relation to day-to-day affairs and then to the
oscillations of cycles in trade.

Wages for Marx *are* subsistence wages, but subsistence wages with
some novelties of form. It remains part of the idea of subsistence that
social forces affect its level and within advanced capitalism cause it to
rise. Subsistence, however, now is a range of levels for different groups
within the working classes, and coexists with incomes below (or far
below) subsistence paid both to human discards among the reserve
army and to many on the fringe between capitalism and the secondary
economies.

Skilled workers, for example, acquire higher standards of subsistence
than do the unskilled. Such differences as are noticed between nations
have counterparts in differences among various domestic categories of
wage laborer. Further, against the expectation of progress in which *all*
share, Marx sets the view that ". . . the greater the social wealth, . . . the

greater is the industrial reserve army,...the greater is official pauperism."[34] Wages are *not* fixed at subsistence because it was inevitable
that only so much circulating capital would be available for advances to
wage labor. On the contrary, the amount of circulating capital produced
is a chosen total, and were it not for competition could easily have been
chosen to provide wage labor with some share in surplus. Marx occasionally declares (overzealously, surely!) that during the period of production it is wage laborers and not their masters who make needed
advances of capital. Somehow they see themselves through by drawing on
small stocks of necessaries until production has been completed and they
are belatedly reimbursed!

So much for orthodox optimism about the relation of wages to subsistence and of unorthodox pessimism: one should not ignore the statements
in which no great emphasis was placed on either optimism or pessimism.
Either a routine equality between wages and subsistence was judged
inevitable and unexciting or other aspects of distribution were regarded
as more promising for theoretical debate than the drab review of
subsistence.

Adam Smith himself expected that the benefits of "natural liberty"
would at some distant date be exhausted, having produced a "full complement of riches,"[35] and with that full complement a population that
could enjoy nothing above a sparse subsistence. The *China* of Smith's
fancies was the nearest example of so wealthy and doleful a society, but
in relation to England its state was remote enough in time not to trouble
so practical an advisor. Petty had taken it for granted that wages are
determined by what the laborer requires "so as to live, labor and generate," and is favorably cited for this opinion by Marx (presumably for
empirical rather than theoretical insight).[36] Turgot was explicit in his
report to his visitors from China. "The mere Workman, who has only his
arms and his industry, has nothing except in so far as he succeeds in
selling his toil to others." And at what price? "The Workmen are therefore obliged to lower the price, in competition with one another. In every
kind of work it cannot fail to happen, and as a matter of fact it does
happen, that the wages of the workman are limited to what is necessary
to procure him his subsistence."[37]

Malthus, Marx notwithstanding, in these matters was not enthusiasti-
cally Malthusian. He describes his famous theses on the contest between
population and sustenance, the contest that is experienced by all living
things, but he distinguishes sharply the nature of the contest as the living
things are human and as they are not. It is possible for humans to resist
the forces that are inescapable for the rest of nature, to modify the

"positive checks" on population that scarcity imposes. Intelligent beings can interpose preventive checks, moral restraint, and the like, and can do so to some effect as individuals, can do so to still greater effect within a well-ordered society, and can supplement these effects by taking advantage of favorable changes in their environment. Sentimental remedies are useless; political upheavals are worse than useless.[38] Still, says Malthus, "...from a review of the state of society in former periods, I would certainly say that the evils resulting from the principle of population have rather diminished than increased, even under the disadvantage of an almost total ignorance of the real cause." How much more successful can policy be now that it is informed about "real cause"! And if Malthus' pious tone still troubles some of his readers, his view of remedies may seem less unctuous when those remedies are preached far more vigorously by John Stuart Mill and Knut Wicksell.

Ricardo, on the other hand, though he hardly brings "enthusiasm" to mind, is *severely* Malthusian and uses the doctrine without any qualification except for acceptance of subsistence as a social rather than physiological datum. Wage labor and services from wage labor are admittedly special commodities, and are produced and maintained outside the walls of manufactories; but produced they are nonetheless and so obtain their *natural* prices as do all other produced objects of trade. "It is the cost of production...and not...supply and demand that must ultimately regulate the price of commodities."[39] Subsistence is the cost of producing labor, and subsistence accordingly must be its price, or at least that natural price which emerges when forces for change have been exhausted. Malthusian adjustments are tolerable in this framework because time for their application has been granted by the analyst. Ricardo has seen his task as exploring the anatomy of natural rates of exchange among commodities of all sorts, and while he does not for a moment concede he has left reality to fend for itself, he is well aware that day-to-day prices (like day-to-day distribution) can be far removed from their natural counterparts. He has approached issues in the spirit many post-classical writers are to adopt.

So wages in the classical system, in all these accounts, are scaled to the technology and fixed capital that are in place, and so in prosperous times will be scaled to fixed capital that is fully employed. So many openings for wage labor will have resulted from that fixed capital operated at capacity levels. Capitalists will compete for whatever totals of workers they need, workers will compete for the employment the capitalists have in the aggregate decided to supply. From one account to another the consequences of these competitions are given different outcomes, for opinion

about the surrounding facts varies from author to author. Wage rates are
determinate, however, under each choice of "surrounding facts," and are
determinate under the interaction of those circumstances with subsistence. Out of wage rates now come predictable results for major determinants of saving and growth, and predictable results about the problems
that will be left for the state and the secondary economies to handle.

Finally, out of the idea of the full employment of capital comes the
correlative idea of periods when capital is unemployed, when times are
not prosperous, when cycles and crises are experienced. Classical theory
has little to say about distribution during these periods, at least little to
say that is systematic or goes beyond description of particular calamities
(which is not to deny that *description* in the style of Marx and Mill can
transmit important messages!). Attention is then given in the classical
writings to what has caused or threatened chaos, and what will forestall
chaos or bring it to an end. Unemployment (of fixed capital) is not very
often considered as a continuing situation.

Two informal reflections on wages and subsistence can bring this section to a close. From their tone and from their sources they may add a
little flavor to the academic utterances so far cited. If Marx has his
sources right, no less an authority on natural liberty than the formidable
William Ewart Gladstone concluded in his budget speech of 1864 that
"...human life is but, in nine cases out of ten, a struggle for existence."[40]
And then there is the despairing judgment by John Stuart Mill about who
was saved by labor-saving machinery: "It is questionable if all the mechan-
ical inventions yet made have lightened the day's toil of any human
being."

Profits, Rates of Profit, Capital

In the classical theory of distribution wage laborers were certainly *hired*
and were hired by someone who owned or controlled fixed capital and
other factors of production as well. This someone who hired laborers was
in the simpler models either identified as the *capitalist* or, if he was active
in agriculture, perhaps as the farmer or the cultivator; and he and the
wage laborer then shared the stage only with the *landlord*. With the
progress of industry, theorists could no longer ignore that their single
personality who "hired and controlled" was a composite of agents usually
possessed of quite distinct identities in the outside world, persons who
comprised subclasses of the simpler idea, a group of entrepreneurs, for
example, a group of rentiers, a group of industrial capitalists, of merchant

capitalists and so on. What then seemed desirable and sufficient for analytic purposes was to keep wage laborers and landlords sharply defined, to keep one term wholly reserved for the personality (or collectivity) that hired *and* controlled in the productive process, and to be flexible in naming and distinguishing agents outside the three central figures.

The piece of language reserved for the indispensable organizing personality ("indispensable" to the history of things, not to the logic) was usually assigned to capitalists without adorning adjectives, sometimes (though rarely) to entrepreneurs, sometimes to the industrial capitalist. In all of these usages one still encountered an artifact: authority and self-interest were to be given the same domain by being attributed to this organizing agent whatever the real forms of industrial organization might be.

How the "capitalist" would behave (one will stay with the simplest usage) has been partly described in the discussion of wages: in relation to wage labor his decisions are fixed by the patterns just discussed. With subsistence looked after, what is left for distribution over the society as a whole is a *net* surplus. It is net first of all of those taxes the State has imposed to provide (1) for public goods and (2) for public transfers based upon the social policies of the day, transfers to provide some measure of sustenance and relief where the markets fail and assistance from the secondary economies is insufficient. It may be worth recalling that in Quesnay's best known "Tableau"[41] something like a third of surplus goes to the public authorities of church and state, no small adjustment! It is net secondly of whatever already determined portion of surplus may have gone to above subsistence wages.

Within the structure of natural liberty capitalists will have responded to this situation according to the pressures of competition. Since they alone organize production, they alone will already possess, or in any event will now bid for, the use of existing fixed capital, existing stocks, existing land (whether by offering to rent or to purchase). They are driven to do as well as they can, to be efficient in their use of resources, and so, according to the logic of "one price" theorems, are driven to be as efficient as the state of the arts will allow. Existing fixed capital will normally be fully employed (again, full employment has its classical significance, if in a wider context), surplus will be generated in quantities corresponding to the fixed capital employed, and the net surplus becomes profits, interest, and rents. In this respect the bookkeeping we inspected in Petty is the bookkeeping used by classical writers without exception as each takes us through his statement of the "national accounts." One might remark that Marx's provocative account of the "Trinity Formula" in the last pages of *Capital*[42] *is* successful provocation, only it manages to present a strict orthodoxy in accounting-for-surplus as though it were unorthodox.

Capitalists obtain profits as the portion of net surplus they are able to retain as residual claimants. In relation to payments of interest the amount of profit (at least within the broad classical categories) is of concern only to two bodies of competitors, those who are organizing capitalists and those who have advanced savings and lent money. With due regard to the kind of natural inequalities encountered in the classical treatment of wages, inequalities of which the principle has already been discussed,[43] the only advantage under natural liberty for one group or the other would be the negligible benefits that knowledgeable competitors can extract from arbitrage. Payments of rent, true, are another matter (not *that* different, really), but can be left to the closing section. What does offer something new is the translation of profits into rates of profit, and the creation of denominators then required so that those rates will have been defined, denominators that accordingly have to be thought of as a homogenized *capital*.

For much of the path from profits to rates of profit one encounters only renamed features that have been noticed in the analysis of wages. Capitalists live within their various particular, inherited constraints, and make their choices about production and investment under the pressure of competition from their fellow capitalists. They both choose *and* are driven to make profits as large as possible, on the one hand seeking surplus just as Robinson Crusoe would, but also seeking surplus in order to retain their rank as capitalists. They are surrounded by profit-seeking neighbors, and know that they will have to match the lowered costs those neighbors will shortly finance from profits, profits those neighbors will similarly have felt compelled to pursue.[44] The capitalists of classical theory ("capitalists" with human faces, one might say) here again have a *personality* that will vanish when post-classical economics introduces its actors who bear only labels (persons "1, 2, . . ., *n*")!

It is all one whether the capitalists are described as maximizing the portion of profits they retain from surplus or as maximizing surplus itself. Both usages are found, and are from time to time (and legitimately) intermingled[45]: given the effectiveness attributed to arbitrage, these organizers of production can maximize the residuals that come to them only by maximizing the total they must share, and from which the residuals accrue. However rates of profit gain their denominators, such rates will have been forced by competition into equality with each other, and to the extent that they arise from mere ownership of capital, into equality (of that portion) with rates of interest as well. Impediments to this process that have been imposed by policy or other external circumstances the authors leave for commentary of a qualitative, particular kind, just as they set aside causes of inequalities in wage rates.

If profits are to designate surplus that accrues to the industrial capitalist, one must keep in mind that the claim is exercised under two headings. This capitalist who hires, purchases, organizes all other agents of production must for better or worse be the beneficiary of all surplus left over, must be "residual claimant." At the same time the organizing capitalist has contributed capital directly to the enterprise he runs that will be physically indistinguishable from capital for which interest is paid. The organizing capitalist could indeed have obtained interest by leasing his own holdings. The industrial or organizing capitalist of classical writings is a composite, for in one aspect he expects to earn interest as any other *owner* of capital might do, and in a second aspect (made possible by the first!) he expects to have chances at acquiring surplus that can only come to those who have organized production and accepted risk.

A more elaborate taxonomy could be used to distinguish, say, *entrepreneurs* from everyday capitalists, from those who own but do not manage. The distinction is occasionally expressed in exactly those terms (with Turgot, for example). But if wage-laborers and landlords are crisply defined in classical theory, capitalists are not: they are residuals conceptually, just as their shares in surplus are residuals economically. But this flexible definition accorded with reality and the abstractions did not. Profits *did* contain interest, profits *did* reflect the existence of risks and uncertainties, and profits *did* contain whatever surplus was gained or lost by accident.

When there was full employment of fixed capital, then, variations in normalized rates of profit and interest could arise only from the contest between natural liberty and the customs of outmoded economic systems. This is classical theory focused upon natural prices, and classical theory in its most representative form. Nonetheless some of the classicists (and many pamphleteers) acquired fame for disputing the efficacy of natural liberty as an assurance of full employment, and supplemented their dissent with essays on "gluts" and on chronic inefficiency. Malthus in the splendid Book II of his *Principles*[46] and later Marx vigorously argued that crises and stagnation belonged to and might dominate any *complete* discussion of normal economic events. One draws from those far-reaching propositions only a point that matters here, the vulnerability of equal rates (even within natural liberty) to shocks or chronic dislocation.

So the awkward question cannot be deferred. How *did* the classicists envision the denominators in these equalized rates of profit and of interest? Two ideas produce tension throughout the analysis. There is the notion that one could use "denominators" counted in the same material units as the surplus itself, and counted either directly or in terms of real costs poured into base and surplus alike. If in this idealized form profit can be expressed in natural units of its base, then rates of profits and of interest can also take on the quality of natural proportions. Smith, Ricardo, Marx (of value rates of profit) routinely employ calculations of this kind. On the other side, however, there is the conception from Petty, Turgot, Marx (of money rates of profit): the denominators are mere effects, reflections of money rates of interest that have whatever level demand and supply for future income may give them.[47]

Under the technical and behavioral laws that govern the classical model, these competing points of view may be of interest chiefly as a metaphysical bequest to post-classical theorizing, for in the upshot they do not produce operational differences. Consider the givens of the system. With fixed capital being fully employed, with subsistence wages being socially determined and actual wages related to subsistence by other institutional forces, with the propensity to save and invest out of surplus being high (and also socially determined as well as being high), with given tastes generating all consumer demands,[48] with all of this already decided, the measure of all capitals, whether old or new, will have been adapted to these givens of the situation. This adaptation will have been underlined by the little space allowed in the classical scheme to *substitution*. The post-classical authors will see possibilities for marginal adjustments everywhere (error must be put right and the calculus displayed). In contrast, the classicists found fixed proportions their natural choice *almost* everywhere. One can remark again on the exceptional treatment of land, and point to a further exception, the great substitutability within outputs rather casually allowed to consumption goods (even to all finished goods) as a whole.

It might be, of course, that the surplus would have the same physical composition as the goods from which it sprang, or that it would have the same sequence of "real costs" as those goods, and that a denominator for rates of surplus, of profit, of interest, would have natural units. It might even be that some "package" of the particular commodities found in surplus would have the same cross-section of real costs as "input" as it would as "output." Were this Sraffa-like curiosity to be observed, magnitudes given to the denominators to produce equal rates of (say) surplus would certainly reflect the phenomenon, but magnitudes would still ultimately be as derivative here as in any other case.

Behavior of a less passive kind appears only in the allocation of saving to whatever opportunity for creating fixed capital is judged to be most profitable. Among the classicists it was received doctrine that the money rate of interest would arise from an interplay of supply and demand, as between those on the one side who wished to surrender present income for future income on the best terms possible, and those on the other side who saw investment opportunities by which future income could be acquired.[49] That this "interplay" took place within an interdependent scheme was also routinely declared, as the endless reference to falling rates of profit amply shows. In general, however, nothing much was offered about the mechanics of *particular* decisions to invest *except* in periods of glut. Malthus and Marx having separated decisions to save from decisions to invest saw the special significance of new accumulation. Perhaps only Rae and von Thunen (in their very different ways) attempted to *explain* choices of investment when prices were normal.

Rent

From beginning to end of classical distributive theory there is probably greater agreement about the nature of rent than about anything else. One writer will say more than another on analytical matters, and one writer will say more than another about institutional or historical matters; but when authors dispute with each other with respect to rent it is about sins of omission, not of commission. Dispute can be intense because the political basis for rent to be paid is not as easily attached to real costs as it is to inheritance or present power, but even at that it is dispute about justice rather than about what surplus goes to rent after "justice" has been imposed or agreed.

In all of the discussion from Petty to Marx one finds a class of landlords who enter the system of natural liberty having long since appropriated most of the land there is. The state itself is a landlord, and protects property rights for itself and for its land-holding clients. True, there may be land that at some given time is too barren to yield rent, and so may be of little interest to private landlords; and there will often be small-holdings farmed outside natural liberty and so part of the secondary economy. But this is background: the land that counts in the theory is the land that has been appropriated by private landlords and now can be rented to others.

Appropriation was a datum centuries before classical economics existed or could have existed. It was directed to power long before it was directed to rent. Adam Smith remarks that "...the highest jurisdiction both civil and criminal...the power of levying troops, of coining money, and even that of making bye-laws...were all rights possessed alloidally by the great proprietors of land several centuries before even the name of feudal law was known in Europe."[50] To have this immense feature of distribution as a given narrows political economy but certainly simplifies theory!

There is still needed an identification of the *land* that is to provide these appropriators with rent. Ricardo offered the famous abstraction that land was constituted "by the original and indestructible powers of the soil."[51] Against this is the alternative abstraction that treats land as a composite, a bequest from nature combined with capital fixed in that bequest (and perhaps assisted further by ordinary fixed capital). This was the usage of the physiocrats, an easily defended alternative so long as the capital that has been combined with land *is not* forgotten, but very troublesome when it *is*, as the somewhat tattered reputation of the physiocrats testifies.[52]

Within the boundaries of natural liberty classical theory would, at the first level of argument, have capitalists pay for the use of land they do not own just as they pay for the use of, say, fixed capital they do not own. They compete with each other and with the owners of the assets they wish to use. In any given circumstances competition assures landlords that they will receive whatever extra amounts of surplus are attributable to the properties of the land they hold (perhaps modified a little by varying perceptions of the "extra amounts"). Demand determines marginal bushels that are more expensive in terms of labor and capital than any other bushels. All less expensive bushels yield rent to the extent of the difference. Wage rates, rates of profit and rates of interest, will (at least in principle) be the same regardless of the quality of the land that the capitalist uses, and regardless of whether he employs substantial or negligible amounts of land. This leaves differentials over and above wages, profit and interest to those whose land has provided the differentials.

A certain confusion appears among several of the authors as to whether or not such *rent* is tribute paid to monopolists,[53] confusion that originates from their using *monopoly* twice over with different meanings. One might, without offense to the dictionary, speak of any owner of a parcel of land (or of anything clearly distinct) as having a monopoly in supplying such and such services from that land or "anything." One might also look to land in general and imagine the consequences (for distribution) of its being brought under single control. Here is the preferred contemporary usage in technical discussion, although it has not displaced the alternative meaning in everyday speech.

Should monopoly of "land in general" be established one would contemplate situations in which landlords could extract a large proportion of the surplus that natural liberty would otherwise assign to profit and interest. Marx was not the only classical writer to ponder this dramatic possibility (described as "absolute ground rent" in an essay occupying some 25 pages of *Capital*),[54] but he was probably vulnerable to a charge of inconsistency in giving collusive monopoly such weight. Adam Smith, after all, always had a place within natural liberty for those monopolists-in-waiting who well understood how economic power could extract added surplus. The problem for Marx was that if collusion can redistribute surplus and undermine the efficiency of natural liberty, it can also allow capitalists the prospect of collective action to save capitalism,[55] of action preventing "inevitable" collapse!

One returns to *rent* under natural liberty but at the second level of argument. Let fixed capital give employment to particular complements of circulating capital and of wage labor, determinate amounts for each separately controlled packet of fully employed capital. Apart from capital already fixed in the soil it is still an open question how land and these other agents of production will be combined in particular enterprises, in particular "farms."[56]

Here are new lines of argument and of the first importance. The novelties originate in the heterogeneity of land and the variety of ways capital can be used with land. Accordingly there must exist a multitude of techniques for producing "corn." When the classical writers recorded how the agents of production might be combined in agriculture, one index would usually have been logically just as good as another. Nevertheless their almost invariable choice was to consider the disposition of a homogenized wage-labor from one farm to the next, an allocation decided as always in classical theory by the capitalists in response to competition. Wage-labor would bring with it capital (fixed *and* circulating) to each farm, and would have commended itself doubly as the measure of everything the capitalists would combine with land. Theorists in the first place had built upon the "toil and trouble" notion of value, and in the second, had assigned to labor an objective dimension.

As capitalists contemplated the allocation of labor (always in its role as index for the factors whose level of use it determined), they would see more or less surplus accruing to each *successive* choice under their control. A given allocation could be directed to one packet of land rather than another, and under the classical convention would always be directed to where the effect on private surplus (and public — in this case, the same thing) is largest. But in describing this behavior the theorist is compelled to use a *marginal rule*, and to use it in two applications. That rule was largely understood and partly expressed by classical writers before Ricardo, but given an authority few rules in economics have ever enjoyed by the quality of his sponsorship.[57] Successive allocations on any particular holding of land add less and less to surplus; and if a given (total) allocation on one holding is more productive than it is on another, so too is any other given allocation. The most fertile land is always "most fertile."

This is almost enough to close the story. Fixed capital already in existence will be combined with land in an efficient way in relation to whatever the overall activity of the economy may be. That overall level is "normally" fixed by the full employment of fixed capital, and will establish a particular level of activity for production using land. More generally, overall activity at any level is indexed by wage-labor as is activity at the level of particular "farms." As was remarked earlier, not much is generally said in classical theory about the assignment of demand from one kind of output to another, but this silence is broken by one very important exception. It belongs to the present discussion. For the classical writers, farms were preoccupied with the production of necessaries, of those commodities from which the bulk of *subsistence* was obtained. A large fraction of consumer spending would have an unchanging destination.

In post-classical economics the development of this marginalist technique is to become an obsession with theorists, applied sometimes to great advantage in explaining economic behavior but also applied in a scholastic spirit to models that exist only because of the technique. The fundamental abstractions, however, always remain as they were with Ricardian rent. What, then, of the application of this classical marginalism to the combination of *investment* with land? It is tempting to let the question pass, treating classical distributive theory as though it dealt only with fixed capital already in place and not with fixed capital now being formed. Surplus from the past, however, had been committed to one farm rather than another, and indeed (for the generalization was immediate) in one proportion rather than another, as between farms and nonagricultural enterprises. Surplus from the past was necessarily affecting present distribution according to how these past choices had been made.

The upshot was an extension of marginalism as an explanation of how existing fixed capital was combined with packets of land. From this beginning with inherited fixed capital and land, marginalist reasoning was inevitably to consider how the *production* of fixed capital would be allocated among the various packets, and then, to consider how the *production* of fixed capital would be allocated among uses of all kinds. The industrial capitalists who organized production of surplus within the existing stocks of fixed capital became the capitalists-entrepreneurs who sought out the most promising outlets for additional fixed capital, and did so on precisely the same *marginalist* principles that guided them in their humbler incarnation. By its nature investment is a marginalist activity and so, not surprisingly, a principal bridge from classical to post-classical argument.[58]

Rent and Physiocracy

And finally? Before turning to closing remarks, something must be said about those classicists to whom *rent* and *surplus* were one and the same, about the school of physiocracy, the amateurs who out of zeal created a profession. One could not comfortably dismiss writers for whom Smith *and* Marx had such high regard! Little is needed, though, to confirm that the distributive system of the physiocrats is after all the distributive system of their successors. True, one encounters many empirical points on which physiocratic evidence is suspect (not an unlikely encounter in highly political economy), some semantical problems that are curiosities rather than theoretical issues, and some assertions of a meta-physical kind that may be indefensible but are logically redundant.[59] Against these blemishes one might set the substance of an argument that has supplied ideas for almost every discussion of distribution since.

The capitalistic economy within France of the 1750s was certainly *not* the national economy but only a minor "primary" system set in a vast "secondary" economy. For physiocracy the point of public policy would be to enlarge the primary economy until its foundation, large-scale farming making heavy use of capital, could support the society as a whole. "We are not speaking here of small scale cultivation...[that] thankless type...which reveals the poverty and ruin of those nations in which it predominates...[and that] has no connection with the order of the *tableau*, where the annual advances are able, with the aid of the fund of original advances, to produce 100 per cent."[60] Side by side with these capitalistic farms there would coexist a multitude of artisanal, manufacturing enterprises, half in and half out of the primary sector, and a greatly reduced secondary economy engaged still in primitive agriculture and marginal labors in the towns.

Through the hands of the capitalist-farmers would flow the subsistence wages advanced to farm-laborers, and would also flow depreciation funds to restore circulating capital, fixed capital in the private domain, and the infrastructure of fixed capital placed in the public domain; and over and above all this would flow the surplus from which rent would be transferred *under competition* to the landlords. Rent would be transferred but would not really have exhausted surplus. Profits and interest would remain as residuals that would go to the enterprising farmers who had organized production and joined stocks of capital to land. *Rent*, like the profits of Smith and Marx, is in some degree a composite term: "... it is the land and the advances made by the farmers for purposes of cultivation which constitute the source of the revenue of agricultural nations."[61]

Should the profits and interest received within the primary sector — urban as well as rural — have been given the same place in surplus as rent? One is reviewing a vocabulary chosen for its political message. What was damaging to theory would help politically, so the hope seems to have been (in years when hope was rarely to turn out well). Even on the theoretical side the advocates of capitalistic farming could argue that by the time the great reformation is complete their physiocratic Utopia would have become a stationary state. Profits and interest could still be large in absolute amounts but would then be negligible as rates, and negligible when measured against rent.

Such simplification is not peculiar to physiocracy. To understand circular flows the theorist has often and understandably shown affection for the repetitive world of the stationary state. He has usually paid a price in clarity, though, and a very large price in relevance. Smith chose well when he deliberately rejected illustrations from physiocratic heaven. The physiocrats had found themselves with an urban economy that had to be denied prominence, and so had restrained their artisans *by assumption* from adopting the institutions of rural capitalism. This might not have been of much practical significance in the France of 1750, but it was to prove very awkward in gaining credibility for the general principles of their system.

Where there is a deeper error, though, was in the attribution of surplus to land as a single source. It is an error of the kind that invites use as a warning and illustration of how seductive error can be. But it was an error that could be accepted or rejected (like Marx's theses on service industries) without consequences for anything in the domain of policy.

With a totally interdependent system it is *meaningless* (and for this reason harmless!) to attribute *surplus* to land or to any other separated source. But why, then, was a question defined that could have no answer? No doubt part of the reason was political expediency. Like many of us, however, the physiocrats seemed to have meditated too long upon initial conditions from the Garden of Eden.

By Way of Conclusion

Just as this classical theory of distribution emerged directly from the world its authors inhabited, so should its empirical verification. The theory is eminently operational. In principle it should be easy to tell whether or not wage-labor is paid by a formula based on subsistence, whether or not fixed capital is employed according to its designed capacity, whether or not the laboring class saves, whether or not the supply of wage-labor is always greater than the demand, and whether or not there is a large secondary economy and a large transfer economy. In principle it should not be difficult, if and where the theory is confirmed, to construct derivative descriptions of distribution, for example, tables connecting individuals and income, tables connecting families and income, tables showing individual or family income over time.

For some of these tests one would expect no great gap to appear between "in principle" and "in practice." Studies in developmental economics suggest, for example, that the classical treatment of subsistence has stood up very well. In general, though, the institutions of the classical world interfere with gathering statistics ready for immediate interpretation. It is no small thing that the markets of a classical system were imbedded in social arrangements far wider and quite as complex as the markets themselves. It is no small thing that the classical industries allowed for so little substitution. It is no small thing that the theory is directed in the main to times when fixed capital is fully employed, and to economic activities that are almost entirely competitive.

One is skeptical that the advance to a neo-classical theory of production added much to what is easy in principle or subtracted much from what is difficult in practice, but will not step over the boundary of this essay to justify that distrust. Instead one will remark in closing, that the theorist today who would follow the classicists in deferring to reality must notice at least one great change in the structures that determine distribution. There is an ever-widening difference between the private and the social wage, between the private and the social share of surplus.[62]

In the economies that are successors to those of the classical theorists, the distribution of earnings is less and less a successful proxy for the distribution of surplus. The state has superimposed its own programs upon distribution and has done so under complex processes and on a very large scale. Surely it is the distribution of surplus that counts; but theorists have spent much more time with marginal conditions than with the logic of the new programs.

Notes

1. "Secondly, [a capital] may be employed in the improvement of land, in the purchase of useful machines and instruments of trade, or in such things as yield a revenue or profit without changing masters or circulating any further. Such capitals, therefore, may very properly be called fixed capitals" [Adam Smith, *Wealth Of Nations*, Modern Library Edition (Random House, 1937), Book II, ch. I, p. 263]. The interpretation of "fixed" varies from author to author without much effect on the resulting inventory. One reads the adjective as indicating fixed in form rather than fixed in place (pointing to durability as a necessary quality rather than location). It would otherwise be unreasonable to imagine the proportion between fixed capital and land on a given "farm" being a matter of choice rather than of history. In the nature of things, of course, this flexibility cannot be as great as that available when some wholly new farm is organized.

2. In speaking of a "dominating account," one does not intend to suggest that other accounts were of negligible theoretical interest. Dupuit on measureable utility, say, Cournot on the calculus of maximization, Rae again but on "Austrian" periods of production, and von Thunen again but on distribution by way of marginal products — these and others had anticipated in their scattered writings many of the principal themes of the new orthodoxy of the 1870s. But something of this kind is almost always true of arguments that become received doctrine: they turn out to have had parents and grandparents with similar features.

3. P.A. Samuelson, "Economists And The History Of Ideas," given to the Association at its New York meetings (December 27, 1961), and reprinted in *Collected Scientific Papers*, Vol. II (M.I.T. Press, 1966). See p. 1502.

4. In Karl Marx's *Capital* (Moscow: Progress Publishers, 1974), one finds in the analysis of "the transformation of the values of commodities into prices of production" (Vol. III, part II, ch. IX, pp. 154ff) a model of general equilibrium that even with its technical flaws is more comprehensive than, say, Leontief's tables from the 1930s. All the formal rules are explicitly reviewed simultaneously, so that consistency and completeness of the interdependent scheme can be readily tested.

5. Where marginalism forced itself upon the classical writers there naturally had to be choice, not only a margin but a margin with (say) diminishing marginal returns.

6. See Adam Smith, *The Wealth of Nations*, Modern Library Edition (Random House, 1937). In popular discussion Smith is automatically associated with that "free trade" of which our government claims to have become a committed advocate. It is true that Smith's program gives scores of pages to international markets, but it does so only as a leading example of policy that should free *all* trade under a single principle. With Ricardo domestic and international trade are *distinct* processes.

7. In speaking of a literature spread over two centuries one is prepared to make firm statements about opinion in the literature without pretending to have discovered every

exception or to have reported every minor qualification discovered. Mill, for example, does speak of a world where every person could be employed, but by way of Utopian arrangements for family planning.

8. Adam Smith, *The Wealth of Nations*, Modern Library Edition (Random House, 1937), Book I, ch. 5, p. 30.

9. See David Ricardo, *Principles of Political Economy and Taxation*, ch. VII, 3rd edition (London, 1821) on "value" set against the "sum of enjoyments," illustrated, for example, by his famous discussion of foreign trade.

10. Marx, *Capital*, Vol. I. See in the first few pages of the work (as in many pages throughout the work) "use-value" that is *explicitly* an aspect of utility, that is *explicitly* the purpose to which surplus is directed, and that has no measure beyond counts (one by one) of the various commodities that people see as useful.

11. Smith, *The Wealth of Nations*, Book II, ch. II, p. 271.

12. Smith, *The Wealth of Nations*, Book II, ch. III, p. 321.

13. Smith, *The Wealth of Nations*, Book V, ch. II, p. 777.

14. In the compilation of the "Petty Papers" by the Marquis of Landsdowne. (New York: Augustus M. Kelley 1967), see Item No. 51, pp. 155ff.

15. William Petty's "Political Arithmetick," from about 1676, one of the items in C.H. Hull's two-volume collection of "Economic Writings of Sir William Petty," first published by the University Press, Cornell, in 1899 but here taken from *Reprints of Economic Classics* (New York: Augustus M. Kelley 1963). See Vol. I, pp. 233–313.

16. See the review of interpretations in John Stuart Mill's *Principles of Political Economy*, Book II, ch. XI, beginning on p. 346. (The edition in hand is that prepared by W.J. Ashley in 1909, republished by Longmans, Green and Company, 1917, and containing Mill's "7th edition" of 1871.) Mill paraphrases Ricardo: "...he [Ricardo] assumes that there is everywhere a minimum rate of wages, either the lowest with which it is physically possible to keep up the population, or the lowest with which people will choose to do so." Mill then debates this thesis: "...it is necessary to consider that the minimum of which [Ricardo] speaks, especially when it is not a physical, but what may be termed a moral minimum, is itself liable to vary."

17. The thesis was an offshoot of the search for an invariable standard of value. Malthus thought he saw the grail in the form of a wage-unit, an expression of real costs that might link early or distant societies to his own [Malthus, *Principles of Political Economy*, Book I, ch. IV, pp. 217ff].

18. See T.R. Malthus' *Principles of Political Economy* (2nd edition, reprinted by the New York Lithographing Company) for the historical record as it was perceived by a leading classical writer. In Book I, ch. IV, he offers a "review of the corn wages of labor from the reign of Edward III," and observes in a recapitulation that there was an interval "of nearly 500 years...[in which] a peck of wheat may be considered as something like a middle point [for] the corn wages of labor..." [p. 254]. See, in addition, Smith, *The Wealth of Nations*, Book I, ch. VIII, p. 74, who writes that "...there are many plain symptoms that the wages of labor are no-where in this country regulated by the lowest rate which is consistent with common humanity," and who then points out in the next two pages that wages in the Scotland of his day are much lower than wages in England — "...the difference, however, in the mode of their subsistence is not the cause, but the effect, of the difference in their wages" — and immediately goes on to borrow from Gregory King and others statistics showing that over time there has been a considerable improvement in wages for both kingdoms.

19. "Competition, however, must be regarded, in the present state of society, as the principal regulator of wages, and custom or individual character only as a modifying

circumstance, and that in a comparatively slight degree" [J.S. Mill, *Principles of Political Economy*, Book II, ch. XI, p. 343].

20. One will rely below on the classical treatment by Adam Smith. For the moment one might appeal for a full "statement in principle" to the discussion of "working classes" in A.R.J. Turgot's "Reflections on the Origin and Distribution of Riches" (originally published by Du Pont de Nemours in the *Ephemerides* for November, 1769). See especially "Reflections" XV to XX.

21. See Smith, *The Wealth of Nations*, Book I, ch. X, pp. 99–143, for an exposition that was as influential as it was carefully detailed on both nominal and real inequalities. Expositions of similar drift are provided by precursors and by a multitude of successors (both classical and post-classical, as readers of Keynes or Leontief or the Canada Year Book are well aware).

22. Malthus, *Principles of Political Economy*, Book I, ch. II, Section 5, "Of the Labor which a Commodity will command, considered as a Measure of Value in Exchange" [pp. 93–111].

23. Marx, *Capital*, Vol. I, part III, ch. VII, on "the Labor Process," especially pp. 196–198. "All labor of a higher or more complicated character than average labor is expenditure of labor-power of a more costly kind, labor-power whose production has cost more time and labor, and which therefore has a higher value, than unskilled or simple labor-power."

24. See Smith, *The Wealth of Nations*, Book I, ch. X, "Of Wages And Profit in the Different Employments of Labor and Stock," say, page 99: "The whole of the advantages and disadvantages of the different employments of labor and stock must, in the same neighborhood, be either perfectly equal or continually tending to equality. . . . This at least would be the case in a society where things were left to follow their natural course, where there was perfect liberty. . . ."

25. Smith, *The Wealth of Nations*, Book II and especially Book III, ch. III, in which the theoretical core of "The Wealth of Nations" is displayed.

26. That proto-Austrian, John Rae, had this same view, as did his truly Austrian successors a half-century later. See his *New Principles on the Subject of Political Economy* (Boston, 1834), and more specifically his Book II, ch. III, pp. 95ff. For Rae and the later "Austrians" the *interesting* question was not how much of maturing "capital" provided the subsistence fund but how maturation occupied one interval of time rather than another. Production used time, but a variable, socially chosen amount of time.

27. For Smith's extended discussion of propensities to save see *The Wealth of Nations*, pp. 320ff.

28. Smith [p. 324] goes so far as to say ". . . every prodigal appears to be a public enemy, and every frugal man a public benefactor." Society's savings contribute to its stability. So the argument ran and still runs.

29. In qualitative terms most theorists of a socialistic kind shared some or much of Marx's appraisal of how regimes of natural liberty were likely to fix wages. Engels himself showed this clearly in his *Conditions of the Working Class in England* (first published in German, Leipzig, 1845), but he confesses just as clearly in later prefaces to the study that he then regarded such work as no more than raw material for Marx's powerful abstractions. One may not agree that this is how the rankings of originality should have been made, but this is certainly how they were made.

30. One will sometimes speak of "industrial capitalism" narrowly, where there is some need to distinguish, say, "merchant capitalism," but generally will allow the one phrase to serve for all variants from Petty to Marx.

31. Ricardo *Principles of Political Economy and Taxation*, ch. XXXI. One might remark here on two much debated aspects of the empirical issue. First, if machines displace workers, the construction of machines recruits workers. What, then, is the net effect? Second, if workers are displaced in one area they may be recruited in some other area or they may not. If recruited, they may or may not be recruited on equal terms. What is their experience in actual histories?

32. See Marx, *Capital*, on the "Accumulation of Capital" and especially chs. XXIV and XXV of Vol. I. Argument with the same focus is often repeated in *Capital* and elsewhere in the Marxian canon, but is here given definitive treatment. The "reserve army" has already appeared in Engels, *Conditions of the Working Class in England*, and is colorful enough language to have still earlier antecedents. Notice, as Marx makes clear, that the reserve army is a wider notion by far than the involuntary unemployment of Keynes, for it contains ordinary wage laborers in the most prosperous of periods and contains large contingents from the secondary economies. One repeats, that with only a handful of exceptions classical arguments had no use for, and made no reference to, full employment of labor.

33. While this text was being edited, one encountered a paper prepared for the annual meetings of the Canadian Economics Association, A.M.C. Waterman's "On The Malthusian Theory of Long Swings" (Winnipeg, May 31, 1986), an interpretation of cycles in real wages causing and being caused by cycles in population. Waterman shows very well, it seems to me, how for a classical writer subsistence wages at conventional levels can be a function of subsistence wages of a physiological kind, and shows how cycles with a long-run basis coexist with — and so must be distinguished from — cycles and crises tied to miscalculation and gluts. One has mildly objected that he uses, but does not need, full employment of labor; and that he similarly uses, but does not need, saving-and-accumulation that has a complex behavioral base (instead of being the required reinvestment of almost all surplus). Waterman's cycles take place within "full employment," but of fixed capital; and his "gluts," like those of everyone else, have the employment of fixed capital variable.

34. Marx, *Capital*, Vol. I, ch. XXV, section 4, p. 644. "This is the absolute general law of capitalist accumulation."

35. Smith, *The Wealth of Nations*, Book I, ch. IX, pp. 94ff.

36. One relies on Marx to have the citation correct. It comes from "The Political Anatomy Of Ireland," 1672, p. 64, and is given in *Capital* in Vol. I, part IV, ch. XII, p. 313. As was seen above, Petty performs his political arithmetic according to this measure of wages.

37. A.J.R. Turgot, "Reflections on the Origin and Distribution of Riches," Reflection No. 6.

38. In all of this the source is T.R. Malthus' *Essay On Population* (the 8th edition, say, of about 1817 though from 1803 editions change very little). Malthus as heartless hypocrite, Malthus as political simpleton, Malthus so pictured by Marx has been painted from such passages as these. One remarks again on the reservations one feels about the picture and the reasons accounting for its violent coloring.

39. Ricardo, *Principles of Political Economy and Taxation*, ch. XXX, p. 382. The "Principles" abound in such tributes to natural price.

40. One quotes at second hand. The item appears in Marx, *Capital*, Vol. I, part VII, ch. XXV, section 5, p. 652. Gladstone would then have been Chancellor of the Exchequer for several years, and so would not seem to have had much of a political interest in bleak utterances directed to Gallup polls.

41. Francois Quesnay, "Tableau Economique," published with extensive explanations

and maxims, and republished in 1894 (in its incarnation from 1759) by the British Economic Association.

42. See Marx, *Capital*, Vol. III, part VII, ch. XLVIII, pp. 814ff.

43. See Rae, *New Principles on the Subject of Political Economy*, Book II, ch. IX, pp. 198n; "...on the effects resulting from the diversities of strength in the accumulative principle, in members of the same society." The argument is "Austrian" but comes to the same conclusion on this particular issue as do virtually all other writings of the classical period. "It thus happens, that all instruments capable of transfer, are in the same society, at nearly the same orders."

44. There are references everywhere in the classical canon, but in especially vigorous form with Marx. For one somewhat formal statement see Vol. III, Book I, part I, ch. I, p. 37: "...the fundamental law of capitalist competition, which political economy had not hitherto grasped, the law which regulates the general rate of profit and the so-called prices of production...rest...on [the] difference between the value and the cost-price of commodities, and on the resulting possibility of selling a commodity at a profit under its value."

45. "But it is only for the sake of profit that any man employs a capital in the support of industry..." [Smith, *The Wealth of Nations*, Book IV, ch. II, p. 423], a recipe that depends on the "profits of stock" described at length in ch. IX of Book I. Marx uses a wider reference: "Our capitalist has two objects in view: in the first place, he wants to produce a use-value that has value in exchange, that is to say, an article destined to be sold, a commodity; and secondly, he desires to produce a commodity whose value shall be greater than the sum of the values of the commodities used in its production..." [*Capital*, Vol. I, ch. VII, p. 186].

46. Malthus, *Principles of Political Economy*, Book II, and especially sections 7 and 10 of the single chapter Book II contains. In section 7 Malthus points with remarkable prescience to economically backward economies that might remain backward for generations, held back from full employment in any sense by custom and inheritance with respect to land tenure. In section 10 he reviews the post-Waterloo stagnation that peace brought to the advanced English economy.

47. Turgot, "Reflections on the Origin and Distribution of Riches," "Reflection" number LVIII among others [p. 49]. "Every capital in money, or every sum of value whatever it may be, is the equivalent of a piece of land producing a revenue equal to a definite fraction of that sum."

48. Consumer behavior is based upon given tastes that will then produce whatever "demands" (or consumer "supplies") are consistent with the distribution of surplus. Wage labor buys such and such necessaries in particular proportions, the others buy necessaries *and* luxuries in particular proportions. Tastes are stylized by class, so that classical writers do not spend much time on the effect new relative prices might have upon demand. Even if this were not so, the factors of production used to produce one output are treated as though over a considerable range they could equally well produce other outputs. Allocation of household spending is given very little space.

49. See again Turgot for as direct a statement as any (but direct statements abound).

50. Smith, *The Wealth of Nations*, Book III, ch. IV, p. 387.

51. Ricardo, *Principles of Political Economy and Taxation*, presented twice over in almost identical language. See, say, Book II, p. 69.

52. Quesnay at one point tells us that "...the advances of a kingdom's agriculture ought to be regarded as if they were fixed property which should be preserved with great care in order to ensure the production of the taxes and revenue of the nation" [p. 5], at another emphasizes that he is talking only of "large scale cultivation" based upon "the wealth

necessary to make the original advances" [p. vi] but then finds the "total of the wealth of the sterile expenditure class" to be "18,000,000,000 livres" [p. xi]. He manages at the end to find a distinction within a *wealth* he has just made homogeneous!

53. "The rent of land, therefore, considered as the price paid for the use of the land, is naturally a monopoly price" [Smith, *The Wealth of Nations*, Book I, ch. XI, p. 145]. He has earlier noticed the monopolists of modern textbooks: "The monopolists, by keeping the market constantly under-stocked, by never fully supplying the effectual demand, sell their commodities much above the natural price, and raise their emoluments, whether they consist in wages or profits, greatly above their natural rate" [Book I, ch. VII, p. 61]. Similar mixtures are common in the classical writings.

54. Marx, *Capital*, Vol. III, part VI, ch. XXIV, pp. 748–773. Conventional "differential rent," however, has occupied almost all of the preceding hundred pages.

55. Marx at times permits stronger capitalists and capitalists engaged in "centralisation" to capture surplus from their less aggressive brethren, and *Marxians* have at times given monopoly a large place in their derivative expositions (Lenin, Ernest Mandel being notables from a longer list). There is always the danger of theory that describes everything and explains nothing.

56. One may as well use the overwhelmingly important special case rather than search for a general term.

57. His successors in the classical tradition usually are content with paraphrase, though some (Rae, Clay, for example) write against Ricardo in Ricardian terms. The debt to Ricardo owed by the marginalists of post-classical orthodoxy and of countless contemporary writers is well known.

58. It is not that classical writing was static and post-classical writing dynamic, for on balance just the opposite was true. The dynamics of classical theory, however, turned upon saving almost automatically invested, whereas even in the smoothly advancing Austrian schemes, investment was the separated result of complex marginal calculation.

59. "Not only does there not exist nor can there exist any other revenue than the net produce of lands, but it is also the land which has furnished all the capitals which make up the sum of all the advances of agriculture and commerce." But how could the economic facts of eighteenth century France be fitted into such a doctrine? "It was that [land] which offered without tillage the first rude advances which were indispensable for the earliest labors; all the rest is the accumulated fruit of the economy of the centuries that have followed one another since man began to cultivate the earth" [Turgot, "Reflections on the Origin and Distribution of Riches," "Reflection C", pp. 96–97]. One should not attempt to dispute this on analytic or theoretical grounds for it is *neither* analytic nor theoretic, but the kind of poetic tautology from which policy can be imagined to flow.

60. Quesnay, "Tableau Economique," "Explanation," p. 6.

61. Quesnay, "Tableau Economique," Economic Maxims, footnote attached to Maxim #9, p. 7.

62. One has in mind the enormous "post-war" expansion of the welfare state, especially in the industrialized world, and so is pointing to contemporary national accounts. Statistics on the secondary economy and on transfers based on custom would add still another level to the problem of reporting distribution in a complete way. One would not be at all surprised, incidentally, to learn that the ratio of social to private wage declined from Petty to Marx, and that its rise in this century has been a return to the much earlier proportion.

3 MARX'S THEORY OF INCOME DISTRIBUTION

David P. Levine

Marx treats the determinants of income distribution within the framework laid out by his classical predecessors, especially Smith and Ricardo. The classical framework did not, however, provide Marx with a single, logically consistent argument upon which he could base his own analysis. Instead, it incorporated elements of several distinct theories which lead in different directions. Marx continues along the different paths first cleared by Smith and Ricardo, at some points following one, at some points another. In this chapter, we investigate the different paths followed by Marx, seeing how they sometimes cross, sometimes meet, and sometimes take us in opposite directions.

Marxian Concepts

While our analysis of the Marxian theory of distribution will not depend heavily on concepts peculiar to Marx, we cannot present the salient features of that theory without assuming familiarity with the terms "value," "surplus-value," and "value of labor-power." In this section, we briefly discuss these concepts.

For Marx, the concept of value connotes a sum of labor time needed by society to produce a given commodity. The idea of such a sum raises difficulties which need not concern us here [see Steedman, 1977, and Levine, 1978, pp. 305–312]. We can capture Marx's intent, at least with regard to the determinants of relative shares, using a broader interpretation of the concept of value.

For classical political economy, the specification of a value unit appropriate to the analysis of distribution required a separation of the determinants of distribution from those of the magnitude of the net product. This separation allowed the classical economist to isolate the forces which determine income distribution from those which determine the value of output. Given the problems implied by the use of labor time as the value unit, classical theory employs an alternative connected to the specification of a system of what Marx terms "prices of production." Marx's price of production is equivalent to the "long-period" or "natural" price of modern versions of the classical theory [Mainwaring, 1984]. The price of production covers all costs of production and returns profit on capital advanced at a rate which is equal for all capitals. Within such a system, value is measured in units of the commodity chosen to act as numeraire. Such a unit will not in general assure independence of the value of output from its distribution.[1] But, unless we are specifically interested in comparison of equilibria, the implied difference need not be a matter of concern. In the following, the term value will refer to price of production in units of a given numeraire.

In contrast to the value of commodities, their "market price" connotes their rate of exchange with the monetary unit when we allow that rate to depend on supply and demand. The market price, determined by supply and demand, need not yield profit at the normal or average rate, or even cover costs of production.

Marx divides the value added by current production into the "value of labor-power" and surplus-value. The value of labor-power refers to the sum of the values of the wages goods when wages are at their "normal" or "subsistence" level. Surplus-value refers to what remains of value added once the value of labor-power has been subtracted. Thus it includes not only profit but also (at a minimum) interest and rent. In the following we will subsume interest and rent into profit and therefore treat surplus-value as the equivalent of profit.

For Marx, each of these categories applies both at the level of the individual (worker or producer) and of the economy as a whole. He assumes virtually throughout that wage and profit rates are uniform (except that wages may vary with skill levels) and does not concern himself with relevant distinctions between what we now refer to as microeconomics and macroeconomics.

Income Distribution

When we view the exchange of commodities from the standpoint of the seller, the transaction realizes revenue for him in the form of money. In the first instance, the category income simply refers to the money realized by the seller of a commodity. In a pure capitalist or private enterprise economy, all property (wealth) is privately held so that all revenue arises out of private transactions in the form of exchange contracts. This implies that all income results from the use of private property and eventually from its sale. Wages refers to the money realized from the sale of labor (or labor services which Marx terms labor-power). Rent arises from an exchange contract trading money for the use of a fixed asset such as land. Interest arises from the use of money as finance and profit from the sale of output produced by capital (and by extension from gains resulting from the buying and selling of assets).

These observations lead naturally to the idea that the prices of commodities relative to their costs of production together with the volume sold determine income for their sellers. In this very general sense, income and price refer to two aspects of the same thing. If we stop here, the theory of income distribution disappears into the general theory of prices.

What could make income a special category (or set of categories) distinct from price? For Marx, the answer has to do with the interconnected processes of social reproduction and capital accumulation. Different types of commodities enter into the accumulation process in different ways. This means that their prices bear upon economic growth (and vice versa) in different ways. The central distinction separates commodities destined for use as means of production from those destined for use as means of consumption: "No society can go on producing, in other words, no society can reproduce, unless it constantly reconverts a part of its products into means of production, or elements of fresh products.... Hence, a definite portion of each year's product belongs to the domain of production. Destined for productive consumption from the very first, this portion exists, for the most part, in the shape of articles totally unfitted for individual consumption" [*Capital*, Vol. I, p. 566], In the case of capital accumulation, or "expanded reproduction" as Marx calls it, this division of the product also involves a division between consumption and net investment as a natural extension of the division between consumption and production.

The division of output into two parts according to its destination suggests a link between income distribution and social reproduction. The scale on which reproduction occurs is directly linked to the way in which the revenue stream is divided. In particular, the division of the revenue stream can affect economic growth by affecting how much of current income can be used to enhance society's capital stock.

One element of the Marxian theory, the one which we will emphasize in the first part of our analysis, seeks to establish how the division of the revenue stream directly determines the proportion of current output available for investment. Marx assumes that the use of income depends entirely on its source. Income realized from the sale of labor is entirely devoted to purchase of means of consumption (i.e., there is no saving out of wages). Income realized from the ownership of capital is devoted (aside from a given margin for "capitalist's consumption") to the acquisition of new means of production. On these assumptions, it follows that the greater the proportion of revenue going to profit, the more rapid the accumulation of capital.

Following the classical economists, Marx gives this conclusion a striking interpretation. According to Marx, "...the magnitude of the capital accumulation clearly depends on the absolute magnitude of the surplus-value" [*Capital*, Vol. I, p. 559]. When Marx states that the magnitude of surplus-value determines accumulation he means (at least in part) that the size of the aggregate pool of profit determines investment. This follows, however, only if we assume (1) that, aside from the fixed margin for consumption, capitalists invest all of their profit in new means of production, and (2) investment decisions do not affect the magnitude of the profits pool. On these assumptions, it follows that a prior determination of the distribution of income acts as a primary determinant of the rate of capital accumulation. Further, since Marx considers the wage (or value of labor-power) the primary determinant of the amount of surplus-value, or profit, the rate of accumulation must depend upon the proportion between profits and wages. Since, for Marx, this proportion depends upon the value of labor-power, the analysis of the process of wage determination must be his starting point in the treatment of income distribution.

The Wage Bargain

Marx begins with a simple classical solution to the problem of wage determination. He assumes that the money wage will tend to settle at a level which, given the prices of commodities, will be just adequate to allow the worker to acquire that "quantity of the means of subsistence" required "for his maintenance" [*Capital*, Vol. I, p. 171].

We can interpret this idea in two different ways. First, we can assume that Marx intended to directly subsume the wage under the rules for

determining the values of commodities according to their cost of production. This requires us to treat labor as a produced commodity with a
determinable cost of production which, at least in equilibrium, equals its
price. Alternatively, we can assume that Marx intends only to claim that
the real wage is governed "by conditions (often of a conventional or
institutional kind) that are *distinct* from those affecting the social product
and the other shares in it" [Garegnani, 1984, p. 295; see also Marglin,
1984, p. 53]. The second is the more general assumption and subsumes
the first as a special case. While I think it fairly clear that Marx had the
first, narrower assumption in mind, that assumption raises severe difficulties of interpretation which need not concern us here. While Garegnani
reserves the term subsistence for the determination of the wage in the
first, narrower case, we will use the term to refer to Garegnani's broader
interpretation. This focuses attention on the idea that a subsistence wage
theory is essentially one which takes either the real wage or the value of
labor-power to be given so far as the determinants of prices and growth
are concerned. We will generally employ this interpretation in our analysis of the Marxian theory.

   Once we have fixed the real wage, the classical assumptions concerning
the net product directly solve the problem of relative shares. Marx generally assumes that technical constraints and the amount of capital determine the magnitude of the net product. The amount and technical specification of the capital stock determine unit labor requirements (n) so
that if Y represents the value of the net product, v the value of labor-
power per unit of labor time, L total labor time, and s the surplus-value,
then

$$Y = \frac{L}{n} = s + vL.$$

If we let e represent the ratio of aggregate surplus to the aggregate value
of labor-power, vL, then, it follows that

$$e = \frac{1}{nv} - 1. \tag{3.1}$$

   Since the worker actually bargains for and receives a money wage rate,
the real wage and value of labor-power presuppose a determinate relationship between money wages and prices. Thus, in order to establish the
validity of the notion of subsistence, we need to show how the prior
determination of an appropriate real wage enters into the determination
of prices and profits. Formally, this is readily established within a steady-
state framework [Mainwaring, 1984, pp. 36–47]. However, the analysis of

the process by which the given real wage constrains and ultimately determines the relation between money wages and prices raises significant issues.

Marx's theory applies two sets of concepts to the analysis of distribution. One set involves value or production price and focuses on a real wage determined prior to the determination of commodity prices. The second involves monetary magnitudes and market prices; it focuses on a dynamic process by which the money wage rate adapts to supply and demand. In order to establish the validity of his analysis of distribution on the basis of the "value of labor-power," Marx must show how the predetermined real wage ultimately controls the fluctuations of money wages (in relation to the prices of wages goods) in response to market circumstances. We now turn to Marx's treatment of this problem.

Marx's only attempt at a systematic analysis of the relationship between money wages, real wages, and prices occurs in his polemical essay on *Value, Price and Profit* [see Levine, 1973, pp. 186–211]. The essay concerns the implications of a successful effort on the part of workers to achieve a higher money wage and poses the question: Can the social and material prospects of the working class be in general improved by wage increases? In order to answer this question Marx needs to find out the impact of a change in money wages on the prices of means of subsistence.

In analyzing this problem, Marx introduces a set of assumptions which turn out to be characteristic of Marxian wage theory:[2]

1. The bargain over the money wage affects all groups of workers uniformly. Differences in wages stem from skill differences and have no bearing on the dynamics of distribution and accumulation. This justifies the treatment of the wage rate as a single magnitude.

2. The productivity of labor does not change in the course of the process of wage determination. One might say that the process of wage determination occupies enough time to assure an equilibrium, but not enough time to allow changes in technique.

3. The amount of capital does not change during the wage determination process. This last assumption requires Marx to abstract from the effect of fluctuations in demand, wages and prices on the composition of the capital stock. He does this by analyzing the problem within the framework of a two-sector model — luxury goods and wages goods. He in effect assumes that both luxury and wages goods sectors produce their own means of production and under conditions of uniform capital intensity.

On the assumption that workers spend their whole income in acquiring consumption goods, Marx concludes that "...a general rise in the rate of wages would, therefore, produce a rise in the demand for, and therefore in the *market prices* of necessaries" [1933, p. 13]. This increase in the prices of wages goods allows capitalists in the wages goods sector to maintain, to a greater or lesser degree, their profit rates in the face of rising wages. However, this does not hold for capitalists in the luxury goods sector where wages have also increased but where demand has not risen and therefore prices remain at their original level.

Given zero net investment, the demand for luxury goods moves directly with the amount of profit, which under these conditions varies directly with its rate. The fall in the profit rate for luxury goods producers means a fall in demand so that not only do prices fail to rise with money wages, they may even tend to fall: "In these branches of industry, therefore, *the rate of profit would fall*, not in simple proportion to the general rise in wages, but in compound ratio of the general rise in wages, the rise in the price of necessaries, and the fall in the price of luxuries" [Marx, 1933, p. 14].

Even though the wage bargain affects money wages uniformly across sectors, it leads to a differentiation of profit rates. In Marxian theory, the differentiation of profit rates across sectors stimulates the movement of capital from lower to higher profit sectors [see Levine, 1980]. The investment of a greater proportion of the social capital into the higher profit sector (wage goods) increases the supply relative to demand in that sector. The process continues until supply and demand equilibrate in both sectors at prices that yield a uniform profit rate.

According to Marx, market prices will eventually settle at the level of the original prices of production. Since "the whole derangement originally arose from a mere change in the proportion of the demand for, and the supply of, different commodities," it follows that this "cause ceasing, the effect would cease, and prices would return to their former level and equilibrium." On more general assumptions, prices at the end of the process will only equal those at the outset under conditions of uniformity of capital to labor ratios [see Mainwaring, 1984, pp. 77–79]. Any implied differences in prices outside of this assumption do not, however, bear on the specific issue under investigation.

Since money wages rise permanently while prices rise only temporarily, the process leads to a higher real wage. In this way the bargain over the money wage is the immediate determinant of real wages which are given independently of prices. The adjustment process brings about a redistribution of output from luxury goods to wages goods appropriate to the higher wage and lower profit rate.

The process described by Marx constitutes a mechanism for fixing distribution rather than a theory of distribution. It makes the value of labor-power depend upon the ability of workers to demand and maintain levels of the money wage rate. Unless we introduce a further specification of the context within which the wage bargain takes place, the value of labor-power and profit will depend upon externally given circumstance. This conclusion accords well enough with Garegnani's notion of "institutional" and "conventional" conditions, but it does not accord well with the larger framework of Marx's theory. We now turn to that larger context.

The General Law of Capitalist Accumulation

Marx analyzes the relationship between wages and capital accumulation in chapter XXV of the first volume of *Capital*. There he specifically concerns himself with "the influence of the growth of capital on the lot of the laboring class" [p. 612]. It becomes clear that the conditions which define a growing economy place limits on distribution which go beyond those associated with the relative bargaining power of the two parties to the wage contract.

Marx considers the influence of accumulation on wages under two different assumptions. First he considers accumulation with a given technology and fixed labor productivity. He then takes up the problem of wage determination once "the development of the productivity of social labor becomes the most powerful lever of accumulation" [*Capital*, Vol. I, p. 621].

If we assume unchanging productivity and analyze the impact of accumulation on wages under the previously discussed assumptions with regard to money and price determination, we arrive at a long-run version of the analysis of wage determination presented in the previous section. The only modification which economic growth on the basis of given technology introduces into that analysis has to do with its impact on the demand for labor. The analysis of this impact fixes an important part of the context within which the wage bargain takes place.

For Marx employment depends upon the amount of capital, unit labor requirements, and the ratio of capital to output (k) both of the latter assumed to be technically given:

$$L = \frac{K}{\dfrac{K}{L}} = \frac{K}{\dfrac{K}{Y} \cdot \dfrac{Y}{L}} = \frac{nK}{k},$$

where K equals the value of the capital stock. Capital intensity (k) is measured at an assumed "normal" level of utilization. The proportional rate of change of employment, in this case its rate of growth (γ), equals the sum of the rate of accumulation ($\alpha = \dot{K}/K$) and the difference between the rates of change of unit labor requirements and capital intensity:

$$\gamma = \alpha + \left(\frac{\dot{n}}{n} - \frac{\dot{k}}{k}\right) \tag{3.2}$$

where the ($\cdot$) indicates a rate of change with respect to time. Thus, when the productivity of labor and technical specification of the production process are given

$$\frac{\dot{n}}{n} = \frac{\dot{k}}{k} = o,$$

and employment grows at the same rate as the capital stock ($\gamma = \alpha$). "Accumulation of capital is, therefore, increase of the proletariat" [*Capital*, Vol. I, p. 614].

For Marx this implies that growth in the demand for labor due to capital accumulation leads to a "rise in the price of labor" [*Capital*, Vol. I, p. 618]. Given his own analysis of the wage bargain, this conclusion only follows if the demand for labor increases more rapidly than the supply; but Marx nowhere specifies the determinants of the supply of labor.[3] Since Marx only analyzes half of the relevant conditions in the labor market, he leaves us to infer the other half from the conclusions he draws.

One inference that gains support from his subsequent analysis of the "reserve army of the unemployed" is that he tends to think of the supply of labor as coming out of a pool so that it is determined by a stock rather than a flow. This pool may include unemployed or semiemployed workers and workers employed outside of the capitalist sector. The latter classification includes what classical economics termed "unproductive" labor.

Adam Smith identified the process of capital accumulation with the transformation of unproductive into productive labor. By this he had in mind the movement of labor out of noncapitalistic employment (petty producers, peasants, servants, etc.) and into the capitalistic, or wage labor, sectors of the economy. The growth of society's capital stock feeds on the existing stock of unproductive workers shifting them into the capitalist sector and increasing the proportion of labor "productively" employed.

Smith interprets the supply of labor as a fixed quantity, a stock (or pool), and the demand for labor as a growing quantity. Marx's use of this method causes difficulties throughout his theory since we cannot make a stock of labor do the analytical work required to fully specify the dynamic relationship between demand and supply over time. Prior to the depletion of the pool of unemployed and unproductive labor, the excess supply of labor should not only prevent its price from rising but tend to push it down. Yet, both Smith and Marx draw the conclusion that capital accumulation works to the advantage of labor by placing upward pressure on the wage so that for workers, "the circle of their enjoyments" expands [*Capital*, Vol. I. p. 618].

Marx assumes that at some point in the growth process the accumulation of capital depletes the pool of available labor to the point where the bargaining position of labor allows it to demand a higher wage. At this point, the wage acts as an adjustment mechanism [Marglin, 1984, pp. 63–66]: ". . . accumulation slackens in consequence of the rise in the price of labor, because the stimulus to gain is blunted" [*Capital*, Vol. I, p. 619]. Marx does not clearly indicate what he means by the "stimulus to gain" but we can assume, consistent with the other parts of his analysis, that he has the expected rate of return on new capital in mind. Marx generally treats the current rate of profit as the primary guide to future rates of return, and this would certainly be the case under conditions of unchanging productivity and full capacity. Under these conditions current and expected profitability depend upon the real wage. As the real wage rises, the expected rate of return falls. As a result of this, "[T]he rate of accumulation lessens; but with its lessening, the primary cause of that lessening vanishes, i.e., the disproportion between capital and exploitable labor-power" [*Capital*, Vol. I, p. 619].

At this point, the treatment of labor supply as a fixed stock clearly breaks down since, given the depletion of the stock, the disproportion between capital (demand for labor) and supply of labor can only disappear if capital accumulation ceases. The wage can only settle at a determinate level with positive accumulation if the supply of labor grows at a rate equal to the rate of growth of demand. But, insofar as we treat the wage as a theoretically determinate magnitude, this forces us to conclude that the rate of growth of labor supply determines the rate of accumulation, which then determines an appropriate level of real wages. Marx argues that, as a result of the decrease in the rate of capital accumulation due to a fall in the stimulus to gain, "[T]he price of labor falls again to a level corresponding with the needs of the self-expansion of capital, whether the level be below, the same as, or above the one which was normal before the rise in wages took place" [*Capital*, Vol. I, p. 619].

As Josef Steindl points out [1952, p. 231], this means that the wage is determined by an independently given long-term rate of accumulation. By so doing, Marx in effect gives up the ideas of subsistence and the value of labor-power and makes the determination of income distribution a part of the theory of output, pricing, and investment.

While Marx does not explicitly recognize the fact that this argument requires him to give up his theory of wages *and* to make distribution and growth determined by the (undetermined) rate of expansion of labor supply, it is nonetheless the case. Formally, let r represent the rate of profit (s/K), then it follows from equation (3.1) that

$$r = \frac{e}{(K/vL)} = \frac{env}{k}. \tag{3.3}$$

On the assumption that the rate of accumulation bears a fixed proportion (b) to the rate of profit — aside from a fixed margin for capitalist's consumption, profits are automatically invested in new capital equipment — then

$$\alpha = br.$$

For equilibrium, the rate of growth of capital must equal that of the labor supply (η):

$$\alpha = \eta,$$

from which it follows that

$$ev = \frac{\eta k}{bn}.$$

Combining this last expression with equation (3.1) allows us to express the value of labor-power as a function of the parameters of the model:

$$v = \frac{b - \eta k}{bn}. \tag{3.4}$$

Expression (3.4) allows the following interpretation: The real wage tends to a level which, given the proportion of profit consumed and the technical conditions, yields profit at a rate just sufficient to finance expansion of capital at the rate η.

The conclusion that the rate of growth of labor supply determines capital accumulation accords very poorly with Marx's overall approach to the problem. Marx places the accumulation process at the center of his analysis and requires subordination of the natural environment to the requirements of capitalist expansion. We can begin to retrieve the spirit of Marx's method only by giving up either the assumption that labor productivity is given, or the assumption that the wage adjusts with demand for and supply of labor. In the second part of his analysis of the impact of accumulation on the condition of the working class, Marx relaxes the first of these assumptions.

In order to analyze accumulation with technical change, Marx introduces a special interpretation of the productivity of labor. Apart from natural conditions "the degree of productivity of labor, in a given society, is expressed in the relative extent of the means of production that one laborer, during a given time, with the same tension of labor-power, turns into products" [p. 622]. Thus Marx defines the productivity of labor as the ratio of capital to labor rather than the ratio of output to labor. He does so because of a prior assumption that in order to increase output per worker each worker must be provided with more capital. This assumption arises, in turn, out of a special conception of technical change.

Marx employs a peculiarly classical notion of technical change and productivity growth. The archetype for this conception appears in Adam Smith's analysis of the division of labor [1937, ch. 1]. Smith focuses his attention on the way in which a change in the organization of the production process leads to an increase in the productivity of labor. For Smith, the technical specification of the production process involves its division into a series of discrete "tasks," each of which brings about a change in the material inputs and all of which taken together lead to the transformation of those inputs into a given product. Smith argues that productivity will rise when, rather than having a single worker perform each of the needed tasks in sequence, several workers divide up the tasks among themselves specializing in one part of the overall process. When this happens, each worker becomes more adept at his assigned labor, and output of the final product increases for any given amount of labor. Under this form of technical change, the nature of the product and the structure of its production process (its division into tasks) remain the same while productivity increases.

Marx takes the logic of this process a step further (already suggested by Smith) by considering the introduction of machinery. Again, the structure of the process (its division into tasks) and the product remain the same. Instead, however, of all the tasks being done by labor, some are now done by machines. The more tasks done by machines, the fewer left for labor, the more productive the remaining labor, regarding both output and capital per worker.

When productivity rises through an increase in capital intensity, it alters the relation between capital accumulation and the demand for labor. Indeed, Marx goes so far as to argue that it reverses that relation. The specific argument intended by Marx is somewhat uncertain on this point. First he states that "[S]ince the demand for labor is determined not by the amount of capital as a whole, but by its variable constituent alone (the wages bill), that demand falls progressively with the increase of the total capital, instead of, as previously assumed, rising in proportion to it" [*Capital*, Vol. I, p. 629]. The growth of demand depends upon the accumulation of capital. If capital intensity rises $\left(\dfrac{\dot{k}}{k} > o\right)$ and unit labor requirements fall $\left(\dfrac{\dot{n}}{n} < o\right)$, the rate of growth of the demand for labor will fall short of the rate of accumulation. This need not imply, however, that the demand for labor will diminish.

Further on in the same paragraph Marx comes somewhat closer to the correct statment when he claims that "[W]ith the growth of the total capital, its variable constituent or the labor incorporated in it, also does increase, but in a constantly diminishing proportion." This second statement allows for continuing growth in demand for labor but in a "diminishing proportion" (presumably to the amount of capital).

Depending upon the rate of growth of labor supply, if the growth in capital intensity is rapid enough, it can offset the positive effect of accumulation on employment sufficiently to create what Marx calls the "industrial reserve army." The process of capital accumulation "constantly produces, and produces in direct ratio of its own energy and extent, a relatively redundant population of laborers, i.e., a population of greater extent than suffices for the average needs of the self-expansion of capital, and therefore a surplus population" [p. 630].

This analysis allows Marx to place the wage bargain into a determinate context. If Marx is correct, it follows that the process of economic growth assures that the supply of labor will grow more rapidly than demand regardless of the rate of population growth or other determinants of what we usually think of as the "natural" rate of growth of labor supply. This leads Marx to his permanent excess supply of labor theory of wage determination which, because it takes pride of place within Marxian theory, we quote at length:

> The greater the social wealth, the functioning capital, the extent and energy of its growth, and, therefore, also the absolute mass of the proletariat and the productiveness of its labor, the greater is the industrial reserve army. The same causes which develop the expansive power of capital, develop also the labor-power at its disposal. The relative mass of the industrial reserve army increases therefore with the potential energy of wealth. But the greater this reserve army

in proportion to the active labor army, the greater is the mass of a consolidated surplus-population, whose misery is in inverse ratio to its torment of labor. The more extensive, finally, the lazarus layers of the working class, and the industrial reserve army, the greater is official pauperism. *This is the absolute general law of capitalist accumulation.* . . . Accumulation of wealth at one pole is, therefore, at the same time accumulation of misery, agony of toil, slavery, ignorance, brutality, mental degradation, at the opposite pole, i.e., on the side of the class that produces its own product in the form of capital [pp. 644–645 italics in original].

Marx employs the "General Law of Capitalist Accumulation" to solve a problem solved by the Malthusian population theory in pre-Marxian classical political economy. In order to establish the reality of the subsistence wage the classical theory argues that pressure from excess labor supply will press the wage down to its minimum level. The permanent excess supply theory of the labor market combined with the idea of a minimum below which the real wage cannot fall for any period of time resolves the problem of the distribution of the net product between capital and labor.

The Marxian solution constitutes a genuine subsistence wage notion of our first type since it claims to establish that the real wage, in the last analysis, must settle at a level predetermined by the costs of producing labor assuming that we can equate those costs with the "minimum" of the wage referred to above. Contrary to Garegnani, this claims much more than simply that the wage is determined by conditions distinct from those affecting the total product and the other shares in it. Garegnani's more general interpretation remains, however, safer ground for the classical approach since it need not depend upon the validity of the permanent excess supply theory. As we have seen, that theory rests on special assumptions concerning the relationship between the rate of increase in productivity, the rate of change of capital intensity, and the rate of capital accumulation. Marx's argument for this relationship is suspect at best.

Only on the basis of Marx's special definition of productivity and special construction of the process of technical change does it follow that an increase in productivity requires an increase in capital intensity. If we drop the special construction, we cannot assume that capital intensity will rise with accumulation and offset the favorable implications of accumulation for the demand for labor. Even when capital intensity increases, it does not imply that it will grow rapidly enough to sufficiently offset the favorable effects of accumulation so as to assure the creation and expansion of the reserve army of the unemployed. If we cannot assure this, then we cannot assume that downward pressure will force the wage to its minimum level. This leaves us without a theory of wages and throws us back to the analysis of the wage bargain in isolation from a determinate context. If, taken as a whole, "the general movements of wages are exclusively regulated by the expansion and contraction of the reserve army, and these correspond to the periodic changes of the industrial cycle," [p. 637] does this mean that wages vary with contingent historical circumstance?

Again, we encounter two distinct theories embedded in the Marxian analysis. One provides nothing more than a mechanism for making the wage responsive to conflict in the labor market and assures an outcome sensitive to the relative bargaining power of the contending parties. The other seeks to place the wage bargain into a determinate context so that its outcome does not, in the long run, depend upon bargaining power. The second theory appears in two versions. The first resolves the problem of distribution by fixing the value of labor-power independently of output, pricing, and investment. The second reverses the determination implied by the first, and fixes wages according to the demands of ongoing accumulation of capital. Before continuing our evaluation of these contending elements of the Marxian theory, we will consider some implications for the rate of profit.

The Rate of Profit

Under the conditions assumed by the General Law of Capitalist Accumulation, profit appears as a residual fully determined once we know the real wage (minimum or subsistence level) and the productivity of labor as expressed by n and k. So much is clear from equation (3.3) which, combined with equation (3.1) implies:

$$r = \frac{1 - vn}{k} \tag{3.5}$$

The rate of profit in equation (3.5) refers to a condition of equilibrium in which prices are at levels appropriate, given the money wage, to provide all workers with the value of their labor-power and all producers with a uniform rate of return on capital invested. In this sense, only one rate of profit exists, and it applies equally to the economy taken as a whole and to all particular units of capital [see Mainwaring, 1984, p. 36].

As we have seen, Marx assumes that capital intensity rises with the development of technology attendant upon capital accumulation. This leads him to conclude that "...the gradual growth of constant capital in relation to variable capital must necessarily lead to a *gradual fall of the general rate of profit*, so long as the rate of surplus-value...remains the same" [*Capital*, Vol. III, p. 212; italics in original]. For our purposes we will assume that the rate of surplus-value is adequately expressed by the ratio of profits to wages (*e*). Marx's conclusion plays a prominent role in his analysis of the historical limits of capitalist expansion. Since profit fuels the accumulation of capital and the rate of profit directly determines the rate of accumulation, the fall in the rate of profit must slow the accumulation process. Furthermore, since the cause of the fall in the profit rate is the growth in productivity resulting from accumulation, we can say that capital accumulation erodes its own foundation. Thus, Marx concludes that "[T]he *real barrier* of capitalist production is *capital itself* " and that the "capitalist mode of production is, for this reason, a historical means of developing the material forces of production and creating an appropriate world market and is, at the same time, a continual conflict between this its historical mission and its own corresponding relations of social production" [*Capital*, Vol. III, p. 250; italics in original].

This follows only as long as capital accumulation proceeds on the basis of a given real wage, given unit labor requirements, and rising capital intensity; in other words, as long as technological change affects capital intensity but not output per worker. Such an assumption seems hardly plausible and in any case contradicts Marx's own analysis of technical change, especially in Volume I of *Capital*. For purposes of his analysis of the rate of profit, Marx tends to assume that the value of labor-power remains constant in the face of falling unit labor costs and rising capital intensity. This would imply a fall in the rate of profit due as much to an increase in the real wage as a rise in capital intensity. These difficulties lead even sympathetic students of Marx to abandon his theory of the long-run determinants of the rate of profit [Sweezy, 1956; Robinson, 1942].

Marx does not provide an analysis of price determination which would support the conclusion that the real wage rises in proportion to the fall in unit labor requirements so that any rise in unit capital requirements leads to a fall in the rate of profit. Such an analysis would require the profit margin to act as a fixed point which determined appropriate levels for the real wage, rate of profit, and rate of accumulation given the technical conditions of production [see Kalecki, 1965]. While an analysis of this sort might apply under particular historical circumstances [see Levine, 1975] it cannot do the work required by Marx of his profit theory: to show how the real barrier to capital is capital itself.

A reconstruction of the theory of distribution which treats the profit margin as the independent variable makes the real wage depend upon productivity and thus cannot reasonably be reconciled with the idea of a subsistence wage, value of labor-power, or cost of production of labor. It does not allow us to separate out the determinants of the real wage and treat them independently as Garegnani rightly suggests we need to do in a properly classical analysis; although it would allow us to treat the wage share as independent (given capacity utilization), thus capturing a significant element of the classical theory emphasized by Garegnani.

In certain respects, Marx's theory leaves us with a contradiction. On one side, it claims that the idea of a minimum wage enforced by the conditions which govern the wage bargain plays a central role in determining income distribution in capitalist economies. On the other side, it attempts to show that, consistent with this, the accumulation process leads to a fall in the rate of profit which marks ultimately the historical limits of capitalist accumulation. This contradiction expresses the presence of a number of conflicting theories of income distribution in Marx's work:

1. The cost of production theory supported by the permanent excess supply theory of the labor market. This theory treats the real wage as a minimum wage, profits as a residual and accumulation as the *result* of distribution.

2. The wage bargain theory. This theory treats the real wage as a direct result of the bargain over the money wage and assumes that the results of the bargain over the money wage depend upon the particular circumstances of the wage bargain ("expansion and contraction of the industrial reserve army" corresponding to "the periodic changes of the industrial cycle").

3. The profit margin or relative shares theory. This theory treats the value of labor-power as an independently determined variable to which the profit rate, real wage, and rate of accumulation must adjust.

4. The rate of capital accumulation theory. This theory treats the accumulation of capital as the "independent variable" and the wage as the "dependent variable" [*Capital*, Vol. I, p. 620]. Distribution must accommodate the needs of accumulation. This theory, while in many ways the most interesting, is the least well developed by Marx. It is arguably the most consistent of the four with Marx's notion of capital as the organizing process of a modern market economy [see Levine, 1978, pp. 115–124], but it is also the least consistent with the idea that the relation between capital and labor (especially profits and wages) determines the accumulation of capital.

All of these theories except the fourth adopt an income distribution approach to the theory of accumulation. That is, each treats the determinants of the distribution of income between profits and wages as logically prior to the determination of capital accumulation. Such an approach is arguably central to Marx's method (but see Steindl [1952, ch. XIV]).

The first three theories establish the independence of distribution in either of two ways: (1) they allow the wage bargain to directly determine real wages because it is a bargain in terms of real wages; and (2) they simply take the value of labor-power to be given. Neither of these two assumptions proves altogether satisfactory. The first requires a set of assumptions concerning money and prices which are difficult to reconcile with the nature of a monetary economy and with forms of industrial organization characteristic of modern economies. The second remains too formal to provide the real basis for the theory of distribution; it, in effect, negates the theoretical issues by making distribution a parameter. In the next section, we consider a modern reformulation of the Marxian theory which analyzes the determination of wages without the classical assumptions regarding prices and the monetary unit.

The Inflation Barrier

The primary modification introduced by modern analysis of the process of wage determination along broadly Marxian lines has to do with price determination. Recall that Marx assumes market prices determined by supply and demand and production prices determined by technology and distribution. He therefore does not take into account the pricing policy of firms operating under conditions within which they exercise decision-making responsibility. This, together with his assumptions concerning the monetary unit, allows him to conclude that the wage bargain directly determines the real wage and thus the distribution of income between wages and profits. Modern analysis attempts to retrieve the idea that the wage bargain plays a primary role in determining the wage share without Marx's special assumptions regarding wages and prices. The specific approach stems from the idea of an "inflation barrier" first introduced by Robinson [1956] and recently given a more systematic formulation by Rowthorn [1980].

The analysis of distribution on the basis of the inflation barrier maintains Marx's assumption of given productivity, but drops the assumption that the rate of exchange between money and commodities depends upon their respective "values" and makes the purchasing power of money vary with independently determined variations in the prices of commodities.

Prices, given the elements of prime cost other than labor, depend in turn primarily upon two factors: the money wage rate and planned levels of investment on the part of firms.

Assume that firms establish profit margins on the basis of their plans for investment and the need for internal funds implied by those plans [Eichner, 1976]. This means that, in the aggregate, firms follow a pricing policy intended to provide them with what Rowthorn terms a "target share" of income [1980, p. 150]. This pricing policy must include some assumption concerning money wages. On their side, workers enter into a wage contract effective simultaneously for their entire group (continuing the classical assumption of a uniform wage) with the intent of achieving gains in their real wages, and, given productivity, in their share of income. Just as the plans of firms when they set prices depend upon assumptions regarding money wages, plans of workers when they enter into money wage contracts depend upon assumptions regarding prices. These assumptions depend upon the ability of each party to anticipate changes in the larger context in response to their actions.

Any plans involving an increase in the share of one of the parties must imply a reduced share for the other and/or an increase in prices. Assume that firms raise prices in order to increase their rates of investment. They can do so under appropriate market conditions, i.e., where demand for their products is strong and utilization of capacity high. Workers can only prevent a reduction in the wage share by demanding and receiving a higher money wage. If conditions in the labor market — especially demand conditions — encourage this outcome, the success on the part of workers frustrates the plans of firms to increase investment and requires that they either give up their plans or raise prices once again. As long as workers maintain pressure on money wages adequate to frustrate the efforts of firms to increase profit margins, they have in effect established a minimum real wage and wage share by translating downward pressure on money wages into upward pressure on prices.

Under conditions of robust demand and near full employment, the inflationary spiral provides a dynamic determination of adjustments in relative share according to the respective rates at which the two parties adjust to wage and price changes. These rates of adjustment depend on various factors including: structural determinants such as the length of wage contracts and the relative ease or difficulty associated with changes in prices, more or less favorable demand conditions in product and labor markets, and ability of the parties to anticipate responses to wage demands or price adjustments.

Like Marx's wage bargain analysis, the analysis of the inflationary process deals with a mechanism for fixing income distribution, but does not explicitly consider the determinants of the context that govern how (and whether) that mechanism works. Because of this, given the assumption of unchanging productivity, the analysis of the inflationary process parallels Marx's own treatment of the labor market and leads to similar conclusions. When productivity does not change, distribution depends upon those institutional or historical factors that determine the relative bargaining position of workers and capitalist (or firms). When productivity increases, this conclusion need not hold. As we have seen, Marx attempts to argue that technological change leads to a permanent excess supply of labor which presses the wage down. This makes the real determinant of wages the minimum sustainable level rather than the bargaining process which only acts as a mechanism for enforcing that minimum. How does productivity growth alter the consequences of the inflation barrier analysis? The outcome, in this case, will depend upon the extent to which the opposing parties anticipate changes in productivity, and especially on the extent to which workers anticipate productivity gains in the formulation of their wage demands.

An increase in productivity makes it possible for real wages to increase without pushing up the wage share (as measured by e). Indeed, rapid enough technical change can allow real wages to increase while the wage share falls. If the value received by the worker in exchange for his labor (v) falls, the real wage can rise as long as productivity increases more rapidly. When workers fail to anticipate productivity changes in forming their wage demands, firms have the opportunity to establish profit margins according to investment plans while acceding (at least up to a point) to the money wage demands of workers without risk of inflationary problems. Firms find themselves limited in their response to money wage pressure by conditions of demand when they assume that demand for their products is price elastic. As long as growing productivity allows them to finance investment at planned rates without an increase in their share of national income, acceding to money wage demands without a proportional increase in prices increases real wages without impeding capital accumulation or undermining demand for products. When workers do not anticipate changes in productivity, distribution tends to follow the rate of accumulation that depends upon investment plans.

When workers anticipate productivity gains, this conclusion no longer holds. In this case the margin provided to firms by productivity growth to determine investment independently of relative shares is eliminated and the rate of accumulation possible for firms depends upon the way in which the wage bargain distributes the benefits of technical progress. In other words, when the distribution of the benefits of productivity growth become an explicit object of the wage bargain, the wage bargain becomes the primary determinant of relative shares even under conditions of technological change.

The analysis of the inflation barrier establishes price adjustment as a mechanism for mediating conflict over the distribution of income where productivity does not change or where the contending parties take changes in productivity into account in formulating their demands. When a capitalist economy operates near full capacity and under conditions of labor scarcity, the price mechanism bears the burden of mediating conflict over shares, and the outcome depends upon specific circumstances (e.g., institutional and historical) which determine the relative ability of the contending parties to respond to erosion or prospective erosion of their shares. To this extent, the inflation barrier analysis continues the central theme identified by Garegnani which we have termed the income distribution approach.

It also allows for a reinterpretation of the subsistence notion along the following lines: Assume that the term subsistence refers to a "normal" level of remuneration based upon prevailing standards of living under given historical circumstances. This is consistent with the idea that the subsistence includes "a historical and moral element" [*Capital*, Vol. I, p. 171]. Workers establish ways of life consistent with their real incomes. The longer their experience of these ways of life, the more they establish themselves as normal and even necessary [see Levine, 1981, pp. 137–145]. Workers enforce the necessity of the associated wage bundle through the mechanism of the wage bargain and possibly the inflation barrier. The implied "subsistence" moves to a higher level when either productivity growth allows increases in real wages consistent with planned rates of investment and the implied profit margins of firms or conditions in product markets weaken the bargaining positions of firms. The inflation barrier limits capital accumulation to rates consistent with the established real wage while the rate of change in the real wage depends upon the ability of firms to execute their plans for growth and innovation. Thus the level of the real wage depends upon bargaining power, whereas changes in that level depend upon capital accumulation and productivity growth.

When productivity improves steadily and the implied gains are not made part of the conditions of the wage bargain, the wage bargain can fix the real wage while simultaneously allowing the wage share and changes in the real wage to depend upon capital accumulation. We can, in this way, reconcile the income distribution approach with Marx's notion that the wage must be at that level "corresponding with the needs of the self-expansion of capital."

It is productivity growth that allows the capitalist economy to subordinate income distribution to the requirements of accumulation without running up against the barrier implied by a minimum real wage. Given capacity utilization, in the absence of sufficiently rapid technological change, contingent conditions of the wage bargain subordinate investment decisions and directly limit the feasible rate of economic growth. The wage bargain determines the wage share; what remains as profit determines the rate of economic growth. This makes profit, or surplus-value, the residual. Once the "development of the productivity of social labor becomes the most powerful lever of accumulation," the wage bargain need no longer determine relative shares. Adjustments of profit margins in accordance with investment plans determine the wage share given the money wage. A robust capitalist economy, confident in the execution of its historical mission, can thus reverse the relation of wages to accumulation and treat the wage as the residual. Viewed from a standpoint outside of this process, we might reasonably conclude that to increase this residual "is precisely the purpose of the whole production process" [Pasinetti, 1981, p. 144], but for the process itself the growth in wages only takes on importance insofar as its effect on demand facilitates the accumulation of capital [see Levine, 1981, pp. 215–233].

The treatment of the wage as a residual works well as long as productivity improves steadily *and* workers do not anticipate productivity growth when formulating their wage demands. Maturation of capitalist economy undermines both of these conditions. When workers treat the benefits of productivity growth as a normal object of the wage bargain, the wage bargain once again asserts itself as a real determinant of the feasible pace of economic growth.

Concluding Remarks

The larger the role played by the wage bargain in determining relative shares, the narrower the scope for the theoretical treatment of distribution. To the extent that distribution depends upon the circumstances of the wage contract, the determinants of distribution must be contextual so that only by limiting the influence of the wage bargain can a systematic determination be introduced.

As we have seen, Marx pursues the problem in two directions. The first emphasizes the wage bargain and its specific historical context. The second emphasizes the "needs of the self-expansion of capital" and therefore the logical implications of economic growth for income distribution and price determination. The idea that income distribution results from a struggle between opposed classes has firm roots in Marx's theory, but so also does the idea that the outcome of that struggle, while depending immediately on the relative power of the combatants, depends ultimately on the requirements of capital accumulation over the long run.

Marx appeals to the accumulation of capital as a process capable of pinning down the distribution of income. This foreshadows the more systematic analysis in neo-Keynesian theory which argues that the level of wages must be appropriate, given technology, to yield profit adequate to finance accumulation at an independently determined rate. Insofar as the rate of accumulation depends upon factors other than the prior determination of distributive shares, that rate replaces the bargaining power of the parties in determining profits and wages. Of course, for this to happen, the outcome of the wage bargain must determine something other than the wage share which requires that the money wage rate fail to govern real wages. The ability of producers to shift prices in response to changes in money wages assures that the determination of the money wage does not determine the wage share and leaves the determination of that share open to factors connected to investment. Thus, the scope of the theoretical treatment of income distribution depends upon the relationship between wages, prices, and investment, especially the direction of determination between them.

As we saw in the previous section, this direction of determination depends upon circumstances linked to the level of development and degree of maturation of the economy including the rate of productivity growth, the organization of product markets, and the extent to which productivity gains become an explicit part of the wage bargain. The extent to which income distribution depends upon the wage bargain depends upon the level of economic development. Roughly speaking, our investigation of Marx's theory suggests three stages of development which define the role of the wage bargain differently.

In the first stage, the low level of development of product markets results in significant dependence of price on supply and demand. The less the ability of firms to set prices in relation to costs, the less responsive prices will be to money wages. The less the responsiveness of prices to money wages, the greater the impact of the wage bargain on the real wage and the wage share. Marx reconciles these circumstances with the accumulation of capital by introducing his permanent excess supply theory of the labor market. Permanent excess supply of labor gains support from, and helps to assure, a low level of development of labor organization and of the labor market. Weak productivity growth implies that capital accumulation presupposes a low level of the real wage.

In the second stage, the organization of product markets allows for a significant degree of "passing along" of cost increases into prices. This prevents the wage bargain from directly determining the wage share, which depends upon profit margins determined by the needs of capital's self-expansion. This is the stage dominated by capital accumulation. Such domination depends upon specific attributes of product and labor markets. Rapid accumulation with technological change makes a steady increase in real wages consistent with profit margins adequate to investment needs. The wage bargain assures that the real wage at a point in time establishes itself as an objective fact and effective minimum and thus as one of the objective structural conditions of the growth process.

In the final stage, the anticipation of productivity gains and price effects of the wage bargain allow the wage bargain to reassert itself as a primary determinant of distribution. Such anticipation assumes well-organized labor markets and an orientation of workers toward the market which goes beyond immediate money wage demands. Because of this, and insofar as these circumstances tend to emerge in mature economies exhibiting weak productivity growth, the third stage tends to make capital accumulation problematic. At this point, we no longer require an economic theory of distribution since circumstances force us to approach the problem of how society disposes of its wealth on a different basis.

Marx leads us to this conclusion in the course of his discussion of the historical limits of capitalist accumulation. Our third stage is one in which the orientation of the parties to the wage bargain takes them beyond their immediate, narrow concerns and leads them to place the wage bargain into a broader context subsuming what were previously prerogatives of property owners, especially firms. To this extent, the wage bargain takes on attributes of a conscious determination of the basic conditions of investment, distribution, and price determination.

Our third stage arises as the agent takes on an awareness of the broader system of relations that determines him, and acts in a way inconsistent with his subjection to anonymous economic laws whose effects he experiences, but which he neither directly perceives nor understands. This development disrupts the organization of the economy on the basis of the idea of individuality found within the framework of the self-ordering market. Marx terms the subjective aspect (or self-understanding) of the individual within this framework "the illusion about competition as the so-called absolute form of free individuality." He goes on to assert that when this illusion vanishes, "this is evidence that the conditions of competition, i.e. of production founded on capital, are already felt and thought of as *barriers*, and hence already *are* such, and more and more become such" [*Grundrisse*, p. 652].

For Marx, the end of the illusion about competition presumes the "unconditional development of the productive forces of society" [*Capital*, Vol. III, p. 250] accomplished during our second stage. "Further development appears as decay," however, once the agent grasps "his own history as a *process*." Thus, as Marx suggests, it is the change in the orientation of the agent to his own history which leads to our third stage. This new awareness leads naturally according to Marx, to "socialized man, the associated producers, rationally regulating their interchange with nature" [*Capital*, Vol. III, p. 820]. Whether Marx is correct in this remains to be seen. An important part of the issue involves the way in which income distribution is determined. While the wage bargain hardly constitutes "rational regulation," it does constitute an arena within which decisions are taken with regard to the disposition of social wealth. When the needs of accumulation determine the distribution of income, the disposition of social wealth depends upon objective and anonymous laws of economic development. To this extent, the greater the role played by the wage bargain and the broader its effects across groups of firms and workers, the greater the potential for rational regulation in economic affairs.

What the inflation barrier analysis suggests is that this potential comes into conflict with the principle of private accumulation as the regulator of the market. This conflict engenders instability rather than rational regulation since the wage bargain encompasses both a degree of rational regulation and the conflict of opposed private interests. This makes both rational regulation and the achievement of private interests difficult. The resulting instability suggests structural problems in the organization of economic affairs. Explicit consideration of these structural problems should be the next step in the theory of income distribution.

Notes

1. An option more in keeping with the classical project involves specification of a composite commodity capable of measuring the net product independently of distribution [see Sraffa, 1960, chs. IV and V].

2. Marx also assumes that the wage bargain does not affect the "value of money wherein the values of products are estimated" [Marx, 1933]. By value of money, Marx has in mind its labor cost. Since this implies that money is a produced commodity whose purchasing

power depends upon its cost of production, it obviates the need for an analysis of the money wage and price adjustment process.

3. Marx does present some general comments on the supply of labor in chapter 30 of *Capital*, Volume I, but does not attempt to develop a specific conception appropriate to the theoretical determination of wages.

References

Eichner, A. (1976). *The Megacorp and Oligopoly*. Cambridge: Cambridge University Press.

Garegnani, P. (1984). Value and distribution in the classical economists and Marx. *Oxford Economic Papers* 36 (June): 2.

Kalecki, M. (1965). *The Theory of Economic Dynamics*. London: George Allen and Unwin.

Levine, D. (1973). *Accumulation and Technical Change in Marxian Economics*. Ph.D. dissertation, Yale University.

──────. (1975). The theory of the growth of the capitalist economy. *Economic Development and Cultural Change* 24 (October): 1.

──────. (1978 and 1981). *Economic Theory*, Two vols. London: Routledge & Kegan Paul.

Mainwaring, L. (1984). *Value and Distribution in Capitalist Economies*. Cambridge: Cambridge University Press.

Marglin, L. (1984). *Growth, Distribution, and Prices*. Cambridge, MA: Harvard University Press.

Marx, K. (1933). *Value, Price and Profit*. New York: International Publishers.

──────. (1967). *Capital*, three vols. New York: International Publishers.

──────. (1973). *Grundrisse*. Harmondsworth: Penguin Books.

Pasinetti, L. (1981). *Structural Change and Economic Growth*. Cambridge: Cambridge University Press.

Robinson, J. (1942). *An Essay on Marxian Economics*. New York: St. Martin's.

──────. (1956). *The Accumulation of Capital*. New York: St. Martin's.

Rowthorn, R. (1980). Conflict, inflation and money. In R. Rowthorn, *Capitalism, Conflict and Inflation*. London: Lawrence and Wishart.

Smith, A. (1937). *The Wealth of Nations*. New York: Modern Library.

Sraffa, P. (1960). *The Production of Commodities by Means of Commodities*. Cambridge: Cambridge University Press.

Steedman, I. (1977). *Marx After Sraffa*. London: New Left Books.

Steindl, J. (1952). *Maturity and Stagnation in American Capitalism*. Oxford: Blackwell.

Sweezy, P. (1956). *The Theory of Capitalist Development*. New York: Monthly Review Press.

4 DISTRIBUTION: NEO-CLASSICAL
Allan J. Braff

The Marginalists

The marginalist writings of Jevons [1871], Walras [1874], and Menger [1871], early in the decade of the 1870s, represent the beginnings of the neo-classical paradigmatic shift from the classical orthodoxy of Smith, Ricardo, Mill, Marx, and others, whose work represents the thesis to which the triumvirate who compose the "marginal revolution" of the 1870s (Jevons, Walras, and Menger) posed their antithesis.

The new focus on the marginal was perfectly adapted to the mathematical method of the calculus with its derivatives, its maximizing or minimizing subject to constraints. Marginal utility, Jevons' "final degree of utility," became the new source of value with primary focus on the subjective desires of individuals seeking to maximize satisfaction. This reversed the classical order of causation which placed the source of value in labor time and the conditions of production.

I am much indebted to A. Asimakopulos for his comments and suggestions on early drafts of this chapter.

The individual's subjective choice displaced the classical concern with socioeconomic classes with their exclusive ownership of land, labor, and capital; with conflicts over distributive shares, involving capitalists and landowners, and then later laborers and capitalists. Any individual in neo-classical theory could own or sell any type of factor input. The classical economists tried to discover natural laws governing change in distributive income shares as population grew and income accumulated. Surplus to landowner or to capitalist was to the classicist, the result of privilege, ownership, and exploitation. The neo-classicists shifted the main concern from distributive shares to the allocation of scarce resources, and to the linking of input rewards to productive contributions.

W.S. Jevons [1871] breaks with classical theory in developing a theory of value based on the subjective notions of utility, but he does not take the second necessary step into the neo-classicists' world. This second step is the linking of distributive shares to subjective value, George Stigler writes:

> It is apparent that Jevons does not depart far from the classical theory [of distribution]. His conception of capital and its rate (of interest) is basically the same as that incorporated in the wages-fund doctrine. The fundamental difference, in fact, is that the classical theory assumes a fixed period of production (one year), and, therefore, resorts to the notion of a subsistence wage in order to divide the produce-less-rent between labor and capital. Jevons merely adds one further element, the variability of the production period, to provide a determinant [increase in value through time without any additional expenditure] of the rate of interest [Stigler, 1941, p. 29].

Wesley Mitchell notes that Jevons, in his preface to the *Theory of Political Economy* [1871], provides a hint that distribution is entirely subject to the principles of value, but "Jevons did not succeed in working out that hint" [Mitchell, 1949, p. 42]. While writing in the older classical tradition on distributive shares where distribution is not derived from value in exchange, Jevons begins the breaking away. Stigler concludes that "Jevons' theories of distribution contribute little to the solution of the problem of distribution, although they contain germs of some important later developments. Rent theory is improved by the implicit inclusion of "fixed" capital; interest theory receives a partial explanation in terms of marginal productivity; wages remain a residual" [1941, p. 35]. After Jevons, diminishing marginal utility applies to all commodities, and maximizing utility becomes the primary economic objective.

In their early work the marginalists emphasized the one-way order of causation from marginal utility to factor price. In Walras' later revisions of his general equilibrium framework, in Marshall's partial equilibrium, and in Wicksell's three-sector analysis, value is the result of the balancing of subjective marginal disutilities (supply) against marginal utilities (demand). When the assumption of given factor supply is relaxed, a theory of factor pricing becomes a theory of factor demand. The prices of the factors of production constitute the costs of production of the producing firm. In spite of an awareness of the influence of supply, the dominance of marginal utility prevails; the primary objective remains utility maximization.

> The marginal utility principle now covers the cost phenomenon and in consequence also the logic of the allocation of resources (structure of production), hence the "supply side" of the economic problem *so far as all this is determined by economic considerations*. And it means on the other hand, that, in as much as costs to firms are income to households, the same marginal principle, with the same proviso automatically covers the phenomena of income formation or of "distribution", *which really ceases to be a distinct topic*, though it may, of course, still be treated separately for the sake of convenience of exposition [Schumpeter, 1954, p. 913; italics in original].

This point of view neglects the dependency of exchange value and derived demand on some prior distribution of income, perhaps determined outside the sphere of market exchange.

León Walras, while recognizing the principle of marginal productivity as early as 1876, did not replace his fixed input coefficient production equations with marginal productivity theory until the third edition of *The Elements* [1896]. However, by relating product price to changes in output, he was able "to secure a determinate solution (input prices) to the distribution problem in terms of productive contribution even with fixed input coefficients under conditions of general equilibrium" [Stigler, 1941, p. 170].

Stigler credits Walras with "a general statement of the problem of production with reference to the allocation of labor to maximizing utility...(but) the entire analysis (on joint production) is rendered superficial and worthless by the assumption that the jointly produced commodities can be produced only in fixed ratio" [Stigler, 1941, p. 18].

The Austrians and Imputation

Of special concern to the Austrians, Menger and his successors, Wieser and Böhm-Bawerk (and to the American, J.B. Clark), was the legitimatization of income to private property in response to the Marxian theory of exploitation and surplus value. These contributors to the neo-classical paradigm viewed the pricing of factors of production as a derivative from the market for final goods, a part of the exchange process.

Carl Menger developed "...the essential notion of the marginal productivity theory, but the fundamental element of this theory, the variability of the proportions in which production services combine (to secure the same product) was completely lost to his followers" [Stigler, 1941, p. 4]. The principle of variable proportions leads directly to the marginal productivity theory, yet, says Stigler: "Quite surprisingly, Menger fails even to mention explicitly the technical principle of diminishing returns from an increasing proportion of any agents in a combination, and, accordingly, to realize its importance for his theory of distribution" [p. 151]. Although he fails to develop a marginal productivity theory, "Menger was the first economist...to suggest...how a given product may be imputed to the resources which cooperate in its production" [p. 152].

In Menger's terms, goods of the higher order exist to produce goods of the first (lowest) order, which directly satisfy consumer wants. Goods of the higher order derive their "value" from goods of the first order. Joseph Schumpeter [1954, p. 913] called Menger's extension of the principle of marginal utility over the whole area of production and distribution "a genuine stroke of genius".

Grappling with the question how the value of each of the cooperating higher-order goods derives value from scarce first-order goods, Menger [1871] suggested the "difference principle" with value equal to the loss sustained if a higher-order good were withdrawn from the group co-producing the lower-order good. The loss in value is net of any additions to product by the other co-producing factors. The difference principle may have served well enough as a restatement of the argument that goods of a higher order derive their value from goods of a lower order, but it was not a satisfactory measure of value. Menger's successor, Friedrich von Wieser, was the first to argue that there are too many cases of joint production where the difference principle attributes more value to the cooperating higher-order goods than the lower-order good possessed.

Wieser [1889, Book. III, ch. 8] moves closer than Menger to an explanation of derived demand for the means of production in terms of marginal productivity. Wieser applied the notion of marginal utility, "grenznutzen," at the margin of production according to the principle of "imputation." By imputation the value of the means of production — the higher-order good — is measured by varying the proportion by which higher-order goods are used in the production of the lower-order goods.

The value imputed to the higher-order good varies according to contribution to marginal utility at the boundary of use of the first-order good. Varying proportion by varying the levels of use of discrete techniques that are used to produce the lower-order goods and employing a system of simultaneous equations is not unlike the dual solution to the linear programming model of more recent vintage.

Assuming fixed supplies of productive factors, zero-elastic supply, the new direction of causation tied value to final demand in terms of marginal utility. Value was imputed to the factors of production without resorting to real costs — the subjective sacrifices associated with the supply of labor or capital. Under the opportunity cost principle, independently elaborated by Wieser and even earlier by Walras, cost is the value of a resource unit determined by utility foregone in some best alternative use.

Wieser preferred his theory of imputation to Menger's because without continuous variability in proportions between factors (which he did not think likely) it was almost impossible to separate the marginal physical contributions of individual productive services and estimate their share of the value product. Wieser's imputation solution holds constant both product prices and input coefficients as output changes.

Fixed input coefficients sacrifice the principle of diminishing returns and "...the assumption of constant product prices which underlies Wieser's distribution theory automatically eliminates the problem of the relation of physical to value productivity, and consequently ignores also the problem of effects of variations of factor supplies on their relative shares of the product" [Stigler, 1941, p. 177]. Using fixed input coefficients it is possible to get a determinate solution to factor prices for the economy as a whole, but the values imputed to the factors are general equilibrium values and bear only a formal relationship to marginal productivities.

Marginal Productivity

In the nineties the marginal productivity theory finally appeared [implicit in Ricardo's theory; also von Thünen, M. Longfield].... Walras at Lausanne, Marshall and Wicksteed and others in England, Wicksell in Sweden, Clark in the United States, and Barone in Italy — all appeared in the nineties with theories which incorporated the substance of the marginal productivity approach to the problem of distribution. However, the simultaneity with which the marginal productivity theory was finally formulated by so many economists is less astonishing than is the fact that it had not been clearly formulated at the same time as the theory of subjective value and become an integral part of the general body of doctrine [Stigler, 1941, pp. 4–5].

Philip Wicksteed [1894] "extended marginal analysis to all parts of man's rational life; he developed a cost theory which was consistent with the general application of the utility theory; he gave the first detailed and reasonably satisfactory statement of the general marginal productivity theory" [p. 39]. His theory of production made extensive use of the principle of substitution. All productive factors are put on equal footing with much more detail than the classical tripartite division. "...managerial ability and land are treated as quantified factors which are exactly comparable with other resources...no distributive share, not even 'profits', can be a residual since there is complete substitutionality" [p. 48]. Wicksteed is often credited with first demonstrating that Ricardian rent as a residual is not inconsistent with rent as the marginal product of land.

The classical interest in the progress of relative income shares to distinct socioeconomic classes appears to expire, at least temporarily, with the marginal revolution of the 1870s. In its place was forged a marginal productivity theory of factor pricing or, more accurately, a marginal productivity theory of factor demand applicable to any factor. The conditions of class ownership and supply that revealed so much to the classicists regarding relative income shares receive little attention in the neo-classical writings that dominate late nineteenth and much of twentieth century economic thought. The functional distribution of income to particular input categories was investigated by J.B. Clark [1899] in aggregative terms. Clark justified the shares to functional income categories in terms of factors' productive contributions. Clark's marginal productivity theory of distribution describes how in an ideal static world (no changes in technology, resources, and growth), capital and labor are justly rewarded according to their productive contribution. Stigler [1947] resurrected the neglected contribution of Clark's contemporary in America, Stuart Wood [1889]. Wood chose a Walrasian-like general equilibrium framework to present his marginal productivity theory of wages, but it was Clark's aggregate production function approach that captured the interest of his contemporaries.

Clark posits a perfectly competitive stationary state with a single wage and a single rate of interest on a homogeneous fund of capital prevailing throughout the economy. Many of his conclusions implicitly assume a linear homogeneous production function. He does not address the problem of measurement of capital. He interprets Ricardian rent as applicable to any asset in the short run, with land much like any other concrete capital good, completely variable for any single industry. The supplies of all productive services are taken as fixed in his analysis of the stationary state.

Most of Clark's message...could be accepted only against a back-drop of completely inelastic input supplies.... Anything less — any acknowledgement of elasticity in input supplies — reduces marginal productivity from a theory of input pricing to a theory of input demand alone [Bronfenbrenner, 1985, p. 368].

James Tobin elaborates on the dependency of marginal productivity on the relative supplies of labor and capital, and on Clark's recognition of some of the intricacies involved in employing an aggregate two-factor production function where marginal productivities determine interest and wages:

> In describing marginal productivity as a function of inputs, Clark is at pains to distinguish between variations of labor relative to existing capital goods and variations relative to a constant stock of capital (the fund) with capital goods appropriately adjusted to each situation. Clark calls the returns to existing capital goods, including land, rents. They will be equal to interest, the marginal productivity of capital, in full equilibrium, when the capital-goods composition of capital is appropriately adjusted. For durable but mortal capital goods these rents seem to be like Marshallian quasi-rents [Tobin, 1985, p. 31].

Clark attempted to raise marginal productivity theory to a principle of ethical justice. Under static competitive conditions with zero economic profits, factor price was determined by a factor's marginal productivity which was equated with the owner's contribution. Clark's "...'law of final productivity' tends to give to labor what labor creates, to the capitalists what capital creates, and to entrepreneurs (businessmen) what the coordinating function creates" [Robinson and Eatwell, 1973, p. 42].

Whether or not it was simply assumed by many neo-classicists toward the end of the nineteenth century that a factor's contribution and the owner's contribution were identical, that an individual was entitled by virtue of ownership to the earnings from the sale of owned factor services, and that under conditions of static competitive equilibrium factor earnings or reward equalled the factor's value of the marginal product, there remained an issue which preoccupied those who held that in competitive equilibrium each factor earned its marginal product.

> The completion of the marginal productivity theory of distribution was achieved only with the development of the proof that if all productive agents are rewarded in accord with their marginal products, then the total product will be exactly exhausted. This exhaustion-of-product problem is of course unique to the general marginal product theory [Stigler, 1941, p. 320].

Wicksteed had explicitly raised the question of product exhaustion and attempted to prove that marginal productivity theory did imply exhaustion of the product.

One point, obviously crucial to all marginal theories of distribution, is that the sum of the marginal contributions of productive factors must equal the total product. Wicksteed (1894) evolved a mathematical proof of this proposition but abandoned it on Edgeworth's criticism that the form of productivity function which it required was not plausible. This form of function was essentially static, involving no change in efficiency with change in the scale of production [J.M. Clark, 1951, pp. 65–66].

Exhaustion of the Product

Knut Wicksell [1900] was the first to give an acceptable formal mathematical statement of a general marginal productivity theory. Maximizing profit under competitive conditions and with a homogeneous and continuous production function, each cooperating agent of production receives a share of the product regulated by its marginal productivity. Diminishing returns applies to all factors; factor proportions vary with changes in their relative pay — the direction of causation can go both ways; no real economic distinction is made between labor and land. He refines Böhm-Bawerk's concept of capital and interest. Capital is "almost always a product, a fruit of the co-operation of the two original factors: laborer and land" [Wicksell, 1901, p. 149].

Wicksell thoroughly reworked Böhm-Bawerk's capital theory and transformed it into an explicit marginal productivity theory that made interest as the marginal productivity of waiting completely coordinate with wages and rent as the marginal productivity of labor and land. By discarding Böhm-Bawerk's one-sector model in favor of a multi-sector treatment, Wicksell went far toward bridging the gap between the Austrian and Walrasian schools [Blaug, 1978, p. 577].

The direction of neo-classical thinking by the end of the nineteenth century is clearly away from income shares to socioeconomic classes and toward the explanation of pay to factors of a particular type, homogeneous within a category, according to their marginal contribution to production at the margin of production. Neither class nor ownership is integral to neo-classical analysis. Robinson and Eatwell [1973, p. 41] present an interesting illustration from Wicksell [1901, p. 109]: "... workers and the means of production are separate factors but all on the same footing, without regard to the differences in their social relationships.... The level of wages and rents would be the same whether a landowner hires laborers for a wage, or laborers hire land for rent."

Apparently A.W. Flux, in a review of Wicksteed's 1894 *Essay on the Laws of Distribution*, was the first to point out the applicability of Euler's mathematical theorem on homogeneous functions to the problem of product exhaustion. If a function is linear homogeneous, the sum of the arguments of the function, each multiplied by its partial derivative, equals the value of the function. In economic language, if a production function exhibits constant returns to scale (if each input changes by a certain proportion output will change by that same proportion) and if each input is paid by an amount equal to its marginal product, the product will be exhausted with no residual or surplus. Euler's mathematical theorem concerning partial derivatives reinforced the marginal productivity theory of factor pricing, although its impact and influence would have been more restricted, limited to linear homogeneous production functions, but for Sir John Hicks' extension of the theorem's result.

The exhaustion-of-product results from the application of Euler's theorem had been seen to depend on the production function being linear homogeneous (constant returns to scale), and on the competitive result that payments to factors equal their marginal products. The exhaustion of the product is not implied where a surplus results from a monopoly or other circumstances, such as price regulations, where factor prices are not expected to equal their marginal products.

Hicks' [1932, pp. 233–239] extension of the applicability of Euler's theorem on homogeneous functions to zero-profit long-run equilibrium, where the production choices of firms must resemble choices under constant returns to scale, is significant in that product exhaustion is no longer seen to depend on the shape of the production function. The same result is now seen to obtain in conditions of long-run perfectly competitive equilibrium where product price equals minimum average cost. Competitive profit-maximizing behavior makes a factor's price equal to the value of its marginal product in the vicinity of firms' minimum average cost levels of operation where constant returns to scale are approximated.

Any "apparent" surplus to more efficient firms in perfectly competitive equilibrium can be attributed to the marginal productivity of superior resources. Whether an owned or hired resource, the higher opportunity cost reflecting the higher productivity equalizes firms' costs and insures the absence of a surplus.

The Ricardian concept of an unearned surplus, which derives from ownership of superior land or from the Marxian rate of surplus value or exploitation in the capitalist mode of production, is associated in neo-classical writing with imperfect markets or competitive markets in disequilibrium where a residual remains since one or more inputs earn less than the value of marginal product. A.C. Pigou [1932] is credited with the notion of monopolistic exploitation due to monopoly power where the price paid for the input service is less than the value of the marginal product because of monopolistic restrictions in the product market. E.H. Chamberlin [1932] and J. Robinson [1933] are given credit for the notion of monopsonistic exploitation where the input is paid less than its marginal revenue product or value to the firm. In both cases something greater than a normal rate of profit may result not because of departure from linear homogeneity in the production function but because of monopoly or monopsony power in the sale of product or the hiring of inputs.

Martin Bronfenbrenner distinguishes between neo-classical micro-distribution, concerned with the pricing of productive inputs, and neo-classical macrodistribution, concerned with the relative shares in functional income distribution. The latter "...has been based on two major notions aggregated from microdistribution, namely the production function and the elasticity of substitution. It also uses some form of the marginal productivity theory of input demand" [Bronfenbrenner, 1971, pp. 386–387]. Bronfenbrenner quotes R.M. Solow's view of aggregate production functions in his 1966 review of J.R. Hicks' *Capital and Growth*:

> I have never thought of the macroeconomic production function as a rigorously justifiable concept. In my mind it is either an illuminating parable or else a mere device for handling data, to be used so long as it gives good empirical results, and to be abandoned as soon as it doesn't, or as soon as something better comes along [Solow, 1966, p. 1259].

Cobb-Douglas Aggregate Production Function

The widely used Cobb-Douglas aggregate production function was developed in the 1920s by Paul H. Douglas and his collaborator, the mathematician C.W. Cobb, from time series of labor, capital, and manufacturing output for the United States and the State of Massachusetts [Cobb and Douglas, 1928]. It was a linear homogeneous function of $Q = bL^kC^{1-k}$ form with Q, L, and C representing homogeneous output, labor, and capital, respectively, and with b and k statistical constants. The function provided a surprisingly close least-squares fit to the data. If it is assumed that the inputs' rates of pay are equal to their marginal products or partial derivatives, the exponents have the convenient property of being equal to the labor and capital income shares. Bronfenbrenner reports that the "Cobb-Douglas function's use for macrodistribution theory may have been something of an after thought. Douglas did, however, compare observed labor shares...with theoretical shares computed along marginal productivity lines, and expressed satisfaction at the closeness of the results.... With both measured and computed labor shares in the range 0.65–0.70 [Bronfenbrenner, 1971, p. 388].

In the concluding part (posthumously from lectures given in 1948) of his *History of Economic Analysis*, Schumpeter [1954, p. 1142] makes particular mention of the concept of the "elasticity of substitution": "This conception is useful in settling in a few lines many problems that filled pages and even volumes in the past (for instance the problem of the influence of the introduction of machines upon the interests of labor). Corrections have been mainly applied to the old theory of production by means of a closer analysis of the properties of Production Functions." The introduction of this concept is attributed to J.R. Hicks [1932] and to Joan Robinson [1933]. In the years that followed almost all neo-classical theoretical considerations of factor shares have utilized the elasticity of substitution, $\sigma = d(b/a) \,/\, b/a \div d(P_a/P_b) \,/\, P_a/P_b$, the ratio of relative changes in the ratio of input quantities (a and b) to relative changes in the ratio of their prices (inverted to get the *expected* positive values).

If real wage rates rise relative to real interest rates and these changes are accompanied by the expected rise in capital to labor, the effect on relative income shares depends on whether $\sigma \gtrless 1$. If the relative changes in the two ratios, the quantity and price ratios, exactly offset each other, then the relative shares remain constant. If the relative rise in the ratio (real wage/real interest rate) is greater than the accompanying rise in the capital/labor ratio, the elasticity of substitution is less than 1, and the labor share will have increased.

A salient characteristic of Cobb-Douglas type linear homogeneous production functions is that the elasticity of substitution is unity and, therefore, relative inputs vary in the same proportions as their relative prices, implying constant relative labor and capital income shares. Using the marginal productivity theory of J.B. Clark and applying Euler's theorem, it was *convenient* to interpret the close statistical fits of the Cobb-Douglas function to mean that aggregate income shares represent contributions to production, that the key to understanding relative income shares is in the factor's technical contribution to production. The factor production elasticities are the constant exponents, k and $1 - k$, constrained to equal unity.

If J.B. Clark's assertion that pay to an agent of production equals its marginal product is valid, then the exponents (the elasticity of production) of a Cobb-Douglas production function equal the respective shares to labor and capital. k, the exponent of the quantity of labor (L) is the elasticity of production or the relative increase in output associated with a relative increase in labor:

$$k = \frac{\partial Q}{Q} \bigg/ \frac{\partial L}{L} = \frac{\partial Q}{\partial L} \cdot \frac{L}{Q}$$

If real wage, $\bar{w}$, equals the marginal product of labor, $\partial Q/\partial L$, then substituting $\bar{w}$ for $\partial Q/\partial L$, $k(= \bar{w}.L/Q)$ is labor's share of the product. Similarly, exponent $1 - k$ would equal capital's share, if real interest $\bar{\imath}$ equals the marginal product of capital $\partial Q/\partial C$.

The statistical estimates of the exponents of a Cobb-Douglas production function roughly agreed with independent estimates of the income shares to labor and capital, which led economists to infer that factors received their marginal products, and that the marginal productivity theory was confirmed.

The characteristic of homogeneous functions that makes them Cobb-Douglas functions is the constancy of the exponents which implies that the elasticity of substitution is unity. This characteristic forces the result that factor shares are constant and unaffected by changes in labor and capital. The popularity of the Cobb-Douglas production function was due to its capacity to "explain" constant shares over a period when factor shares appeared to hold constant. The constancy of factor shares is supported if technical change is neutral over the period.

For over 30 years from 1928 to the early 1960s, the Cobb-Douglas function was the primary tool used to decribe a causal relationship between production and distribution at various levels of aggregation, of distributive shares in terms of factors' marginal productivity. (A.A. Walters [1963] and Bronfenbrenner [1971] present excellent surveys of this literature.) As the level of aggregation increases, confidence diminishes in the validity and meaning of the result that distributive shares are related solely to technical elasticities of production or to the elasticity of substitution in production, a function of the elasticities of production. At higher levels of aggregation, substitution within broad categories are conceivably as significant as substitution between *labor* and *capital*; indices representing more diverse inputs and outputs are more likely to deviate from the necessary conditions for valid aggregation (discussed below); deflating to generate aggregate real input or output series is complicated by changes in quality, in kind, and in time variance in the production of component products; measurement of capital becomes more complex and problematical; the notion of an aggregate quantity of labor is inevitably lumped together with greater efficiencies due to investment in human capital;

changing prices and product mix can easily distort estimates of a factor's technical elasticity of production. Finally the aggregate production function leapfrogs over the adjustments, partial or complete, by which changes in factor supply affect factor price, product price, product mix, production techniques, and feedback effects. These difficulties associated with aggregation may be set aside if it is clearly established that *aggregate* production functions with homogeneous labor and capital are not related to the heterogeneous world by aggregation but are merely metaphorical extrapolations of microrelationships.

Certainly there are alternative explanations to constant distributive shares other than the offsetting rise in the ratio of wage/interest rate to the observed rising capital/labor ratio implied by the Cobb-Douglas function's unitary elasticity of substitution. It is at least plausible that constant shares could result from some combination of biased technical change, substitution in consumption of more capital-intensive goods, imperfect market structure and behavior, increasing returns to scale, and an elasticity of substitution less than unity.

Distributive Shares: Aggregate Production Function

To analyze distributive shares employing aggregate production functions, problems of aggregation must be confronted. Blaug [1978, pp. 492–493] lists several: (1) W. Leontief's theorem on separable functions which requires for valid aggregation that the marginal rates of substitution between any two variables be independent of a third variable: (2) L.A. Klein's aggregation theorem requires in a Cobb-Douglas type aggregate production function that the exponents be interpreted as the geometric mean of the constituent microfunctions; (3) F.M. Fisher's theorem that the capital of firms can be aggregated if, and only if, the microproduction functions differ from each other by a capital-augmenting technical difference, such that different capital goods in different firms can be represented as more or less the same thing. A similar restriction on aggregation applies to labor and output. This list of aggregation requirements, although extremely stringent, is not exhaustive.

The general view that labor's share was a constant — Bowley's Law — had its origin in Arthur Bowley's empirical research on functional distribution in Great Britain in the period 1890–1913. The constancy of relative shares began to be questioned after World War II. Kuznets [1955] suggested two stages of growth. In the first with capital scarce and a surplus of unskilled labor, capital share rises. In the second stage with capital less scarce relative to skilled labor, labor's share stabilizes and then rises. Kuznets [1959] noted that the observed stability of labor's share in the United States was of wages *and* salaries, and was due to the balancing of conflicting effects of the underlying determinants. Solow [1958], using improved data, found the labor share to be surprisingly unstable within and between industries. Kravis [1959] concluded that labor's share was slowly rising.

The Impact of Technical Change on Factor Shares

The constant elasticity of substitution (C.E.S.) type aggregate production function was used to estimate a constant elasticity of substitution (not necessarily equal to unity) that provided a better statistical fit in cases where distributive shares were changing. With the rapid pace of technical change it became more and more awkward to analyze change in functional income shares within the context of static production functions. Plausibly, even highly likely, some of the observed changes in relative factor utilization and shares were attributable to technical change, new products, and processes. When growth in output brings with it the prospect of biased technical change, the list of possible influences on factor shares clearly lengthens.

Solow [1957] distinguished between embodied and disembodied technical progress, with the latter viewed as separate from embodied changes that enhanced the quality and kinds of factors employed (e.g., new machines and labor skills). Technical change — a cost-reducing shift in the production function — whether embodied or disembodied, could be capital-saving, neutral, or labor-saving. Even casual observation of U.S. economic history in the twentieth century suggests a positive trend in the ratio of real wage rate to the real rate of interest on capital, and in the accumulation of capital relative to the expansion of the labor force, but it has proven difficult to sort out those effects on growth *and on shares* due to substitution or capital deepening within existing production functions and those due to technical innovation or shifts to new production functions. Early suggestions for classifying technical innovations involving shifts in aggregate production functions came from Harrod [1948], Hicks [1932], and J. Robinson [1933].

Hicks' basis for classifying technical progress is represented in figure 4–1. Holding the labor-capital ratio constant at the preinnovation equilibrium ratio L^0/K^0 along a straight-line ray from the origin and holding output to the same preinnovation rate, Hicks compares the slope of the

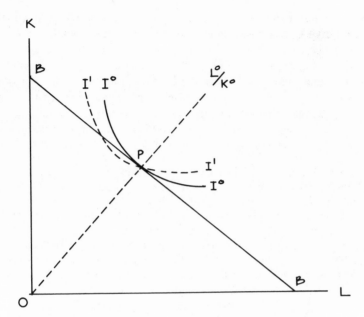

Figure 4-1. Classification of Technical Progress — Hicks.

postinnovation isoquant with the original isoquant at the point (P) where the preinnovation output represented by the original isoquant ($I^0 I^0$) crosses the production ray representing the original labor/capital ratio. The axes represent aggregate labor (L) and capital (K), assumed measurable. The slope of the price line BB, drawn tangent to the original isoquant $I^0 I^0$, equals the relative prices of labor and capital, w/i.

The slope, $\Delta K/\Delta L$, of the isoquant in the vicinity of any particular point, such as P, is equal to the ratio of the marginal products $\Delta K/\Delta L = MP_L/MP_K$. Any cost-minimizing long-run equilibrium in the region where K and L are partial substitutes and the isoquant is convex will occur where the slope (w/i) of the price line (BB) equals the slope of the isoquant (MP_L/MP_K). Hicks classifies a technical innovation as labor-saving if, at point P, the marginal product of capital (MP_K) rises relative to the marginal product of labor (MP_L) — the slope of the isoquant (MP_L/MP_K) at P becomes flatter, as is the case with the dashed isoquant $I^1 I^1$ at the original position, P. If the innovation is neutral, the marginal product of capital and labor rise in the same proportion. If, as was observed, wages are rising relative to interest rate, a steeper price line would reach a new equilibrium tangency position to the northeast of P

along a steeper production ray. The observed more rapid growth of
capital relative to labor is at least consistent with technical change with a
Hicksian labor-saving bias.

Similar to Hicks, Joan Robinson's labor-saving innovation would raise
the relative marginal productivities, MP_K/MP_L, at the initial capital/labor
ratio, but Robinson extends Hicks' basis for classification. In the context
of a comparative equilibrium move to a new full-employment equilibrium, holding constant the rate of interest, the new postinnovation
equilibrium position may differ from the old.

> I analysed the effect of an invention upon the relative shares of the factors in
> the total product, when the amount of capital is adjusted to the new technique
> (so that full equilibrium is attained, with zero investment), in terms of the
> classification of inventions and the elasticity of substitution showing that, with
> a constant rate of interest, the relative shares are unchanged, in equilibrium,
> by an invention which is neutral in Mr. Hicks's sense provided that the
> elasticity of substitution is equal to unity, while if an invention is labor-saving
> or capital-saving in Mr. Hicks's sense, the relative shares are unchanged (in
> equilibrium, with a constant rate of interest) if the elasticity of substitution is
> correspondingly less or greater than unity [Robinson, 1937–38, p. 175].

Harrod classifies technical progress according to how — given a constant rate of interest — it affects his required capital coefficient, which
is an incremental capital-output ratio. Technical progress is said to be
neutral, capital-using, or capital-saving, depending upon whether this
capital coefficient is unchanged, increased, or lowered, respectively. In
the first two cases technical progress must also be labor-saving, with
output per unit of labor higher, but in the third case it is possible to have
a higher labor requirement and for the technical change to be classified as
one of "progress." If technical progress has been neutral according to
Harrod's definition and equilibrium has been maintained with a constant
rate of interest, then the real-wage rate has been increasing at the rate of
technical progress and factor shares are unchanged. With capital-using
technical progress, under the same conditions, the profit share would be
increasing, and the real-wage rate would increase at a slower rate than
technical progress; the reverse would hold for capital-saving technical
progress. Joan Robinson establishes the conditions for Harrod's classification to "dovetail" with Hicks.

> (...with neutral technical change and a constant rate of interest) the relative
> share of capital in the total product is unchanged by the invention; ...if, in
> this case, the elasticity of substitution with the new technique is equal to unity,
> then the invention must be neutral in Mr. Hicks's sense, while if the elasticity

of substitution is less or greater than unity, the invention must be capital-saving or labor-saving, to a corresponding extent, in Mr. Hicks's sense [1937–38, p. 178].

By monitoring the capital coefficient, the new investment in capital required for a change in output, Harrod measures directly whether the economy is becoming more capital-using, capital-saving, or neutral as output changes. Harrod's basis for classification allows for substitution in consumption as changes occur in relative prices of commodities that differ in factor intensities and price elasticities of demand.

Whether technical progress is labor-saving, capital-saving, or neutral, all agree, is associated with whether labor's income share is decreasing, increasing, or unchanged. For these associations to conform to their technical criteria for technical change requires restrictions on the values that the elasticity of substitution may take. Harrod's criterion for neutral change — constant capital/output ratio — does not preclude a labor-bias or capital-bias in technical change — does not, in fact, indicate what type of change will occur.

Any change in relative income shares is likely to result from the balancing of several forces. It cannot be assumed that an expected rise in wages relative to rate of return on capital will necessarily induce technical progress with a labor-saving bias (or that any observed change in relative factor price is the result of a bias in technical progress). In an aggregate context an offset to the rise in the capital/labor ratio is at least as likely to depend on substitution on the demand side, on changes in the prices of products of various factor intensities, and on the elasticities of demand for these products, as on bias in technical progress or substitution in production.

Blaug points out that Harrod's criterion of neutral technical change — stability in the aggregate capital/output ratio at constant rates of interest — furnishes

...only presumptive evidence of neutrality. Leaving aside the consideration that only strongly-biased technical change will show up clearly, the aggregate capital-output ratio is influenced not only by the direction of technical change but also by savings propensities, inter-industry shifts in investment, expectations about the future rate of technical advance, and the cumulative influence of the rate of growth of output. Moreover, the denominator of the ratio includes the end product of spending on education, health and training, while the numerator refers solely to non-human capital. It is always possible to argue that technical change has shown no tendency toward "capital deepening" because of the rise in the ratio of human-to-nonhuman capital over the century. The fact that capital has grown faster than labor may itself be a statistical illusion, the result of measuring labor in man-hours instead of efficiency units. Furthermore, it is not at all clear how capital is to be measured for purposes of verifying the neutrality hypothesis [Blaug, 1978, p. 505].

In a recent account of the role of technical progress, Kaldor [1985, p. 67] writes:

> But while the capital/labor ratio increased enormously, the capital/output ratio did not, as it necessarily would have done if the increase in labor productivity was a matter of substituting capital for labor along a neo-classical production function.... The capital/labor ratio is a by-product of high productivity resulting from large production; it has nothing to do with marginal productivity or marginal rates of substitution, concepts that only make sense under the wholly artificial assumption of constant returns of scale.

Kaldor attributes the rising demand for capital relative to labor to expanding markets that permit higher productivity with lower unit costs from technical innovations involving more capital-intensive techniques and greater division of labor. Research on aggregate production functions has not been decisive on the sources, the extent or the direction of bias in technical change, or on the influence of technical change on relative factor prices or income shares.

The Measurement of Capital

The problem of measurement of capital has been a thorn in the neo-classicists' side. Capital as a quantifiable entity has generally been employed in microproduction and macroproduction functions. Wicksell [1901] drew a distinction between disparate concrete man-made capital goods and the value "capital." While capital goods yielded quasi-rents, the value of any capital asset is given by the discounted flow of the expected net income generated by the asset. The rate of discount is the rate of interest, but Wicksell suggests that increasing capital by lengthening the period of investment may affect the rate of interest on capital. Increasing capitalistic production involves a lengthening of the period of production which constitutes an increase in capital, subject to diminishing returns and associated with a fall in interest rate and rise in wages. Whether labor's share rises or falls depends on the nature of the production function.

Assuming no change in technology, widening the capital structure without changing its average period of production would reduce the rate of interest in much the same way that Ricardo's addition of circulating capital (labor and tools) added to land is subject to diminishing returns (declining marginal product). The variable factor is the widening of the capital structure by the increased application of primary factors, land and labor, embodied in the stock of capital goods. This tends to reduce the marginal product of capital as primary factors expand with the average time of their application fixed. The prices, real wages and rent, of the primary factors are bid up, lowering the rate of interest — the ratio of the marginal product of capital to the marginal cost of the embodied primary factors.

A deepening of the capital structure increases the average period of production, reduces the annual replacement requirement of primary factors, and partially counteracts the tendency for interest rates to fall relative to wages. The net effect of new investment is to cause a decline in the real rate of interest. Wicksell noticed that if primary factors earned compound interest, any measure of capital in terms of average period of production is not independent of the rate of interest. What is now commonly called the "Wicksell effect" derives from Wicksell's observation that net capital investment which reduces the real interest rate requires a reevaluation of capital invested.

It is a short leap from Wicksell to Joan Robinson's [1953–54] unequivocal statement that the stock of capital cannot be measured unless the rate of interest is known. Therefore, the use of capital (the value of) as an argument in a production function to determine the rate of interest is circular and illogical. The response to this problem that changes the axis in a production function from capital to the rental of productive service of capital good(s) is a nonsolution.

The rent (R) on a capital asset is derived from the asset's adjusted value ($\bar{V}$) (taking into account changes due to depreciation, obsolescence, capital gain, or loss) and the interest rate, both of which are to be determined. The logical problem of circularity is compounded. Another alternative is a retreat into disaggregation so each distinct item of capital or labor skill becomes an argument in the production function. This avoids problems of aggregation, but quantification and measurement become overwhelming. This alternative is not very useful except as a formal exercise.

The concepts of reswitching and capital-reversing cast doubt on the inverse relation in factor demand, and suggest that a decline in interest rate may not be associated with change to more capital-intensive techniques. Changes in interest rate may raise or lower the value of capital, and there may even be multiple switch-points which depend on the age pattern of labor applications. Piero Sraffa provides a clear illustration of these concepts and also shows the impossibility of aggregating periods of production to represent the quantity of capital [1960, pp. 37–38].

An Attempt To Resurrect the Aggregate Production Function

Samuelson [1962] attempted to demonstrate that an aggregate production function with a single homogeneous product, homogeneous labor, and homogeneous capital was a surrogate for the heterogeneous real world, and that the aggregate function, though not related in any precise way by aggregation, could be interpreted as if derived from perfectly malleable heterogeneous capital goods. He attempted to show that there is but a single switch-point and thereby rescue the monotonic inverse relation between the interest rate/wage rate ratio and the capital intensity of the technique (capital per man), but he succeeded only in demonstrating that the inverse relation holds if, and only if, the identical capital/man techniques hold throughout the economy.

The Microproduction Function and Factor Demand

Neo-classical economics has always tended to believe input prices are determined endogenously within the market, the result of supply and demand, but whether input prices are determined in response to market forces, or exogenously in response to bargaining, custom, political influences, etc., elasticity of substitution is the arbiter of income shares in the microsetting whenever there is a change in relative input prices. In the extreme case of elasticity of substitution equal to zero, the perfectly complementary input case preferred by the Austrian school, marginal product is not a meaningful concept.

The notion that the functional distribution of income may be explained simply by invoking the principles of marginal productivity as enshrined in an aggregate production function for the economy as a whole was broached for the first time in Hicks' *Theory of Wages* (1932). Until Hicks there was, in fact, no theory of the share of wages and profits in total income that commanded universal assent and 19th century writers like Wicksteed, Wicksell, Walras and Marshall analysed the problem of factor pricing without appealing to the concept of an *aggregate* production function, making homogeneous output a function of homogeneous capital and homogeneous labor, much less an *aggregate* production function of the Cobb-Douglas variety with its unitary elasticity of substitution. So strong has been the hold of Hicksian thinking on recent writings about income distribution that it comes as something of a shock to realize that only J.B. Clark and possibly Böhm-Bawerk among the great 19th century neo-classical economists ever operated with a simplistic marginal productivity theory of distribution applied to the economy as a whole, conceived, as it were, as one giant firm [Blaug, 1978, p. 487].

In the microeconomics of the individual firm, as an implication of cost-minimizing and profit-maximizing, with the elasticity of substitution a measure of technical substitutability, the firm chooses the input mix for any relative factor prices by equating the ratio of factor marginal products (slope of isoquant, the marginal rate of substitution) with the factor-price ratio. The elasticity of substitution is a measure of technical substitutability embedded in the particular microproduction function, in the shapes of its isoquants. The firm's responsiveness to changes in relative factor prices depends on substitutability in production, as summarized by the elasticity of substitution.

The competitive firm produces that rate of output where marginal cost of production equals product price, a necessary condition for profit maximization. This implies, according to the cost-minimizing equi-marginal principle, that factor services are employed at that rate where their prices equal their values of marginal products; and it provides a first approximation to a factor demand curve. In the short run with at least one factor fixed, the inverse relation between factor price and factor quantity demanded depends largely on diminishing returns to the variable factor(s), or more generally on the law of variable proportions. As the ceteris paribus condition, holding constant product price and the quantities of other factors, is relaxed, Marshall's partial equilibrium framework is strained or at least stretched by interdependencies between a factor's marginal product and the optimal levels of use of cooperating factors, whether complements or substitutes. Factor demand in the market is further modified by the lack of independence between product price at which marginal product was valued and the rate of factor employment. On the microlevel and under competitive conditions, the curve representing the value of the marginal product, modified by change in product price and rates of hire of cooperating factors, becomes the factor's market demand curve. In equilibrium, as an implication of profit maximization, the quantity of the factor demanded will be such that factor price will equal value of marginal product somewhere along this demand curve, whatever the factor's price or however that factor price is determined.

Given a situation where all factors are variable (as in long-run analysis) the completed cost-minimizing adjustment to an initial change in relative

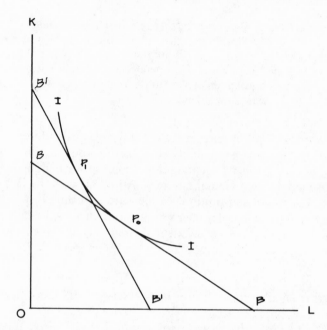

Figure 4-2. Substitution Effect of Change in Relative
Factor Price.

factor prices (within the limits of technical substitutability as summarized
by the production function and the shapes of its isoquants) will bring all
relative factor prices (= slope of price line) back into equality with the
ratio of their marginal products (= marginal rate of substitution between
inputs, the slope of the isoquant II in figure 4-2). We ignore any scale or
budget effects of the change in relative factor price, and confine our
attention to the substitution effect along the isoquant, assumed to be
continuous, differentiable, and convex. The inputs are flows of productive
services assumed measurable in physical units.

An increase in w/i, the relative price of labor (L) to the interest rate on
capital (K) — measured in physical units — is represented in figure 4-2
by the change in slope of the two price lines, BB and $B'B'$, both drawn
tangent to the isoquant at point P_1, the point of tangency northeast of
initial cost-minimizing equilibrium at P_0. In long-run equilibrium after the
completed adjustment to the change in the relative factor price, the factor
price ratio (w/i) equals the ratio of factor marginal products (MP_L/MP_K).
In general, factor market demand would be less elastic if adjustment to

long-run competitive equilibrium is incomplete than would be the case where all firms in all product markets employing the particular factor had completely adjusted.

Hicks judges it "much the best" to restrict the marginal productivity theory of factor demand to the ratio of factor marginal products that define the slope of the isoquants under conditions of full equilibrium where continuous substitution among factors is possible:

> Since the whole conception of marginal productivity depends upon the variability of industrial methods, little advantage seems to be gained from the attempt which is sometimes made to define a "short period marginal product" — the additional production due to a small increase in the quantity of labor, when not only the quantity, but also the form of the cooperating capital is supposed unchanged [Hicks, 1932, p. 20].

Of special interest is the perfectly complementary factor case which allows no substitution within the microproduction function. Although marginal productivity is not meaningful where fixed production coefficients apply, the effect of a change in factor price on product price, and substitution in the form of changing product mix, feeds back and contributes to factor demand. Technical change (induced and independent) also contributes to factor demand.

The production function in a microdistribution context remains the basis for neo-classical estimates of factor demand. That factor employment and factor pricing is best understood in a supply-demand framework is not to concede that factor demand or factor price is necessarily related to marginal productivity, as the neo-classical textbook would have it, nor that factor price is necessarily endogenously determined within the market.

Except in instances where it is useful to suppose the supply of factor services is zero-elastic, factor supply has a role in the determination of factor pricing. Factor supply curves, based on individuals' choices between income and leisure or on time preferences concerning consumption now or later, do affect factor price. Individual and market factor supply curves shift with respect to endogenous forces such as changes in prices or income, and to exogenous (often noneconomic) forces such as wars, earthquakes, or technological change.

Where factor price is determined independently of marginal productivity by custom, legislation (e.g., minimum wage), collective bargaining agreements, central bank policies, among others, this creates a range of infinitely elastic supply, as in figure 4–3. The factor price, w, though determined exogenously, will nevertheless equal the marginal product, if

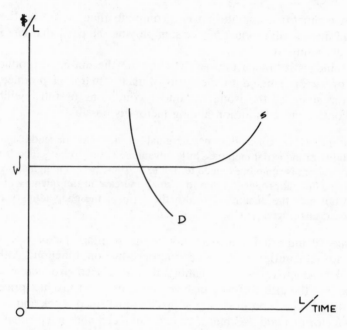

Figure 4–3. Exogenously-determined Wage Rate.

the factor-hiring decisions are ruled by competitive profit-maximizing choices based on marginal productivity. This, of course, need not be the case as in situations of perfect complementarity where marginal product is meaningless, or in regulated or imperfect markets. Neither is it true that market prices of factors of production are immune from market forces reflecting their scarcity. Even the medieval "just price," and the classical subsistence wage could be influenced by market forces when market demand intersected the less than infinitely elastic sections of supply generating market shortage, putting stress on price to reflect scarcity. The possibilities of infinitely elastic or backward-bending supply curves and the *supply-relative* nature of market price, where supply and demand are not independent, have been well known for over a century and contribute to the body of criticism of marginal productivity theory as a theory of factor price. An interesting example of this criticism, particularly of the dependency of factor pricing on the strong assumption of zero-elastic supply and of the lack of independence of supply and demand, is offered by Maurice Dobb:

...the Austrians (as also Walras in the main) simplified their problem by assuming that one started from *given* supplies of productive factors, whose "services" entered into the exchange-process by commanding a "hire price". This is indeed, a basis for what was to become the fashionable reduction of the cost-concept to the shadowy and contingent notion of "opportunity cost" (i.e. the cost of foregone production opportunities for creating utilities). But if this assumption of given factor-supplies is relaxed, the difference that this makes is merely to substitute, in Marshallian fashion, a series of rather vaguely defined and subjectively conceived "factor-supply schedules" of questionable realism and independence (questionable because dependent on some kind of distribution-relative "real cost" of "efforts and sacrifices") [Dobb, 1973, p. 170, italics in original].

A general theory of factor demand remains central to neo-classical distribution theory, but the comfortable connection between factor price and productive contribution has been loosened; any presumed moral advantage to market pricing based on marginal productivity has been undermined. Once disabused of the notion that the complex connection between factor price and "contribution to production" has any moral or normative connotations, neo-classical economics can go back to basics and extend its domain. First the basics: that the supply-and-demand concept is very helpful in understanding factor pricing; that sometimes in some markets with supply zero-elastic, demand will mainly determine factor price; that sometimes in some markets with supply infinitely elastic, demand will mainly determine the rate of factor employment with price exogenously determined; and sometimes in some markets both blades of the Marshallian scissors will act on factor price and employment.

Analytical Income Categories

The price and employment of factors of production by type has, of course, a direct relation to the distribution of income shares by type, whatever the level of aggregation or type of classification. Neo-classical economics has drifted to the newer classification of analytical income categories, which permit any factor price or share to be analyzed into wage, rent, profit, and interest components. This makes the older classi-cal classification according to ownership by socioeconomic class more remote. Not only may an individual own any factor of production in-dependent of any class identification but now, with the analytical basis for income categories, any given factor of production can earn a rental surplus above contractual costs, or costs necessary to ensure supply, with interest rate as an expected rate of return linking current income flows to their source (past investments in human or nonhuman capital), and profit a residual gain (loss) from the expected rate of return of investment in the capital source. Harry Johnson clarifies the distinction between the classical and the analytical income categories:

> Clearly the division between the opportunity cost or "wage" element and the surplus over the necessary cost or "rent" element depends on the size or the level of aggregation of the particular factor considered. . . . From the longer-run point of view, all specific factors can be considered to be the result of the investment of resources in the past in a specific form. . . . The current earnings of a specific factor can accordingly be regarded as a return on past investment involved in creating it or maintaining its productive existence. Conceptually, the "quasi-rent" involved can be divided into two components which parallel the distinction between necessary cost and surplus in the short-run analysis. The first is interest at the prevailing market rate on the past investment that created the factor; the second is a surplus or deficiency of that actual income in relation to that imputed interest charge. . .[Johnson, 1973, pp. 30–31].

The critical problems of political economy relate more to the older classification of distributive shares than to the analytical income categories. The analytical classification distances distributive shares from any classical association with class conflict.

Refocusing attention on income shares to traditional categories — wages, rent, interest, and profit — is a useful direction for future research. Many problems associated with income shares have yet to be addressed. The impact of changes in factor prices and income share on the size distribution of income is not well understood, nor are the dynamics of the distribution of factor endowment and property ownership. A precarious balance exists between the distributive shares required to support acceptable rates of growth and employment, and acceptable degrees of inequality in the size distribution of income.

Equilibrium and Factor Demand

The equilibrium adjustment mechanism varies in different markets. Price rigidities seem to make quantity adjustments to equilibrium or non-equilibrium positions more likely. Where social costs of high rates of unemployment are perceived as lower than social costs of high inflation, the forces operating to clear labor markets may be so weak as to permit continual surpluses, or redefinitions or rejection of "equilibrium." Malinvaud suggests that equilibrium need not imply market clearing prices, that alternative definitions of equilibrium may involve rationing of available supply with a balance achieved between product and factor markets:

> Economists have been brought up to think that the very notion of equilibrium implies that, for each commodity, supply must equal demand which of course cannot be the case for labor if some involuntary unemployment remains. But a general equilibrium is an abstract construct that has no logical obligation to assume equality between supply and demand [Malinvaud, 1977 p. 5].

In the context of static equilibrium the *simplistic* demand curve seen to depend on the marginal productivity of a variable input must be set aside in any real-world view when other cooperating inputs, their adjustments in quantity, form, and price, as well as product price changes are taken into account. Together with short-run partial equilibrium adjustments, cost-minimizing long-run equilibrium adjustments in factor quantities also contribute to what is really a *hybrid* factor demand that includes factor quantities at all stages of adjustment in the production process.

Conclusion

Neo-classical economics has traditionally contained factor pricing and distributive shares within the limited sphere of market exchange. It has relied on individual profit- and utility-maximizing within a competitive market structure, on the production function, on the unifying concept of equilibrium, with distribution derived rather mechanically within this "analytic" framework.

Over time, in an effort to understand a changing world and to deal more effectively with its problems, increasing recognition has been given to the importance of market imperfections, externalities, the institutional framework, new notions of equilibrium and the adjustment process, the objectives that control choice, bargaining power, social relations, constraints imposed by national priorities, and so forth. As neo-classical economists break away from one or another of the traditional neo-classical concepts and conditions, presumably at some point they go beyond the domain of neo-classical economics. Or does the domain of neo-classical economics expand; does neo-classical economics become a more powerful analytical tool in the wake of the criticisms and critical analysis associated with the "capital controversies"; does it accept at least to a degree the classical order of causation with greater emphasis on distribution of income, on ownership and property rights? With historical change, a world dominated more and more by noncompetitive markets in dynamic disequilibrium may no longer be a neo-classical world. Neo-classical analytical techniques cannot be used to explain everything. To be useful, they must be adapted to deal with this changing world.

References

Blaug, M. (1978). *Economic Theory in Retrospect*, 3rd edition. Cambridge: Cambridge University Press.

Bronfenbrenner, M. (1971). *Income Distribution Theory*. Chicago: Aldine, Atherton.

————. (1985). Marginal productivity, a rehabilitation. In G.R. Feiwel (ed.), *Issues in Contemporary Economics & Distribution*. Albany, NY: State University of New York Press.

Chamberlin, E.H. (1932). *The Theory of Monopolistic Competition*. Cambridge, MA: Harvard University Press.

Clark, J.B. (1899). *The Distribution of Wealth*. New York: Macmillan.

Clark, J.M. (1951). *A.E.A. Reading in the Theory of Income Distribution*. Homewood, IL: Irwin.

Cobb, C.W., and Douglas, P.H. (1928). A theory of production. *American Economic Review* (May).

Dobb, M. (1973). *Theories of Value and Distribution*. Cambridge: Cambridge University Press.

Edgeworth, F.Y. (1881). *Mathematical Psychics*. London: Kegan Paul.

Flux, A.W. Review of Wicksteed's 1894 *Essay on the Laws of Distribution*, reprinted in Baumol and Goldfield (eds.), (1968). *Precursors in Mathematical Economics*. London: London School of Economics and Political Sciences.

Harrod, R.F. (1948). *Towards A Dynamic Economics*. London: Macmillan.

Hicks, J.R. (1932). *Theory of Wages*. London: Macmillan.

————. (1946). *Value and Capital*, 2nd edition. Oxford: Oxford University Press.

Jevons, W.S. (1871). *Theory of Political Economy*. London: Macmillan.

Johnson, H. (1973). *The Theory of Income Distribution*. London: Gray-Mills.

Kaldor, N. (1985). *Economics Without Equilibrium*. Armonk, NY: M.E. Sharpe.

Kravis, I. (1959). Relative income shares in fact and theory. *American Economic Review* (December).

Kuznets, S. (1959). Quantitative aspects of the economic growth of nations, IV: Distribution of national income by factor shares. *Economic Development and Cultural Change* (April).

————. (1955). Economic growth and income inequality. *American Economic Review* (March).

Malinvaud, E. (1977). *The Theory of Unemployment Reconsidered*. Oxford: Basil Blackwood.

Marshall, A. (1890). *Principles of Economics*, 8th edition. London: Macmillan.

Menger, Carl. (1870). *Grundsatze der Volkswertschaftslehre*, Vol. I, Reprint No. 17. London: London School of Economics.

Mitchell, Wesley C. (1949). *Lecture Notes on Types of Economic Theory*. New York: Augustus M. Kelley.

Pigou, A.C. (1932). *Economics of Welfare*, 4th edition. London: Macmillan.

Robinson, J. (1933). *Economics of Imperfect Competition*. London: Macmillan.

————. (1937–38). The classification of invention. *Review of Economic Studies*, reprinted in *A.E.A. Readings in Income Distribution*. Philadelphia: Blakiston, 1951, 175–180.

————. (1953–54). The production function and the theory of capital. *Review of Economic Studies*, 1953–54. Also in *Collected Economic Papers*, Vol. II. Oxford: Blackwell, 1980.

Robinson, J., and Eatwell, J. (1973). *An Introduction to Modern Economics*. London: McGraw-Hill.

Samuelson, P. (1962). Parable and realism in capital theory: the surrogate production function. *Review of Economic Studies* 39: 193–206.

Schumpeter, J. (1954). *A History of Economic Analysis*. Homewood, IL: Irwin.

Solow, R.H. (1957) Technical change and the aggregate production function. *Review of Economics and Statistics*, 39 (August): 312–320.

————. (1966). Review of J.R. Hicks' *Capital and Growth*. *American Economic Review*, 56, (December): 1257–1260.

Sraffa, P. (1960). *Production of Commodities by Means of Commodities*. Cambridge: Cambridge University Press.

Stigler, George J. (1941). *Production and Distribution Theories*. New York: Macmillan.

————. (1947). Stuart Wood and the marginal productivity theory. *Quarterly Journal of Economics* 61 (August): 640–649.

Tobin, J. (1985). Neo-classical theory in America: J.B. Clark and Fisher. *American Economic Review* 35 (December): 28–38.

Walras, L. (1890). *Elements of Pure Economics*. Translated by W. Jaffe. London: Allen & Unwin, 1954.

Walters, A.A. (1963). Production and cost functions: an econometric survey. *Econometrica* (Jan.–April).

Wicksell, K. (1900). On marginal productivity as the basis for economic distribution. *Ekonomisk Tedsksift* II.

————. (1901). *Lectures on Political Economy*. Translated by E. Classen from second Swedish edition 1911. London: Routledge, 1934.

Wicksteed, P.H. (1894). *An Essay on the Coordination of the Laws of Distribution*. London: Macmillan.

Wieser, F. von (1889). *Natural Value*. London: Macmillan, 1893.

Wood, Stuart (1889). The theory of wages. *Publication of the American Economic Association*, No. 4.

5 THE DISTRIBUTION THEORY OF MARSHALL'S *PRINCIPLES*

John K. Whitaker

Alfred Marshall's *Principles of Economics* [Marshall, 1890] is well known for its contributions to the theory of value.[1] It is less widely appreciated that the book also contains a well-developed theory of distribution. Just as Marshall's value theory retained a strong classical infusion, especially in its treatment of supply, so too did his distribution theory preserve much of the classical viewpoint. This was especially the case in the treatment of rent and factor supply, but also in the concern with secular changes. It was only when dealing with the demand for labor and other factors that Marshall came to diverge crucially from his classical forebearers and must be classified as essentially a marginal-productivity theorist. Much interest attaches to the intellectual processes leading from Marshall's earliest and distinctly classical formulation of distribution theory to the mature version embodied in the *Principles*. However, concern here will be restricted to describing and assessing the latter, leaving the earlier versions aside.[2] Only the long-period aspects of Marshall's distribution theory will be considered. There are hints — no more — of a short-period theory of distribution over the trade cycle, but no attempt will be made to follow out this train of thought.[3]

The dense complex texture of Marshall's *Principles*, and the extensive revisions it underwent, make a straightforward statement of its treatment of distribution difficult. It seems best to consider the separate facets *seriatim*, before attempting an overview. The exposition is based mainly on the final version of Marshall [1920]. The existing interpretive literature on Marshall's distribution theory is surprisingly scant, and there will be limited occasion to advert to it.[4]

The *Principles* treats distribution in two distinct phases. These correspond broadly to the division between Book V and Book VI, although the division is not watertight. The Book V approach is partial-equilibrium, considering only a single industry or a small group of interrelated industries, and it treats factor supply only cursorily. Emphasis is entirely on the derived-demand link from final demand to factor prices, ignoring the reciprocal link from factor incomes to final demands. The Book VI treatment differs from this partial approach in one or both of two ways. The first is that factor-supply conditions and the institutional framework are treated "realistically" on lines already commenced in Book IV. The second is the adoption of a general-equilibrium — or, more precisely, a macroeconomic — formulation, based on the concept of the "national dividend." It was the Book VI treatment alone which Marshall regarded as dealing with "Value, or Distribution and Exchange" in its entirety. He saw Book V as concerned more narrowly with the technicalities of "The Theory of the Equilibrium of Demand and Supply."[5] "It deals with abstractions; and refers to realities for the purpose of illustration only" [Marshall, 1898; reproduced at Guillebaud, 1961, Vol. II, p. 72].

Factor Demand

The theory of factor demand [Marshall, 1920, pp. 351–362, 403–411, 514–523, 848–849; Guillebaud, 1961, Vol. II, pp. 580–588] is essentially a marginal productivity theory, but this fact is obscured by Marshall's preference for the concept of (marginal) *net product*.[6] The calculation of net product is described in the following way. The businessman estimates "how much *net product* (i.e. net addition to the value of his total product) will be caused by a certain extra use of any one agent: *net* that is after deducting for any extra expenses that may be indirectly caused by the change" [Marshall, 1920, p. 406].[7] Unlike the marginal product concept, which varies the amount of only one input, holding the quantities of all others constant, the net product admits simultaneous variation of the quantities of all inputs. Thus, it can be employed in situations where factor substitutability is limited or nonexistent. This can be important in short-period contexts, which may partly explain Marshall's preference for using net rather than marginal product. But net product is by no means restricted to situations of limited substitutability, as Hicks [1932, pp. 12–14] maintains. There is ample evidence that Marshall used it when full factor substitutability was assumed and, indeed, that this was his dominant long-period assumption. His preference for net over marginal product does not seem to have rested on a perception that the theoretical implications were different or conflicting. Rather, it seems to have stemmed from his desire to make his discussion realistic and palatable to men of business and affairs.

Marshall employed marginal products in the example of the marginal shepherd and in Note XIV of the Mathematical Appendix [Marshall, 1920, pp. 515–518, 846–852]. He explained,

> The supposition that an additional worker can be taken on without a corresponding increase in the supply of capital for plant, raw material, &c., does not alter the substance of the problem of marginal products; but merely simplifies its form a little. In this exceptional case, we have not to dwell upon the need for the appropriate adjustment of various agents of production, each being used up to the point at which any additional use of it would be less efficient in proportion to its cost than the additional use of some other agent [Guillebaud, 1961, Vol. II. pp. 586–587].

He defended his approach against an attack by Hobson which was based on an assumption of nonsubstitutability of inputs:

> He [Hobson] argues that if the marginal application of any agent of production be curtailed, that will so disorganize production that every other agent will be working to less effect than before; and that therefore the total resulting loss will include not only the true marginal product of that agent, but also a part of the products due to the other agents: but he appears to have overlooked the following points: — (1) There are forces constantly at work tending so to readjust the distribution of resources between their different uses, that any maladjustment will be arrested before it has gone far: and the argument does not profess to apply to exceptional cases of violent maladjustment. (2) When the adjustment is such as to give the best results, a slight change in the proportions in which they are applied diminishes the efficiency of that adjustment by a quantity which is very small relatively to that change — in technical language it is of "the second order of smalls" —; and it may therefore be neglected relatively to that change.... A grave error would therefore have been involved, if any allowance had been made for those elements which Mr. Hobson asserts to have been overlooked. (3) In economics, as in physics, changes are generally continuous [Marshall, 1920, p. 409n].

As Marshall implies in his point (2), net and marginal products coincide if there is full factor substitution and profit maximization. The induced changes in the use of other inputs can be ignored by an envelope property which makes the effect on output of these changes only of "the second order of smalls." To demonstrate this formally, assume that a producer obtains output, y, by using n variable inputs, $x_1, x_2, \ldots x_n$, according to the differentiable production function $y = f(x_1, x_2, \ldots x_n)$ and denote $\partial f/\partial x_i$ by f_i, etc. Suppose that the prices $p, w_1, w_2, \ldots w_n$ of output and the inputs are unaffected by the producer's actions. When input j is varied, let other inputs also be adjusted at rates dx_i/dx_j for $i \neq j$. The marginal net product of input j may now be defined (as a rate per unit of j) by

$$(mnp)_j = p\frac{df}{dx_j} - \sum_{i \neq j} w_i \frac{dx_i}{dx_j} = p\left(f_j + \sum_{i \neq j} f_i \frac{dx_i}{dx_j}\right) - \sum_{i \neq j} w_i \frac{dx_i}{dx_j}$$

$$= pf_j + \sum_{i \neq j} (pf_i - w_i)\frac{dx_i}{dx_j}. \tag{5.1}$$

Two properties should be observed. First, starting from a point where profits are maximized, so that $pf_i = w_i$ for $i = 1, 2, \ldots n$, it must follow that $(mnp)_j = pf_j$. That is, the marginal net product of input j coincides with the value of its marginal product.[8] Second, the statement $w_j = (mnp)_j$ is "only a particular way of wording the familiar doctrine that the value of everything tends to be equal to the value of its [marginal] expenses of production" [Guillebaud, 1961, Vol. II, p. 582]. That is, if $(mnp)_j$ is replaced by w_j the first step in equation (5.1) is equivalent to the condition $pdy = \Sigma w_j dx_j$, where the sum includes all inputs.

The total demand for an input by an industry or group of related industries is the sum of the demands of the constituent firms all determined by equating net or marginal product to the input price. This total demand tends to increase as the relative price of the input falls (and this would still be true even if substitution were not smooth at the level of the individual firm: see Marshall, 1920, pp. 406–407n). In particular, the demand for capital rises as the interest rate falls [Marshall, 1920, pp. 519–520, 542]. Little or no attention was paid to the formal derivation and properties of factor-demand functions. The only formal treatment was that carried out in the context of derived demand, where fixed coefficients of production were assumed for simplicity, although it was intimated without much justification that similar arguments applied in cases with factor substitutability [Marshall, 1920, pp. 381–387, 852–856]. Nevertheless, the general notion of demand functions for inputs is present throughout Marshall's treatment of distribution, especially his macroeconomic one.

The macroeconomic treatment of factor demands in Book VI rests on the concept of the "national dividend," essentially equivalent to the modern concept of real net national income or product.[9] The argument is left in a somewhat metaphorical state:

> The net aggregate of all the commodities produced is itself the true source from which flow the demand prices for all these commodities, and therefore for the agents of production used in making them. Or, to put the same thing in another way, this national dividend is at once the aggregate net product of, and the sole source of payment for, all the agents of production within the country: it is divided up into earnings of labor; interest of capital; and lastly the producer's surplus, or rent, of land and of other differential advantages for production. It constitutes the whole of them, and the whole of it is distributed among them; and the larger it is, the larger, other things being equal, will be the share of each of them.
>
> It is distributed among them, speaking generally, in proportion to the need which people have for their several services — *i.e.* not the *total* need, but the *marginal* need [Marshall, 1920, p. 536].

Although imprecise, this wording leaves little doubt that Marshall had in mind here, as in earlier work [see Whitaker, 1974], an aggregate production function which expresses the national dividend as a function of the inputs of labor of various types and capital, the partial derivatives of the function representing the demand prices of the inputs.

The necessity for a macroeconomic approach to distribution was explained most clearly in a passage appearing only in the preface to the second edition of the *Principles*:

> ...though the causes that govern demand, and those that govern supply can be studied separately, in the case of any single commodity, yet this cannot be done for the agents of production as a whole. For the demand for the labor of the various grades of workers, and for that "service of waiting" by which capital is accumulated, all comes from the aggregate National Dividend produced by those very agents of production (acting upon the free gifts of nature): and though they are always competing with one another for the field of employment, yet at the same time those agents provide for one another that field of employment [Guillebaud, 1961, Vol. II, p. 40].

The basic vision of distribution as a whole which is revealed here is essentially the same as that presented in 1879, in many ways more clearly, in the *Economics of Industry*.[10] The main difference is that rent is no longer subtracted from the national dividend to obtain an "earnings and interest fund" available entirely for distribution between labor and capital. This change was explained in a footnote which appeared only in the first edition of the *Principles*.

> Experience has shown that the term "Earnings and Interest Fund" is apt to be misunderstood. For, firstly, a Fund suggests the notion of a reservoir of

stored-up wealth, and not a stream, or flow, of new production: and, secondly, the proposal to put rent aside while we are considering how earnings and interest are determined, has been found to suggest that rent is determined first and then takes part in determining earnings and interest; and this is, of course, the opposite of what really occurs [Guillebaud, 1961, Vol. II, p. 592].

The second point is the vital one in the present context, and it introduces the next topic.

Rent and Producer Surplus

The treatment of land rent in Books IV and VI runs in terms of the surplus from applying variable numbers of doses of labor and capital to a fixed piece of land. It does not advance significantly the treatment in early work [Whitaker, 1975, Vol. I, pp. 224–260; Vol. II, pp. 216, 224–230], and its main purpose is to analyze the consequences of different land-tenure practices. In Book V, however, there is presented a much more complex treatment of rent, producer surplus, and quasi-rent which makes land rent only "the leading species of a large genus" [Marshall, 1920, p. viii]. Quasi-rents, which are due to temporary factor-supply inelasticities, may be left aside here. In the long period all factor supplies are free to adapt fully to demand, and all capital is free capital. Free capital, being homogeneous, cannot earn differential rent, whether invested in real assets or in the training and education of workers.[11] The sources of differential rent lie rather in the heterogeneity of natural resources — "land" in a generic sense — and in the array of human talents and skills which are innate rather than purposively acquired. But while land is perpetual,[12] individual skills are short-lived. In long-period analysis differential rents to skills accrue not to individuals but to the possession of certain traits whose distribution is determined by the population's genetic endowment.

Book V gives a clear, if not very explicit, indication of how hetero-genous land is allocated among uses, each piece going to that use able to pay the highest rent. This rent is not determined by the opportunity cost of the foregone yield in the next-best *alternative* use, but by the differen-tial advantage over marginal production in the *chosen* use. Marginal production is defined as output produced by varying capital and labor of normal skill and ability. The payment to such resources contains no differential rent element, so that the marginal cost which helps determine price can be determined "without reasoning in a circle" and then serves as the basis on which the price-determined rent to "differential advantages" may be calculated. (Average cost, including rent to differential advantage, must just equal the marginal cost of such marginal production.) This is a perfectly valid use of the "envelope theorem." If resource use is optimal initially, the marginal cost of increasing output will be the same whatever input or subgroup of inputs is increased. But it introduces asymmetry where there is basically symmetry. For any one firm, as Marshall readily concedes, the prices of all inputs, including land, enter symmetrically into production costs, and the same might be expected for any one industry, which has to bid land away from other uses, just as it must bid labor away. Marshall's reluctance to treat inputs symmetrically at the industry level must be attributed to two causes. First, there is the desire to treat land as widely heterogeneous, so that the concept of the marginal product of land can be employed only at a very microeconomic level. Second, there is the wish to preserve an appearance of continuity with the classical doctrine that rent to land, which is in fixed overall supply, is price determined rather than price determining. But since the classical doctrine rested on the limitation of land to a single use, corn production, any continuity is more apparent than real.[13]

Differential rent accruing to the innate skills of individuals is to be treated analogously to the rent of land, with one big difference [Marshall, 1920, pp. 577–579, 624n]. Only those skills recognizable in advance of commitment to a particular occupation can be regarded as yielding rent proper. In other cases individuals still remain effectively homogeneous when they commit themselves, more or less irrevocably, to a specific occupation. The possibility of turning out to be exceptionally talented and earning a high income (or the opposite) then influences the occupational choices of all individuals, even those who prove to be of only normal ability. To those who receive them, the high incomes result from a gift of nature and can be viewed as rents. But, although they are rents to the individual, they are not rents to society, or rents proper. For they could not be eliminated or taxed without impairing the supply of workers to the occupation. In long-period equilibrium, the average income in the occupation is no higher than is necessary to maintain supply.

Marshall discounted the significance of the case in which talents are revealed before occupational choice is made [Marshall, 1920, p. 578]. Neglecting such cases, rents accrue in the long-period theory of distribution entirely to natural resources — the nonproduced means of production. Capital and the various types of labor — which Marshall treats as produced means of production — receive only socially necessary rewards. Natural resources obtain as rent or producer's surplus that portion of the national dividend remaining after the produced factors have received their marginal products. The complication that the individuals in each occupation are heterogeneous ex post is evaded by assuming that every individual in an occupation is equivalent to a suitable multiple of a standard individual, i.e., by working in homogeneous efficiency units of labor.

The Supply of Capital

Capital is measured in the same units as the National Dividend (i.e., in money of constant purchasing power). It is produced by labor and waiting with the aid of natural resources, and the interest rate is the return to waiting rather than to capital. Labor and waiting are the real costs (i.e., the human or disutility costs) of production, and land labor and waiting, rather than land labor and capital, are the fundamental agents of production.[14]

Capital accumulation is governed by saving decisions. Say's law is at work, and the demand for capital influences accumulation only by its effect on the interest rate. Despite individual exceptions, saving will be larger in aggregate the higher the interest rate. Some individuals would save at negative interest rates, but most individuals discount for futurity (not necessarily irrationally given the uncertainty of the future) so that a positive interest rate will usually be needed to avoid capital decumulation overall. The rate of saving at any interest rate increases with income per head and also depends upon the way income is distributed among individuals and classes, which to some degree correlates with its distribution among factors. The willingness to save increases over time due to social and educational changes which make individuals more rational and forward-looking in their behavior. The overall supply of capital adjusts only slowly, since new saving is only a small fraction of the accumulated stock, but the supply to any particular use can adjust much more rapidly.[15]

The Supply of Labor

No aspect of Marshall's treatment of distribution is more complex and more in need of exegesis than his treatment of long-period labor supply. To start with, certain basic presumptions may be listed.[16]

1. The family rather than the worker is the basic unit making labor supply decisions.

2. The decision to enter an occupation is usually made by parents on behalf of their children, and once made is largely irrevocable.

3. Entry into an occupation requires a fixed amount to be invested in human capital through education and training, the amount varying with the occupation.

4. Neither parents nor employers, who must provide education and training, have a legal claim on the extra earnings it yields the worker: "free human beings are not brought up to their work on the same principles as a machine, a horse, or a slave. If they were there would be very little difference between the distribution and the exchange side of value; for every agent of production would reap a return adequate to cover its own expenses of production" [Marshall, 1920, p. 504].

5. The choice between occupations takes into accounts the combination of wages, working conditions, normal hours, job security, etc., expected over the lifetime tenure as well as the cost of training.[17] The attractiveness of each occupation is represented by its money-equivalent "net advantages," which are ranked similarly by all individuals.

6. Expectations are myopic, or perhaps extrapolative, and adjustment of supply is very slow, requiring generations rather than years [Marshall, 1920, pp. 571–572].

7. Workers of different efficiency in a given occupation can be regarded as supplying different quantities of a standard kind of labor, which can be measured in homogeneous efficiency units. For the most part, employers do not care what mix of numbers and average efficiency yields a given number of efficiency units.[18] Workers of different efficiency get the same "efficiency wage" per efficiency unit, but "time wages" which differ in proportion to their individual efficiencies.

8. Worker efficiency is endogenously related to consumption and hours.

9. The supplies of managers and businessmen are determined analogously to those of all kinds of skilled labor.

To bring out various aspects more clearly, the discussion will proceed in three stages. In the first stage output and labor, as well as capital, are assumed homogeneous, all workers thus being of the same efficiency. This permits a simplified account of the determination of the average level of labor efficiency, which Marshall took to be endogenous and closely related to consumption levels and patterns.[19]

Denote output by Q, the number of workers by N, and the efficiency of each worker by e, and assume that the capital stock, natural resources, and technology are given. Then Q will be a function of Ne. It will be simplest to start by treating N, like K, as given. It then follows that output per worker is given by

$$Q/N = f(e), f'(e) > 0 > f''(e). \tag{5.2}$$

Thus, on the marginal productivity principle, the efficiency wage, that is the marginal product of an efficiency unit of labor, is $f'(e)$ while the time wage, that is the wage per actual worker, is $w = ef'(e)$.[20] Note that w may rise or fall with e, depending upon the response elasticity of $f'(e)$.

To sustain efficiency each worker needs a certain minimum level of consumption which depends on his efficiency. This level, $c(e)$, rises quite rapidly with e. For it covers not mere physiological needs but also all the conditions (adequate housing, travel, recreation, inviting comestibles, etc.) needed to preserve alertness and morale and to permit children to be raised and educated to their parents' standards. Some of these necessities are "conventional" rather than strictly necessary, but if they were not allowed for, then strict necessities would be stinted with a deleterious effect on future efficiency. Marshall's basic assumption is that efficiency will fall over time, certainly by the next generation, if wages per head fall below necessary consumption per head. But will efficiency rise in the converse case? This depends upon how the surplus consumption is spent. If it is spent wisely in ways which raise the "standard of life" — the physical, behavioral, attitudinal, and cognitional attributes on which efficiency depends — then efficiency will indeed tend to rise. Marshall felt that this outcome would occur in most advanced societies, and in that case we can postulate (in a linear approximation with $\beta > 0$) that

$$\beta(de/dt) = w - c(e) = ef'(e) - c(e) \tag{5.3}$$

$$\beta(de/dt)/e = f'(e) - c(e)/e. \tag{5.4}$$

Providing that necessary consumption per efficiency unit of labor, $c(e)/e$, does not fall as rapidly when e rises as does the marginal product of an efficiency unit, $f'(e)$, then e must on the above assumptions converge monotonically over time to a stationary value e_0 which is defined by $e_0 f'(e_0) = c(e_0)$. An increase in K or a decrease in N will raise f' at any e and increase e_0. An upward shift in the $c(e)$ function will lower e_0. When e_0 is reached, wages are entirely absorbed in necessaries, but these are the expanded necessaries associated with a high standard of life. To Marshall's eyes at least, the worker's true welfare depends more on his e (his "standard of life") than on his w (his "standard of living").

Although sketchy, this simple formulation does help decode some of Marshall's cryptic and otherwise-baffling remarks, such as:

The supply of labor [in efficiency units] corresponds quickly to the demand for it, when the worker's income is spent mainly on necessaries for efficiency.

Any increase in consumption that is strictly necessary to efficiency pays its own way and adds to, as much as it draws from, the national dividend.

In the western world the earnings that are got by efficient labor are not much above the lowest that are needed to cover the expenses of rearing and training efficient workers, and of sustaining and bringing into activity their full energies.[21]

The argument can be rephrased in terms of the demand and supply for labor, providing that labor is measured in efficiency units. The demand price for labor is $f'(e)$ while the supply price is $c(e)/e$. In typical Marshallian fashion, the actual efficiency wage is always determined by the demand price for the given supply quantity, while this supply quantity evolves according to the current discrepancy between the supply price and the wage. In other words, $c(e)/e$ is essentially a supply schedule for labor in efficiency units, given the population.

What if population is endogenous, too? Marshall's early Malthusianism had become diluted, and he increasingly emphasized the looseness and uncertainty of the links from living standards to population growth, although never denying them entirely. In the case where surplus consumption is wisely spent, in efficiency-increasing ways, the "standard of comfort" or conventional Malthusian subsistence level might plausibly be equated to the necessary consumption per worker, $c(e)$. An excess of the wage per man, w, over this necessary consumption will now induce population growth as well as efficiency growth. Holding capital and technology constant, and starting from a point at which $w > c(e)$, the resulting expansionary process will come to equilibrium at a lower wage per worker than would have been attained with population constant, the more so, the more rapid the population response is (see the Appendix). On the other hand, if surplus wages are spent on indulgences of a stultifying rather than elevating type, the efficiency-growth nexus will be broken. The addiction to such "habitual comforts" will keep the population at its initial level of efficiency and, should wages fall for any reason, efficiency might be depressed as necessaries for efficiency are stinted to conserve habitual comforts. The ultimate result may well be a Malthusian equilibrium in which the wage per man is equal to a standard of comfort which is low, despite exceeding the necessary consumption $c(e)$ by an amount reflecting habitual comforts, precisely because e is low. In such a situation wages per man are determined by "the so-called iron or brazen law, which ties them close to the cost of rearing and sustaining a rather inefficient class of laborers" [Marshall, 1920, p. 531].

Worker efficiency can depend on hours of work as well as consumption. Marshall joined the considerable contemporary debate on the desirability of legally restricting hours, viewing standard hours as typically determined by employers. Unless hours are extremely long, lowering them will yield only slow gains in worker efficiency, much of it accruing to the next generation through improved home conditions. Since the employer has no property rights over such gains, his incentive to exploit the hours-efficiency relationship is attenuated — hence the need for collective action [see Marshall, 1920, pp. 527n, 693–702].

In the second phase of the discussion, which we now enter, all changes in efficiency or population are assumed away and the focus is on the subdivision of the labor force into "grades" and "trades" or occupations, ignoring the individual differences among workers in any occupation. Output is still taken as homogeneous.[22] Workers are first divided into broad social groups or "grades." These are never clearly defined, but Giddings' division into automatic manual labor, responsible manual labor, automatic brain workers, and responsible brain workers is cited with approval [Marshall, 1920, p. 218n]. These divisions rest to some extent on broad differences in aptitudes, but these are prominent only for the last category. Much more important are the barriers to upward intergrade mobility posed by the limited knowledge, limited personal connections, and limited means and borrowing abilities of parents. Parents in choosing an occupation for a child are able to choose freely among occupations in their own grade, but are at a disadvantage in choosing an occupation in a higher grade when compared to parents already in that grade. One important reason for this is that the lower the grade, the less able and willing are parents to sacrifice or borrow to invest in education and training for a child. Not only are knowledge and foresight more limited but discretionary income for saving, and loan collateral for borrowing, are less: the value of the skills to be acquired is not acceptable as collateral. The rate of discount attached to the marginal investment in human capital is thus higher the lower the grade. This fact alone would inhibit upward mobility, even if there were no other barriers. However, economic and social advance are tending to diminish this as well as other barriers, so that the sharp boundaries between grades are gradually crumbling.

Each grade is subdivided into many "trades" or occupations, and in long-period equilibrium each trade in a grade must yield the same "net advantages" given that parents can choose freely among them. It should be emphasized that net advantages are adjusted to take into account the cost of the requisite education and training.

The third and last phase of the discussion is to recognize heterogeneity of output, so that trades can be differentiated by product as well as by task. The general lines are fairly self-evident, as far as labor supply is concerned, and little need be added. Again, the crucial point is that within a grade the monetary-equivalent net advantages of all occupations should be equalized, no matter which commodity is being produced.

Organization and Business Power

At an early stage in the *Principles* Marshall remarks that "it seems best sometimes to reckon Organization apart as a distinct agent of production" additional to land, labor, and capital, or waiting [Marshall, 1920, p. 139]. He explains that organization has many forms, exampling "that of a single business, that of various businesses in the same trade, that of various trades relative to one another, and that of the State providing security for all and help for many" [p. 139]. Organization at a level higher than the individual firm is intimately related to Marshall's concept of external economies and, like the land endowment, helps determine the character of the aggregate production function relating the national dividend to labor and capital inputs. But it does not enter otherwise into the question of income distribution, since no one draws an income from supplying such higher-level aspects of organization. Matters are otherwise with the organization of the individual firm, which is created in the expectation of a resulting profit income. This raises the question, glossed over so far, of how Marshall treats profits.

A preliminary answer can be given by making the assumption that it is possible for a firm to borrow freely at a market interest rate which is appropriate to the riskiness of its line of business. Marshall's firms are typically founded and run by a single businessman or entrepreneur. Such individuals must have the ability and training to equip them to supply the requisite "business power," but the necessary innate abilities are sufficiently widespread in the population that business power *of normal ability* can be treated as a produced means of production. For Marshall it is simply a form of highly skilled labor and, in long-period equilibrium, its income is determined analogously to that of any other kind of skilled labor. The demand price for business power is simply the marginal product of business power in augmenting the national dividend. The supply price is that needed to produce a replacement flow of new entrants to the occupation just adequate to maintain the existing supply. In long-period equilibrium, the quantity of business power supplied must be such that demand and supply price are equal to each other. It is true that business power receives its income as a residual surplus from the business while most (but not all) workers receive contractual incomes. This difference is important for short-period questions, but Marshall does not attach significance to it in long-period equilibrium where future incomes, contractual or residual, are all fully foreseen and fully adjusted to.

The above discussion deals only with business power (and businessmen) of normal ability. As usual, exceptional individuals will receive surpluses above the normal return to reflect their differential advantages over businessmen of only normal ability. Such rents form a particularly important part in the return to business power as a whole, as compared to the returns to other types of labor, since business offers an unusually wide scope for exceptional individuals to excel. Thus, "the rent of rare natural abilities may be regarded as a specially important element in the incomes of business men, so long as we consider them as individuals" [Marshall, 1920, p. 623]. The latter qualification reminds us again that rare ability is normally revealed only after occupational commitment, so that there is rent only from an individual viewpoint and not from a social one.

The provisional assumption about borrowing made above must now be relaxed. Control of some capital is often a necessary condition for entering the occupation of businessman, as it is for entering some of the professions. If the capital is borrowed rather than owned, the lender must receive an above-market interest rate, since the loan is backed mainly by the borrower's probity and promise. This premium is a compensation to the lender for "personal risks" which are over and above the "trade risks" of the particular line of business [Marshall, 1920, p. 590]. Those who own their capital will receive a like premium as long as they are in effective competition with those using borrowed capital.

Writing in 1887, Marshall had stated that the supply price of "business ability in command of the requisite capital" is constituted of

> (a) the supply price of the ability itself; together with (b) the supply price of the bringing together of that ability with the capital required to give it scope, or, to look at the same thing from another point of view, Insurance against Personal Risks; together with (c) the supply price of the capital employed, or interest [Guillebaud, 1961, Vol. II, p. 672; from Marshall, 1887].

In the *Principles* the second component is interpreted as a return to "organization." Thus

> the supply of business power in command of capital may be regarded as consisting of three elements, the supply of capital, the supply of business

power to manage it, and the supply of the organization by which the two are brought together and made effective for production [Marshall, 1920, p. 596; also see p. 313].

The last two of these elements comprise "gross earnings of management," "net earnings" being the second element only.

A comparison of these two quotations makes it evident that the difference between gross and net earnings of management is simply the equivalent of the premium for personal risk paid by those working with borrowed capital. It is doubtful whether Marshall was wise to single out this component as the return to pure organization. It does not appear to correspond to a functional separation in the businessman's activities (organizing rather than managing). And similar premia are built into the return to human capital in all skilled occupations because of like difficulties in borrowing against future earnings. It would seem preferable to treat the supply of business power in command of capital in the same way as the supply of workers in command of the particular kind and amount of human capital needed to enter a skilled occupation.[23]

Distribution as a Whole: Long-Period Equilibrium

The components for a unified treatment of "the great central problem of distribution and exchange" [Marshall, 1920, p. 580; also see p. xv] are now collected. Their assemblage into an all-embracing theory of long-period stationary equilibrium comes as something of an anticlimax, for Marshall remained content to describe the outcome only in broad and sketchy terms — not surprisingly, given the intricacy of his treatment of labor supply.

In long-period equilibrium, all changes in background circumstances are excluded, and conditions of demography and thriftiness are assumed such that capital and the population in each grade are constant, at least once equilibrium is reached. The theory can be expressed at various levels of aggregation with respect to either output, labor, or capital. Thus, at the most aggregated level,

Capital in general and labor in general co-operate in the production of the national dividend, and draw from it their earnings in the measure of their respective (marginal) efficiencies [Marshall, 1920, p. 544].

At a somewhat lower level of aggregation, Marshall observes,

We have seen that the national dividend is at once the aggregate net product of, and the sole source of payment for, all the agents of production within the country; that the larger it is, the larger, other things being equal, will be the share of each agent of production, and that an increase in the supply of any agent will generally lower its price to the benefit of other agents [Marshall, 1920, p. 678].

At the completely disaggregated level, the best description of the theory as a whole is the following composite statement.[24]

The tendency of every one to select the best means for attaining his own ends (or, in more technical phrase, the operation of the law of substitution), acting gradually but constantly under almost stationary conditions would then have caused each several kind of labor or machinery, or other agent of production to be used for each several purpose until its further use there was no longer remunerative; each branch of production would have been extended until it so far satiated the wants which it was directed to meet, that no further supply of its products would be sold on such terms as to pay their expenses of production; and meanwhile the employment of each several agent in each branch of production would have been extended until full advantage had been taken of its special fitness for the work; its use would cease only when there remained nothing that could be done by it better or more cheaply than by other means.

There is a constant tendency towards a position of normal equilibrium, in which the supply of each of these agents shall stand in such a relation to the demand for its services, as to give those who have provided the supply a sufficient reward for their efforts and sacrifices. If the economic conditions of the country remained stationary sufficiently long, this tendency would realize itself in such an adjustment of supply to demand, that both machines and human beings would earn generally an amount that corresponded fairly with their cost of rearing and training, conventional necessaries as well as those things which are strictly necessary being reckoned for.

In long-period equilibrium, the determination of the interest rate is described as follows:

...interest, being the price paid for the use of capital in any market, tends towards an equilibrium level such that the aggregate demand for capital in that market, at that rate of interest, is equal to the aggregate stock forthcoming there at that rate [Marshall, 1920, p. 534].

As to the determination of the wages of any kind of labor,

...marginal productivity rules the demand-price for it; and, on the other side, wages tend to retain a close though indirect and intricate relation with the cost of rearing, training and sustaining the energy of efficient labor. The various elements of the problem mutually determine (in the sense of governing) one another; and incidentally this secures that supply-price and demand-price tend to equality: wages are not governed by demand-price nor by supply-price, but by the whole set of causes which govern demand and supply [Marshall, 1920, p. 532].

Beyond this Marshall would not, or could not, go. "All the elements of the great central problem of distribution and exchange mutually govern one another," but unfortunately the mutual interactions are "so complicated that it is impossible to comprehend the whole in a single statement" [Marshall, 1920, pp. 545, 580]. Readers were pointed toward Notes XIV–XXI of the Mathematical Appendix [Marshall, 1920, pp. 846–856], especially Note XXI, but the latter only generalizes trivially the treatment of joint and composite demand in Book V [Marshall, 1920, pp. 381–388], without transcending its partial-equilibrium setting and its restriction to fixed production coefficients. Possibly the reader was meant to import into Note XXI the discussion of variable production coefficients in Note XIV, but precious little guidance was given as to how to do this. The failure is surprising since Marshall had worked out in the 1880s many of the details in rough notes.[25]

Distribution as a Whole: The Adding-up Problem

The only major change in the distribution theory presented in the successive editions of the *Principles* was with respect to rent. In the first two editions, rent was clearly viewed as a residual surplus, as it had been in the *Economics of Industry*:

> While earnings and interest are among the elements that mutually determine one another, rent is not: it is determined by the others.... the central problem of distribution and exchange is concerned with the determination of earnings and interest and the values of commodities. These being known, and the resources of nature and the arts of production being given, the data are supplied from which the producer's surplus afforded by any differential advantage can be calculated by a mere arithmetical process [Guillebaud, 1961, Vol. II, p. 594 marginal note; p. 595].

The third edition of 1895 switched, however, to the view that "the national income or dividend is completely absorbed in remunerating the owner of each agent of production at its marginal rate" so that "the earnings of the several agents of production, according to their marginal services, exhaust the national dividend" [Marshall, 1920, pp. 536, 830; Guillebaud, 1961, Vol. II, p. 828]. Along with this claim of product exhaustion by marginal-productivity imputation went an increased stress on the symmetry between land and other inputs in the eyes of the individual producer. The distinctive feature of land was now found solely in the permanent fixity of its overall supply, although this feature did continue to receive great emphasis.[26] But no proof or theoretical basis was provided to justify the assertion of product exhaustion. It is to be suspected that Marshall, perhaps influenced by the work of Wicksteed and Clark, with its symmetrical treatment of all factors, had superficially revised his own formulation into greater congruence with theirs without exploring fully the logical implications of the change.[27] The result was a weakening of the theoretical coherence and precision of his own distribution theory.

Secular Aspects

The analysis of long-period normal equilibrium is only one of several modes of analysis espoused by Marshall. He distinguished market-period and short-period normal analysis, both versions of equilibrium theorizing, and also — what is of interest here — secular analysis which deals with movements "caused by the gradual growth of knowledge, of population and of capital, and the changing conditions of demand and supply from one generation to another" [Marshall, 1920, p. 379]. The defect of equilibrium analysis, especially its long-period variety, is that "violence is required for keeping broad forces in the pound of Ceteris Paribus during, say, a whole generation, on the ground that they have only an indirect bearing on the question in hand" [Marshall, 1920, p. 379n]. This may not impair the didactic or doctrinal value of long-period normal theory, but it does reduce its value as a tool for prediction or the analysis of practical matters, and this is especially true in the theory of distribution where the long period may be very long indeed due to the long time needed for adaptation of population and labor supply. Marshall explicitly designed Book VI, chapter XII, of the Principles as an exercise in secular analysis, and much of the final chapter XIII of Book VI is in this vein, too.[28] In these two chapters the treatment of distribution tends to switch from a concern with static equilibrium for a closed economy to the analysis of growth and change in an open economy, but unfortunately the treatment is scant and sketchy. The most important element is the discussion of growth in a new country where land is abundant and capital easily imported [Marshall, 1920, pp. 668–671].

Compared to Marshall's previous work on distribution, the Principles emphasizes "statical" aspects and gives less weight to considerations of economic growth and evolution. It should be borne in mind when judging this change that the book is only the first volume of an incomplete work. It consciously concentrates mainly on long-period equilibrium, deferring other matters or treating them incompletely, and its aim is to clarify the roles demand and supply forces play in value and distribution.[29] For this limited, and essentially doctrinal, goal the practical limitations of long-period equilibrium analysis were not vital. But because Marshall's commitment to this form of analysis was tactical rather than strategic, he never embraced it wholeheartedly. For example, he remained reluctant to subscribe firmly to theories of demography and saving which emphasize the choking off of population growth and capital accumulation by low wage and interest rates. Yet, once population and capital are viewed as endogenous, long-period stationary equilibrium cannot be maintained unless population growth and capital accumulation are choked off by diminishing returns to land. A certain ambivalence or tension thus runs through the treatment of long-period distribution in the *Principles*. A critic as acute as Joan Robinson has been led to interpret Marshall's "normal" interest rate as generated by sustained growth rather than by stationary equilibrium.[30] Although hardly justified as a textual interpretation of Book VI, this is, I feel, a correct assessment of Marshall's more general views throughout his life.

In dealing with questions of value theory, Marshall was able to leave the confines of the literal stationary state and use the looser "statical method," which rests on "less violent" assumptions.

> By that method we fix our minds on some central point: we suppose it for the time [hypothetically] reduced to a *stationary* state; and we then study in relation to it the forces that affect the things by which it is surrounded [Marshall, 1920, p. 369].

Such an approximate method might serve well enough in the partial-equilibrium analysis of the demand and supply for an individual commodity, even in the long period. But it could hardly be used in the long-period analysis of income distribution without slighting the factor-supply side by artificially treating variables as if they were constants — a practice for which Marshall was prone to criticize other marginal-productivity theorists strongly.[31] Marshall was aware that in a general-equilibrium context the literal stationary state was a logical implication of the statical method, but he failed to press this point in his general-equilibrium treatment of distribution.[32]

Doctrinal Aspects

As in his treatment of value, Marshall in his treatment of distribution was anxious to inculcate a balanced appreciation of the complementary roles of demand-and-supply influences, to preserve the valid elements from the classical tradition, with its strong emphasis on the supply side, and to rebuke recent writers who had exaggerated the role of the demand side by putting forward as complete treatments theories which would be valid only if all quantities supplied were fixed. Writers in the Ricardian tradition were represented (no doubt overgenerously) as having consciously elected to concentrate on the supply side, which they deemed the more important, while glossing over the demand side, which they nevertheless broadly grasped.[33] Among modern writers Böhm-Bawerk was subject to the most explicit criticisms, but Jevons and Clark must also have been among the implied targets.[34] The new school of marginal-productivity theorists was conceded to have done good work in filling the lacunae left by the classical theorists, but the most important recent development, the truly revolutionary shift from classical preconceptions, was in the treatment of endogenous labor efficiency, pioneered by Walker.[35]

> The new views...of the causes that govern the supply of efficient labor, have not attracted much notice, but are really very important and far reaching. But, on the other hand, the new views on the causes that govern the demand for labor, though they have justly claimed and received a great deal of attention, have not really led to any great substantial change in the theory of distribution [Guillebaud, 1961, Vol. II, p. 553].

Marshall was particularly anxious to dispute the view that the doctrine "wages equal the net or marginal product of labor" is a valid theory of wages. He conceded, however, that it "throws into clear light the action of one of the causes that govern wages" — that is, the demand-side influences [Marshall, 1920, p. 518]. This line of criticism, in conjunction with some of Marshall's more ambiguous wordings, might suggest that he should be regarded as a precursor of modern Cambridge critics of marginal-productivity theory, but this would be unwarranted.[36] Any doubts that he subscribed to the strongest aggregative form of the "neo-classical" theory of distribution should be dispelled by passages like this:

> ...an increase of material capital causes it to push its way into new uses...by its increased competition for employment it will have forced down the rate of interest, therefore the joint product of a dose of capital and labor will now be divided more in favor of labor than before [Marshall, 1920, p. 665].

Practical Applications

The importance Marshall attached to a correct formulation of the determinants of distribution came as much from the practical implications and advice he could extract from it as from the resolution of doctrinal controversy. A full treatment of these matters would take us too far astray, but some central points can usefully be observed. They are made most easily when the theory is formulated in terms of the production of the national dividend, Q, by capital, K, and various kinds of homogeneous labor. Let the numbers of workers of different types be $L_1, L_2, \ldots L_n$, and their efficiencies $e_1, e_2, \ldots e_n$. Then

$$Q = F(K, L_1e_1, L_2e_2, \ldots L_ne_n) \tag{5.5}$$

The rate of interest, r, and the wages $w_1, w_2, \ldots w_n$ *per man* of the various types of worker are given by the marginal products:

$$r = \partial F/\partial K , \; w_i = e_i\partial F/\partial(L_ie_i) , \; i = 1, 2, \ldots n. \tag{5.6}$$

Any residual output accrues as rent to natural resources.[37]

Marshall's predilection for a macroeconomic formulation of distribution is partly attributable to the ease with which it clarifies the mutual interdependence of the different factors, bringing out simply the various ways in which their interests conflict or coincide. A reduction in L_1 (say) will raise w_1, and generally lower r and $w_2, w_3, \ldots w_n$, although the price of an input which is a close substitute for L_1 might rise. On the other hand, an increase in e_1 (say) will generally raise r and $w_2, w_3, \ldots w_n$, although the price of an input which is a close substitute for L_1 might fall. But what will happen to w_1 when e_1 rises? It may rise or fall, depending on whether the reduction in the marginal product of an efficiency unit is in smaller or larger proportion than the rise in the number of efficiency units per man. Marshall was prone to take the optimistic view and emphasize the probability of a rise.[38]

He was thus led to frown on "antisocial" policies for raising wages by restricting numbers, and to applaud policies which rely on increasing labor efficiency. The former tend to harm other factors, the latter to benefit them. Disapproval of the first class of policies was heightened by the thought that the likely reduction in r would retard capital accumulation and perhaps lead to capital export. It was also heightened by the recognition that the traditional argument for population restriction — the pressure against limited natural resources — had largely been eliminated by the opening up of the international economy. Policies which reduced numbers (as a whole or in any occupation) by ways which reduced labor efficiency, or even merely retarded its growth, were represented as doubly vicious.[39]

Concluding Observations

A comprehensive summing up and tying together of loose ends would be difficult and will not be attempted. But three broad points can be made.

1. There are strong threads of continuity running from Marshall's earliest work on distribution right through to the mature version of the *Principles*. In particular, both early and mature versions share a strong emphasis on the classical tradition regarding factor supply. Both also emphasize induced changes in labor efficiency — a post-classical concern which was prominent in the later nineteenth century. Where they differ most is in the treatment of factor demand, but even here the crucial change was not marginal productivity and the "principle of substitution" but the escape from the classical presumption that wages are advanced entirely from capital. Secular change receives less emphasis in the *Principles* than in earlier work, but this seems to be a tactical change, whose effect is exaggerated by the incompleteness of the *Principles*, and not a fundamental change in approach.

2. The distribution theory of the *Economics of Industry*, although it must defer to the earlier work of Thünen, stood head and shoulders above all other competitors in the field. When the *Principles* appeared it was only one of several available treatments of the neo-classical approach to distribution and, although it had many virtues, it was soon neither the most precise nor the most pathbreaking. Marshall's failure to follow up his initial advantage can perhaps be attributed to the wide-ranging nature of his ambitions and his unwillingness to restrict his contributions to a narrow area, but it also reflected his declining interest in doctrinal controversy and pure theory. He regarded economic theory as a rough-and-ready aid to practical discussion, rather than something to be made elegant and precise for its own sake. Given such an attitude, his reluctance to push formal theorizing as far as he could, and as far as others were doing, is understandable. But his evasion of the analytical puzzle of "adding up" is harder to excuse. So is his failure to incorporate into his distribution theory the whole range of issues concerned with increasing returns and the representative firm which played so prominent a part in his value theory.[40]

3. Marshall's criticisms of the neo-classical theory of distribution were internal criticisms, conceding the general framework but arguing for fuller

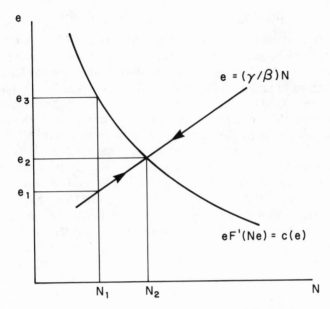

Figure 5A–1. Worker-Efficiency and Size of Population.

consideration of supply aspects. He was not a precursor of modern criticisms of marginal-productivity theory. Where he might justly be regarded as a significant precursor of modern work is in his analysis of human capital, which foreshadows many recent developments in labor economics, and in his stress on induced change in labor efficiency, the importance of which has had to be rediscovered by modern students of economic development.

Appendix to The Supply of Labor: The Case with Both Population and Efficiency Endogenous

Given capital, natural resources, and technology, output is a diminishing-return function $F(Ne)$ of the labor input in efficiency units, N being (working) population and e efficiency per worker. We have $F' > 0 > F''$. The wage per efficiency unit is F' and the wage per worker is $eF' = \partial F/\partial N$. The basic dynamic relations assumed are (in linear approximations with β, γ positive constants)

$$\beta(de/dt) = eF'(Ne) - c(e) = \gamma(dN/dt).$$

Assuming the stability condition of the text (i.e., $\partial(F' - c/e)/\partial e < 0$ always), the condition $eF'(Ne) = c(e)$ for stationary equilibrium defines e as a function of N which is negatively sloped when graphed in (N, e) space as shown in figure 5A-1. If the initial position in (N, e) space is to the left of this equilibrium curve, the economy will follow rightwards a trajectory from the initial point with slope γ/β until it meets the curve. If the initial position is to the right, the trajectory followed will still have slope γ/β, but it will be followed leftwards. These geometric facts imply the result stated in the text. For example, starting at the point (N_1, e_1), where $w = ef'(e) > c(e)$, the point (N_2, e_2) is reached. But if N had been held constant at N_1 then e would have grown to e_3. Since $e_3 > e_2$, since $w = c(e)$ everywhere on the negatively sloped curve, and since $c(e)$ increases with e, it follows that w is lower at (N_2, e_2) than it would have been at (N_1, e_3).

Notes

1. A useful overview of Marshall's work is provided by O'Brien [1981]. The standard biographical reference is Keynes [1924]. Pigou [1925] reproduces this and much valuable background material.

2. In the later editions of the *Principles*, distribution was treated in Book VI and Appendix J, but some preliminary discussions are to be found in Books IV and V. (See Book IV, chapters 1–4, 6, 7, 13, and Book V, chapters 8–11, of the eighth and final edition — Marshall [1920]. This edition is reproduced as the first volume of the indispensable variorum edition — Guillebaud [1961] — whose second volume reproduces variant readings from earlier editions plus related passages and documents.) Besides the manuscripts reproduced in Whitaker [1975, Vol. I, pp. 178–259; Vol. II, pp. 250–252, 275–277, 309–316, 321–335], distribution is discussed in the *Economics of Industry* — Marshall [1879] — and in its replacement, the *Elements of Economics of Industry* — Marshall [1892] — the latter largely a condensation of the *Principles* but adding Marshall's most elaborate treatment of trades unions. The most important of his occasional publications touching on distribution are Marshall [1872, 1885, 1887, 1888, 1893, 1898].

3. See, for example, Marshall [1879, pp. 146–167; 1920, pp. 573–575, 619–620, 664, 709–711; 1923, pp. 234–263]. Marshall's views on money and business cycles are described by Wolfe [1956] and Eshag [1963].

4. The most important treatment is that of Stigler [1941, chapters 4, 12], which is, however, quite selective. Robertson [1970] is more comprehensive, but is primarily concerned with illustrating Marshall's general approach to economics. Whitaker [1974] expounds Marshall's early work on distribution and growth and is supplemented by the exegeses in Whitaker [1975, especially Vol. I, pp. 67–83, 178–184, 224–229; Vol. II, pp. 248–250, 305–309]. Marshall's treatment of the supply of labor is dealt with in Walker [1974, 1975], while aspects of his treatment of labor markets are considered by Hicks [1930] and Petridis [1973]. His views on rent are discussed by Ogilvie [1930] and Hollond [1930].

5. These were the titles of Books VI and V in editions 2–4 of the *Principles*. See Guillebaud [1961, Vol. II, pp. 16–18, 72–73, 77–130]. Book V dealt only with the "theoretical backbone of our knowledge of the causes which govern value on its two sides of distribution and exchange" [p. 72]. Marshall suggested at one point that Book V took factor prices for granted while Book VI explained them, and thus dealt with value as a whole [p. 573]. But this distinction is too sharp.

6. Stigler [1941, pp. 344–356] is reluctant to portray Marshall as an outright marginal-productivity theorist but this seems unnecessarily (and uncharacteristically) cautious. See, for example, Guillebaud [1961, Vol. II, p. 567] where the net product is explicitly identified as the partial derivative of a production function. The term "marginal efficiency" or "marginal net efficiency" was sometimes used instead of "net product." See, for example, Guillebaud [1961, Vol. II, p. 559] and Marshall [1920, p. 826].

7. Marshall recognized that the marginal addition to the value of the product might be less than the value of the marginal addition to the product, and that it would necessarily be so for a monopolist or for a manufacturing firm producing a differentiated product, but he chose generally to neglect this complication [Marshall, 1920, pp. 517, 849].

8. See Bliss [1975, pp. 93–101]. Assuming cost minimization rather than profit maximization, so that $w_i/w_j = f_i/f_j$ for all $i \neq j$, and noting that marginal cost is $mc = w_j/f_j$ by the envelope property, equation 5.1 may be written as

$$(mnp)_j - pf_j = (p - mc)(df/dx_j - f_j).$$

Marginal net product equals the value of marginal product if either $p = mc$ (implying profit maximization) or $df/dx_j = f_j$ (variation of all inputs other than j has a combined zero net effect on output).

9. See Marshall [1920, pp. 79–80, 523–524] and Guillebaud [1961, Vol. II, pp. 588–591].

10. For an account of the distribution theory presented in Marshall [1879] see Whitaker [1974; 1975, Vol. I, pp. 74–80].

11. This is not to imply that the rate of return is equalized in all uses. See section on The Supply of Labor.

12. With the important exception of depletable resources. Marshall was always careful to treat use of these as a form of disinvestment, a feature difficult to build into long-period equilibrium.

13. On the topics dealt with in this paragraph see Marshall [1920, pp. 403–439, 499–500, 535–536]. The producer's surplus or differential rent dealt with here must be sharply distinguished from the producer's surplus of Appendix K, which applies to all factors and is an analogue of consumer's surplus [pp. 830–832].

14. See especially Guillebaud [1961, Vol. II, pp. 637–638, 643]. Marshall mentions elsewhere [1920, p. 139] a fourth fundamental agent "organization" — see section on Organization and Business Power. As Robertson [1970, p. 27] notes, Marshall has a tendency to apply the word "agent" to broad groups of inputs and the word "factor" to specific inputs, but this distinction is not followed through with entire consistency.

15. On the material in this paragraph see Marshall [1920, pp. 232–236, 533–534, 581–582, 680] and Guillebaud [1961, Vol. II, pp. 638–639, 680].

16. See Marshall [1920, pp. 193–219, 525–579, 689–722] and Walker [1974].

17. Workers are not often free to choose their work hours, but when they are the choice between occupations requires an optimal life-time path of work hours to be estimated for each alternative!

18. There is an exception in the case where a man needs the same fixed capital whatever his efficiency. See Marshall [1920, pp. 549–550, 706n].

19. On the general issues dealt with in this first phase of discussion see Marshall [1920, pp. 86–91, 173–203, 591–592, 529–534, 546–550, 689–696], Guillebaud [1961, Vol. II, pp. 40, 313–316, 616–617] and Walker [1974]. The very vague and elliptic nature of much of Marshall's treatment needs to be emphasized.

20. Note that with N fixed $\partial Q/\partial(Ne) = \partial(Q/N)/\partial e$.

21. Marshall [1920, pp. 530–531]. The middle quotation might be interpreted as saying $f'(e) \geq c'(e)$, which is true for $e < e_0$ if $c(e)/e$ is nonincreasing with e so that $c'(e) \leq c(e)/e$.

22. On this phase of the discussion see Marshall [1920, pp. 217–219, 514, 556–557, 562–564, 571–572, 622, 660–663, 680–684].

23. On the issues dealt with in this section see Marshall [1920, pp. 291–313, 596–628]; Robertson [1970, pp. 56–59]. The return to hired managers will be determined in a similar way to the return to any skilled worker. Should a businessman himself perform duties which might have been deputed to a hired manager, then the return to these activities will be the same as the hired manager would have received.

24. The first paragraph, which refers to distribution under "physiocratic" factor-supply assumptions, only appeared in the first two editions of the *Principles*. See Guillebaud [1961, Vol. II, p. 577]. The second paragraph comes from Marshall [1920, p. 577]. For other passages dealing with distribution as a whole see Marshall [1920, pp. xv, 521–522, 525–526, 532, 536–537, 665, 678, 824, 850, 852] and Guillebaud [1961, Vol. II, pp. 40, 559, 578–580].

25. See Whitaker [1975, Vol. II, pp. 322–332]. These jottings remain within a partial-equilibrium framework in which commodity demands and factor supplies depend only on an own-price variable, but they do use differentiable production functions whose partial derivatives serve as the marginal products entering output-supply and input-demand decisions. The notes are suggestive and provide further evidence for treating Marshall as an adherent of orthodox marginal-productivity theory. But because they are sketchy and marred by various slight blunders, they fall short of a decisive resolution of the issues they deal with. Even so, they go further than anything published at the time and would have been a significant contribution had they been polished up and published in the mid 1880s (when they were most probably written).

26. See, for example, Marshall [1920, pp. 430–432, 450, 534–536].

27. See Stigler [1941, chapters 3, 11] for details of the contributions of P.H. Wicksteed and J.B. Clark.

28. See Marshall [1920, p. 380]. Chapter XII, "General Influences of Progress on Value," was essentially unchanged from the first edition. Chapter XIII, "Progress in Relation to Standards of Life," dates essentially from the 1907 edition.

29. See Marshall [1920, pp. xii–xv, 380]. A very good account by Marshall of the nature and limitations of long-period equilibrium is in Guillebaud [1961, Vol. II, pp. 572–576: also see p. 625] and Marshall [1920, p. 379n].

30. See Robinson [1964, pp. 2, 23–26; 1973, pp. 62–63]. Stigler [1941, pp. 62–63] is critical of Marshall's reluctance to espouse stationary-equilibrium methods more decisively.

31. An alternative to keeping quantities of capital and population hypothetically fixed would be to take the interest rate and the wage rate of unskilled workers as fixed. The latter perhaps comes closer to Marshall's general preference for embedding distribution in a setting of sustained growth. But the *Principles* seems to have taken the pragmatic expedient of postulating rather arbitrary supply functions for capital and population.

32. See Marshall [1920, p. 379n] and Guillebaud [1961, Vol. II, p. 625].

33. See Marshall [1920, pp. 525, 543–544, 580, 583] and Guillebaud [1961, Vol. II, pp. 592–594].

34. See Marshall [1920, pp. 410, 532n, 583–584n], Pigou [1925, pp. 412–418], and

Guillebaud [1961, Vol. II, pp. 567, 643]. The last page referenced, written in 1890, lists the following writers as having contributed "during the last few years" to the "difficult and important task" of making clear the various aspects of distribution: Jevons, Menger, Wieser, Pantaleoni, Sidgwick, Walker, Clark, Giddings, Patten, Wood, and Webb.

35. Walker [1876]. The significance of arguments concerning the "economy of high wages" tends to be underestimated in modern histories of the economic thought of the period.

36. There is in particular the well-known remark that "The doctrine that the earnings of a worker tend to be equal to the net product of his work, has by itself no real meaning; since in order to estimate net product, we have to take for granted all the expenses of production of the commodity...other than his own wages" [Marshall, 1920, p. 518]. This seems more radical when taken out of context than it does in context, when it appears as little more than an awkward way of stressing mutual interdependence. See Marshall [1920, pp. 410, 525–526] for less tortuous statements with similar effect.

37. The function F is assumed to have negative direct second-order partial derivatives with respect to all arguments. Cross second-order partials are negative if inputs are "close substitutes."

38. See, for example, Marshall [1920, pp. 666–667n, 670–671n].

39. On such matters see Marshall [1920, pp. 537–540, 666–667, 689–722, 825]. Also see the discussions of trades unions in Marshall [1879, pp. 199–213] and Marshall [1892, pp. 362–403].

40. For mention of increasing returns in connection with distribution see Marshall [1920, pp. 518n, 667n, 849]. In a remarkable footnote, appearing only in editions 3–5 of the *Principles*, Marshall did outline clearly the distinction between social and private net product and its pertinence to the failure of "the doctrine of maximum satisfaction." But this brilliant insight was left to be further developed by Pigou. See Guillebaud [1961, Vol. II, p. 587]

References

Bliss, C.J. (1975). *Capital Theory and the Distribution of Income*. Amsterdam: North-Holland.

Eshag, E. (1963). *From Marshall to Keynes: An Essay on the Monetary Theory of the Cambridge School*. Oxford: Blackwell.

Guillebaud, C.W. (ed.) (1961). *Alfred Marshall: Principles of Economics: Ninth (Variorum) Edition*. Two vols. London: Macmillan.

Hicks, J.R. (1930). Edgeworth, Marshall and the indeterminateness of wages. *Economic Journal* 40: 215–231.

————. (1932) *The Theory of Wages*. London: Macmillan. Citations are of the second edition, 1963.

Hollond, M.T. (1930). Marshall on rent: a reply to Professor Ogilvie. *Economic Journal* 40: 369–383.

Keynes, J.M. (1924). Alfred Marshall, 1842–1924. *Economic Journal* 34: 311–372. Reprinted with slight changes in Pigou (1925) and in J.M. Keynes (1933), *Essays in Biography*. London: Macmillan.

Marshall, A. (1872). Review of W.S. Jevons' *Theory of Political Economy*, *Academy*. Reprinted in Pigou (1925).

—————. (1885). Theories and facts about wages. *Annual of the Wholesale Cooperative Society*. Reprinted in Guillebaud (1961).

—————. (1887). The theory of business profits. *Quarterly Journal of Economics* I: 477–481. Reprinted in Guillebaud (1961).

—————. (1888). Wages and profits. *Quarterly Journal of Economics* 2: 218–223. Reprinted in Guillebaud (1961).

—————. (1890). *Principles of Economics, Vol. I*. London: Macmillan.

—————. (1892). *Elements of Economics of Industry*. London: Macmillan. Citations are of the third edition, 1899.

—————. (1893). On rent. *Economic Journal* 3: 74–90. Reprinted in Guillebaud (1961).

—————. (1898). Distribution and exchange. *Economic Journal* 8: 37–59. Portions are reproduced in Pigou (1925) and Guillebaud (1961).

—————. (1920). *Principles of Economics: an Introductory Volume*. London: Macmillan. The eighth edition of Marshall (1890).

—————. (1923). *Money Credit and Commerce*. London: Macmillan.

Marshall, A., and M.P. (1879). *Economics of Industry*. London: Macmillan. Citations are of the second edition, 1881.

O'Brien D.P. (1981). Alfred Marshall, 1842–1924. In D.P. O'Brien and J.R. Presley (eds.), *Pioneers of Modern Economics in Britain*. London: Macmillan.

Ogilvie, F.W. (1930). Marshall on rent. *Economic Journal* 40: 1–24.

Petridis, A. (1973). Alfred Marshall's attitudes to and economic analysis of trade unions: a case of anomalies in a competitive system. *History of Political Economy* 5: 165–198.

Pigou, A.C. (1925). *Memorials of Alfred Marshall*. London: Macmillan.

Robertson, H.M. (1970). Alfred Marshall's aims and methods illustrated from his treatment of distribution. *History of Political Economy* 2: 1–65.

Robinson, J. (1964). *Collected Economic Papers*, Vol. Two. Oxford: Blackwell.

—————. (1973). *Collected Economic Papers*, Vol. Four. Oxford: Blackwell.

Stigler, G.J. (1941), *Production and Distribution Theories: the Formative Period*. New York: Macmillan.

Walker, D.A. (1974). Marshall on the long-run supply of labor. *Zeitschrift für de Gesamte Staatswissenschaft* 130: 691–705.

—————. (1975). Marshall on the short-run supply of labor. *Southern Economic Journal* 41: 429–441.

Walker, F.A. (1876). *The Wages Question*. New York: Holt.

Whitaker, J.K. (1974). The Marshallian system in 1881: distribution and growth. *Economic Journal* 84: 1–17.

—————. (1975). *The Early Economic Writings of Alfred Marshall, 1867–1890*. Two vols. London: Macmillan.

Wolfe, J.N. (1956). Marshall and the trade cycle. *Oxford Economic Papers* 8: 90–101.

6 POST-KEYNESIAN THEORIES OF DISTRIBUTION

Athanasios Asimakopulos

The factor incomes that appear in post-Keynesian theories of income distribution are profits (a category that includes interest and rent, as well as dividends and retained earnings) and wages (a category that includes salaries, except possibly the salaries of higher business executives that may be considered part of profits). There are three features that distinguish these theories: (1) they consider investment to be an important determinant of profits; (2) they assume that, at least over a wide range of possible values, investment is independent of saving, with saving adapting to investment; and (3) the propensity to save out of profits is assumed to be greater than the propensity to save out of wages.

The three versions of this theory that have received the most attention, those of Kalecki, Kaldor, and Pasinetti, will be examined in some detail. Even though they all contain the three distinguishing features noted above, there are important differences between them. Kalecki's theoreti-

I am grateful, without attaching any responsibility for possible errors or interpretations, to S. Ingerman, A. Roncaglia, L. Soderstrom, and J. Weldon, for comments on an earlier draft.

cal framework for the examination of the distribution of income is similar to that employed by Keynes in his *General Theory*, even though Kalecki developed it prior to the publication of that book. Kalecki's analysis deals only with situations of short-period equilibrium in which the economy is generally characterized by less than full employment of labor and productive capacity, but unlike Keynes, he was primarily interested in explaining the cyclical patterns obtained over a sequence of short periods. Kaldor's version is restricted to situations where, in addition to short-period equilibrium, there is full employment of labor and normal utilization of productive capacity. Pasinetti's version is even more special, since it is concerned with a situation that not only can be characterized by long-period equilibrium for firms with full employment of labor but is also the result of exponential growth at a constant rate for a very long period of time. The relative values of all the variables in the latter model are adjusted to the conditions of this steady state. Kalecki's theory concentrates on the determination of profits and the profit share, and the assumptions made about the degree of competition, market structure and pricing policy, can affect its conclusions. The model used by Kalecki, because it is anchored in a short period that displays important characteristics of modern capitalist economies, is very flexible. For example, it can allow for consideration of the possible effects of trade union pressures on markups and the inflationary potential of attempts to affect labor's income share through this route. The theories developed by Kaldor and Pasinetti are tied to the assumption of full employment of both labor and productive capacity, and this makes the short-period situations they examine more special than those used by Kalecki. For Pasinetti, with long-period equilibrium at the center of his analysis, the key dependent variable is the equilibrium rate of profit.

Kalecki on Distribution

Although "post-Keynesian," or even "Keynesian" is the umbrella term for the theories of distribution presented here — and the former thus appears as this chapter's heading — a more appropriate label would be "Kaleckian," because all three of the main features of theory listed above first appeared in Kalecki's writings.[1] The determination of profits, in the simplified model of a closed economy with no government taxation or expenditure and no workers' saving, is set out in his study of the business cycle that was published in Polish in 1933, and that formed the basis of the paper presented at the Econometric Society meeting in Leyden in

October 1933, and subsequently published in *Econometrica* in 1935. A portion of this study was subsequently published in the first chapter of his *Selected Essays* [Kalecki, 1971]. (A companion piece that also considered the effects of different market conditions on the profit share and real wages [Kalecki, 1935a] was published in French.) There the theory is set out for a situation of short-period equilibrium, even though it is not explicitly identified in this way. Investment expenditure in the period is equal to planned expenditure, and the consumption expenditures of workers and capitalists are in the desired relations to their incomes. The first statement of the theory deals only with "real" expenditures and incomes, and makes use of the national income identity between gross national product and gross national expenditure, as well as the special assumptions already noted, to arrive at the conclusion that profits in the period are equal to the sum of capitalists' expenditures in the period. This can be shown by letting P stand for gross profits, I for gross investment, C_c and C_w for capitalists' and workers' consumption, respectively, and W for total wages. The national income identity can be written as

$$W + P = I + C_c + C_w \qquad (6.1)$$

and given the assumption that $C_w = W$, we obtain

$$P = I + C_c. \qquad (6.2)$$

Equation (6.2) is based on more than a simple manipulation of the identity shown in equation (6.1). The behavioral assumption that the propensity to save of workers is zero has been introduced, as well as two short-period equilibrium assumptions. They are that workers' consumption is in the desired relation to income, and actual investment in the period is equal to planned investment. Kalecki also presents a function for capitalists' consumption expenditures that show them related to current profits.

$$C_c = B_o + \lambda P \qquad (6.3)$$

where λ is a positive constant considerably smaller than 1, and B_o is fairly large. When this expression is substituted for C_c in equation (6.2), we obtain

$$P = \frac{B_o + I}{(1 - \lambda)} \qquad (6.4)$$

Current gross profits are thus proportionate to the sum of the constant part of capitalists' consumption expenditures and the inverse of the marginal propensity to save out of profits. In his discussion of the relation between changes in investment and changes in aggregate production, Kalecki implicitly recognizes that the working out of the multiplier effects of the former requires the passage of time.

> When production of investment goods rises the aggregate production increases directly *pro tanto*, but in addition there is an increase due to the demand for consumer goods on the part of the workers newly engaged in the investment goods industries. The consequent increase in employment in the consumer-goods industries leads to a further rise in the demand for consumer goods. . . . *The aggregate production and the profit per unit of output will ultimately rise to such an extent as to assure an increment in real profits equal to that of production of investment goods and capitalists' consumption* [Kalecki, 1971, p. 12; italics in original].

Kalecki's equations, however, do not refer to the passage of time; they deal only with situations of short-period equilibrium, where the full multiplier effects of any change in investment that might have occurred in this period, as compared to the previous period, have been completed.

Kalecki concludes from equations (6.2) and (6.4) that "capitalists, as a whole, determine their own profits by the extent of their investment and personal consumption. In a way they are 'masters of their fate;' but how they 'master' it is determined by objective factors, so that fluctuations of profits appear after all to be unavoidable" [p. 13]. Even though there is reference here to capitalists "as a whole," it is clear from Kalecki's subsequent statements, both in this quotation and in other writings, that capitalists do not act as a united "class" in determining their expenditures. The determination of profits refers to the macroeconomic effects of the very large number of individual decisions made by capitalists, decisions that in the case of investment often reflect rivalry and struggle for market shares. An entrepreneur sees profits being earned as a result of being in a position to take advantage of favorable market conditions, conditions that he tries to influence by advertising and other expenditures, or even by collusive behavior with potential rivals in particular markets, but he cannot count on his own current investment expenditures automatically increasing his own current profits along the lines of equation (6.2). This equation reflects macroeconomic conditions, conditions over which his own expenditures have a negligible effect.

Kalecki's theory of profits has its basis in his study of Karl Marx and Rosa Luxemburg. He has noted that his profit equations "are contained in the famous Marxian scheme of 'extended reproduction'" [Kalecki, 1939, p. 45, and also Kalecki, 1954, p. 47], but Marx uses this scheme for a different purpose. "He is interested in finding out, with the help of exchange equations, the pace of investment in investment and consumption goods respectively, which is necessary in order to secure a steady expansion of output" [Kalecki, 1939, p. 45]. It is from Luxemburg who "stressed the point that, if capitalists are saving, their profits can be 'realized' only if a corresponding amount is spent by them on investment" [pp. 45–46], that Kalecki obtained the inspiration to turn an accounting identity into a theory of the determination of profits.

   Kalecki turned to a consideration of the determination of the profit share, prices, and real wages in Kalecki [1935a].[2] With profits in real terms in the short-period equilibrium situations examined being fully determined by capitalists' expenditures in real terms, the profit share and real wages depend on the extent to which output responds to changes in the factors that determine profits. Kalecki assumes that there exists a reserve of unemployed labor [1935a, p. 296n] and that the degree of utilization of existing capital equipment can be varied [p. 300]. Under competititve conditions changes in capitalists' expenditures lead to changes in output and prices in the same direction. The higher prices relative to wage costs that result from higher capitalist expenditures, increase the profit share and lower real-wage rates. A decrease in capitalist expenditures results in changes in the opposite direction. Real-wage rates move inversely to output, as higher prices relative to wage costs are required to increase output, given diminishing returns from the operation of existing equipment.[3] Kalecki also examined the case where profit margins, and thus prices, are fixed as a result of cartel arrangements. In this case output varies proportionately to the increase in capitalist expenditures, with the wage share and real-wage rates being unaffected by this increase. With total profits determined by capitalists' expenditures, higher profit margins, given these expenditures in real terms, will bring about lower real-wage rates and a higher profit share as they adversely affect total output.

   The determination of income shares and the real wage bill, in Kalecki's simplified model, thus depend on the assumptions made about competitive conditions in product markets and the conditions of production. With competitive markets it is assumed that the "marginal" equipment is less efficient, leading to rising unit prime costs for increases in output. A different implicit assumption, one without a necessarily noticeable difference in the efficiency of marginal equipment, appears to be made when cartel arrangements are discussed, since a constant profit share is taken to be consistent with higher output and relatively constant prices.

   Kalecki returned to a consideration of the significance of his profits equation in an article [Kalecki, 1942] that was subsequently expanded and incorporated in Kalecki [1954, ch. 3], and reprinted in Kalecki [1971, ch. 7]. He asked of equation [6.2]: "Does it mean that profits in a given period determine capitalists' consumption and investment, or the reverse of this?" [1971, p. 78]. He answers it on the basis of the position that the determinant in any such equation is the element that is subject to the decisions of capitalists. "Now, it is clear that capitalists may decide to consume and to invest more in a given period than in the preceding one, but they cannot decide to earn more. It is, therefore, their investment and consumption decisions which determine profits, and not vice versa" [1971, pp. 78–79]. This answer is not satisfactory because it does not exclude the possibility that the expenditure decisions in a particular period are themselves based on profits in that period. In the latter case there is not a one-way causation from capitalists' expenditures to profits but rather a relationship of mutual dependence. The causal relationship that Kalecki sees thus requires that the period of time considered be sufficiently short so that, given the length of the time lags between investment decisions and expenditures, and between capitalists' consumption expenditures and profits, these expenditures are independent of current profits. The necessary equality between current profits and current capitalists' expenditures (when workers' saving is zero) can thus be read as showing a one-way relationship that goes to profits from expenditures only if the period of time for the equation is short relative to time lags that separate these expenditures and profits.

Kalecki draws attention to a condition that only holds if "the period which we consider is short" [1971, p. 79]; he sees it as necessary, not for the establishment of the direction of causation between current profits and current capitalists' expenditures but for "capitalists' investment and consumption [to be] determined by decisions shaped in the *past*" [1971, p. 79; italics in the original]. He recognizes that past investment decisions "may not fully determine the volume of investment in a given period, owing to unexpected accumulation or running down of stocks" [1971, p. 79], and thus concludes (when there is no workers' saving) "that the real gross profits in a given short period are determined by decisions of capitalists with respect to their consumption and investment shaped in the past, subject to correction for unexpected changes in the volume of stocks" [1971, pp. 79–80].

In the general case of an open economy with government taxation and expenditure, and workers' saving, Kalecki rearranged the expanded number of items that now appear in the national income identity to obtain an equation for gross profits net of taxes. They are shown to be equal to the sum of gross investment, the export surplus, the government deficit, and capitalists' consumption, minus workers' saving. These after-tax profits in a particular period can be said to be determined by the values of the items to which they must be equal, if the latter are independent of current profits. For a short period of time, such as a quarter of a year, this assumption is not an unreasonable one to make. Planned investment expenditures in a particular quarter are independent of actual profits in that quarter, and thus actual investment expenditures in the quarter (even when these values are affected by unexpected changes in inventories) are largely independent of current profits. Even if capitalists' consumption expenditures are directly related to their incomes, these incomes are generally a lagged function of profits. Interest receipts depend on the terms at which placements were made in the past, while dividends tend to lag profits by a quarter of a year. The other items on the right-hand side of the profits equation are also largely independent of the values for current profits.[4]

Kalecki's subsequent discussions of the determination of the labor share in his writings in the 1940s and later, observe the separation of the determination of profits from the determinants of the profit share. The discussion of the latter becomes focused around the "degree of monopoly" which affects the size of the profit margin. "If, for instance, the degree of monopoly increases, and, as a result, so does the ratio of profits to wages, real profits do not change, but the real wage bill falls, first because of the fall in the real wage rate, and secondly because of the consequent reduction in demand for wage goods, and thus of output and employment in the wage-good industries" [Kalecki, 1942, p. 260]. The wage share also depends on the ratio of prices of raw materials to unit wage costs, a ratio that depends on demand conditions. Kalecki distinguishes between "demand-determined" prices — in which category he places primary goods — and "cost-determined" prices, in which category he places manufactured or "finished" goods. He states that "these two types of price formation arise out of different conditions of supply. The production of finished goods is elastic as a result of existing reserves of productive capacity.... The situation with respect to raw materials is different...with supply inelastic in short periods, an increase in demand causes a diminution of stocks and a consequent increase in price" [Kalecki, 1954, p. 11]. It is clear from his discussion of these two types of prices that the nature of market conditions is also an important distinguishing factor, with competitive markets being the typical case for primary goods, and oligopolistic markets for manufactured goods. Firms producing manufactured goods set prices by marking up unit prime costs, costs that are assumed to be constant over some considerable range of output. A firm's markup reflects the average price in the particular industry, and the various elements that protect the firm from competition that Kalecki gathered together under the term "degree of monopoly" [1954, pp. 12–13]. The higher the degree of monopoly, the higher the firm's price relative to its unit prime costs. This cost-based nature of price formation was extended by Kalecki to cover construction, transportation, and services, and he concludes that "the determinants of the relative share of wages in the gross income of the private sector" are "broadly speaking, the degree of monopoly, the ratio of prices of raw materials to unit wage costs and industrial composition" [1954, p. 30].

Changes in this labor share can be affected by changes in average markups in industries whose prices are cost-determined, and by changes in capitalists' expenditures through their effects on the demand for primary goods, and thus on the ratio of prices of raw materials to unit wage costs. Even in Kalecki's simplified model, however, this labor share is only the share of labor prime costs in value added, and not, as Kalecki's statement claims, "the relative share of wages in the gross income of the private sector," [1954, p. 30] because it ignores the wages that are part of overhead costs.[5] With the recognition that overhead costs are in part wages, then it follows that changes in capitalists' expenditures can affect the wage share, quite apart from their effects on the ratio of raw material prices to unit wage costs, as Kalecki had noted in his 1933 study [Kalecki, 1971, p. 11n]. With higher demand, the overhead wages costs are spread over a larger output, and even with constant prices, profit per unit of output is higher.

Kalecki's proposition that the degree of monopoly can affect the profit share but not the level of profits, is not valid in his more general model of an open economy with government taxation and expenditure and workers' saving [Asimakopulos, 1975, pp. 331–332]. Changes in profit margins, given capitalists' expenditures, affect total profits as well as income shares because of their influence on workers' real incomes and thus on workers' saving, as well as, on the economy's international competitiveness, which alters its trade balance. The resulting change in economic activity could also alter the government deficit. Kalecki did not examine the effects of changes in the degree of monopoly on profits in this general model, contenting himself with pointing out "the significance of 'external' markets (including those created by budget deficits) for a capitalist economy. Without such markets profits are conditioned by the ability of capitalists to consume or to undertake capital investment" [Kalecki, 1954, p. 52]. There was no modification to the earlier conclusion in that chapter which gave the degree of monopoly a role only in determining "the workers' income" [p. 47]. This denial of a role to profit margins in the determination of profits has become the accepted way of viewing Kalecki's theory of distribution. For example, Joan Robinson, in her 1976 Michal Kalecki Memorial Lecture, points to the "very striking proposition that firms, considered as a whole, cannot increase their profits merely by raising prices. Raising profit margins reduces real wages and consequently employment in wage-good industries" [Robinson, 1980, p. 192].

Kalecki examines the possible impact on distribution of collective bargaining, in a paper entitled "Class Struggle and Distribution of National Income" that was published posthumously in 1971. This bargaining is seen as changing the labor share if it can change the markups on unit prime costs. Such changes are considered possible when buoyant market conditions for goods and relatively tight labor markets allow "a spectacular wage rise" [Kalecki, 1971, p. 162], a rise that is reflected in a fall in markups because "bargaining is proceeding by industries" [1971, p. 161n]. An industry that is forced by trade union pressure to raise wages substantially will allow some erosion of its markup, because "an industry will not like such a process making its products more and more expensive and thus less competitive with products of other industries" [p. 161]. Assuming, as does Kalecki, that capitalists' expenditures in real terms are not affected by this demonstration of "trade-union power," then this increase in wage rates, through the lowering of markups, "leads — contrary to the precepts of classical economics — to an increase in employment" [p. 163]. Kalecki states that this conclusion "is feasible only if excess capacity is in existence. Otherwise it is impossible to increase wages in relation to prices of wage goods because prices are determined by demand, and functions [determining fixed markups] become defunct" [p. 164]. In addition, there is an implicit assumption that the rising money-wage rates and prices through which this "class struggle" expresses itself, do not adversely affect capitalists' expenditures. Kalecki does not consider the possibility that rising prices adversely affect capitalists' expenditures, but this may occur. For example, consumption in real terms of rentiers whose incomes are largely fixed in money terms (e.g., retired workers) may be reduced when prices increase sharply, and the monetary authorities, concerned by these rising prices, may impose credit restraints that lead to lower investment expenditures.[6]

Mention should also be made of Kalecki's distinction between profits and interest, with the difference between these two items being the earnings of the entrepreneurs. These earnings must always be residuals in the short-period situations considered by Kalecki, with short-term variations in profits — given the contractual nature of interest payments —

being reflected in even sharper variations in the earnings of entrepreneurs. There is a parallel distinction between the prospective rate of
profit on investment and the rate of interest, with the difference between
them being the expected rate of return to entrepreneurs for undertaking
the risks involved in investment in plant and equipment and the organization of production. This appears, for example, in his 1937 paper on
taxation when he considers a tax on capitalists' incomes. He gives as a
numerical example, "the prospective rate of profit of a certain type of
investment is initially at nine percent, let us say, and the rate of interest
at three percent, the entrepreneur planning investment has a differential
of six percent before income tax deduction and 5.1 percent after the
deduction of 15 percent income tax to cover his risk" [Kalecki, 1971, pp.
39–40]. Kalecki has also used the gap between these two rates as ". . . the
key to the problem of amount of investment decisions in a given situation
in a certain period of time. . . . This amount is just so much as will equate
the marginal risk to the gap between the prospective rate of profit and the
rate of interest, both being given by the economic situation of the period
in question" [Kalecki, 1937, p. 85]. For Kalecki the short-term rate of
interest is determined by the value of transactions, which underlies the
demand for money, and the supply of money by the banks, while "the
long-term rate is determined by anticipation of the short-term rate based
on past experience and by estimates of the risk involved in the possible
depreciation of long-term [financial] assets" [Kalecki, 1954, p. 73].

Kaldor's "Keynesian" Theory of Distribution

The theory of distribution presented by Kaldor as "Keynesian" differs
from Kalecki's theory in certain essential points, even though it shares the
view of investment as independent from saving, and the assumption about
the relative values for the propensities to save out of profits and out of
wages. Kaldor states that the principle of the multiplier "could be alternatively applied to a determination of the relation between prices and
wages, if the level of output and employment is taken as given, or the
determination of the level of employment, if distribution (i.e. the relation
between prices and wages) is taken as given" [Kaldor 1955–56, p. 227].
He sees its role in the latter capacity as part of "a short-run theory," or
"in the framework of a static model," and in the former capacity as part
of "a long-run theory" or in the framework "of a dynamic growth model"
[1955–56, p. 228]. Kaldor is here apparently unaware of its use by
Kalecki [1935a, pp. 296–297] to explain both employment and the rela-

tion of prices to wages.[7] With plant and equipment as well as capitalists' expenditures given in the short period, employment and output are pushed, under competitive conditions, up to the point where prices are equal to marginal costs. Higher investment in such a situation would increase employment and lower the real-wage rate.[8] There is an implicit assumption by Kaldor of full utilization of productive capacity — a utilization that arises as a result of "flexible profit margins." Plant and equipment must be just sufficient, under these conditions, to provide full employment in order to arrive at Kaldor's conclusion that "[A]ssuming flexible prices (or rather flexible profit margins) the system is thus stable at full employment" [Kaldor, 1955–56, p. 230].

Kaldor's subsequent reference to Harrod's warranted rate of growth, an entrepreneurial equilibrium rate, implies not only the full utilization of productive capacity in his model but also prices for goods when plant is utilized at this rate that provide a normal rate of profit on investment. The short period in Kaldor's analysis thus displays the special characteristics of a situation of long-period equilibrium, with the investment term being net investment, as in Harrod [1939, p. 16]. In Kalecki's theory, where the short period does not, in general have either full employment or these long-period equilibrium features for firms, the investment term is gross investment, since estimates of depreciation are, in the nature of things, liable to be mistaken when the assumption of continuing long-period equilibrium is dropped.

Kaldor's model is assumed to operate only within a certain range of values for the dependent variables. This range is marked by a certain subsistence minimum for the real wage, and by limits on the minimum permissible value for the rate of profit or the profit share, whichever is reached first [Kaldor, 1955–56, pp. 232–233]. With total output (Y) given by the assumption of full employment, it is the difference in the saving propensities that determines income shares. The propensities to save that appear in Kaldor's model are those relevant to the category of income rather than to the "class" to which individuals belong. He assumes simple proportional saving functions, with the propensity to save out of profits (s_p) being greater than the propensity to save out of wages (s_w). Support for this assumption is provided by the observation "that the bulk of profits accrues in the form of company profits and a high proportion of companies' marginal profits is put to reserve" [1955–56, p. 229n]. Not only is saving necessarily equal to the independently determined value for investment, but in short-period equilibrium the distribution of income between profits and wages must be such as to make this saving that which is determined by the propensities to save. This latter equality can be written as (with total income being exhausted by the sum of wages and profits).

$$I = s_p P + s_w W = s_p P + s_w(Y - P) = (s_p - s_w)P + s_w Y. \quad (6.5)$$

If both sides of this equation are divided by Y, we obtain

$$\frac{I}{Y} = (s_p - s_w)\frac{P}{Y} + s_w \quad (6.6)$$

$$\text{or} \quad \frac{P}{Y} = \frac{1}{s_p - s_w}\frac{I}{Y} - \frac{s_w}{s_p - s_w} \quad (6.7)$$

Kaldor thus concludes that, given the propensities to save, the share of profits in income depends only on the ratio of investment to output, a ratio that is exogenously determined in his model. He notes that the "model operates only if the two savings propensities differ and the marginal propensity to save from profits exceeds that from wages" [1955–56, p. 230]. In the special case of a zero value for the workers' propensity to save, the amount of profits is equal to the sum of capitalists' expenditures, as in Kalecki's model.

Kaldor then considers the determinants of the investment/output ratio that is the independent variable, determinants that must themselves be independent of the profit share if the model is to explain that share. These determinants are expressed in terms of concepts he attributes to Harrod, but they do not appear in this form in Harrod's writings. Kaldor states that the determinants of the investment/output ratio in a situation of long-period equilibrium are "the rate of growth of output capacity (G) and the capital/output ratio, v" [1955–56, p. 231],[9] and he writes

$$\frac{I}{Y} = Gv. \quad (6.8)$$

If K is used to denote the value of capital, then v is equal to K/Y, and for equation (6.8) to hold, G must be equal to I/K. Kaldor identifies G as the rate of growth of output capacity, and it must thus be equal to the ratio of net investment to the value of existing capital. If G is taken to be exogenously determined by the requirements for full employment growth, then it must be equal to the sum of the rate of growth of the labor force and the rate of technical progress. Such a rate of growth will only be "warranted," that is, investment will be justified by the resulting increase in output, if the investment/output ratio derived from equation (6.8) is equal to the desired saving/output ratio in the economy. The latter is shown by the right-hand side of equation (6.6), and equation (6.7) shows the profit share as dependent on the investment/output ratio. "Hence the 'warranted' and the 'natural' rates of growth are not independent of one another; if profit margins are flexible, the former will adjust itself to the latter through a consequential change in P/Y" [1955–56, p. 232].

Kaldor concludes that, subject to limitations on the values that may be taken by the dependent variables in his model and the independence of his capital/output ratio from the profit share, the model "shows the share of profits P/Y, the rate of profit in capital P/vY, and the real wage rate W/L, as functions of I/Y which in turn is determined independently of P/Y or W/L" [p. 232]. With profit margins being a dependent variable, there is not, as in the case of Kalecki's oligopoly model, the possibility of considering the effects of changes in these margins on distribution. There is thus, given the minimum wage rate that constrains the model, no way that money-wage increases can affect the wage share (unless the resulting price increases affect the saving propensities), since they can have no influence on equilibrium profit margins.

Pasinetti on the Rate of Profit

Pasinetti [1962] appears to begin his analysis of the determination of the rate of profit with Kaldor's equation for the short-period equilibrium equality between investment and saving (equation (6.5) above), but there are two important differences. He examines, in addition to the profit share, the determination of the rate of profit, and his analysis is thus more clearly located in a short-period situation that is characterized by long-period equilibrium, where the use of the value of capital is widely accepted. Pasinetti assumes, as does Kaldor, simple proportional saving functions, but he has "class" rather than "category of income" functions. His equation for the rate of profit is thus written as

$$I = s_w W + s_c P = s_w Y + (s_c - s_w)P \qquad (6.9)$$

whence:

$$\frac{P}{K} = \frac{1}{s_c - s_w} \frac{I}{K} - \frac{s_w}{s_c - s_w} \frac{Y}{K} \qquad (6.10)$$

where s_c is the propensity to save of capitalists and s_w is now the propensity to save of workers.

There is, as Pasinetti points out, a logical slip in equation (6.9) since it does not allow for the profit income of workers, income that accrues to them from their past savings.[10] When the model is reformulated to explicitly recognize the split of profits between capitalists (P_c) and workers (P_w), the short-period equilibrium equality between investment and savings can be written as:

$$I = s_w (W + P_w) + s_c P_c = s_w Y + (s_c - s_w) P_c \qquad (6.11)$$

whence

$$\frac{P_c}{K} = \frac{1}{s_c - s_w} \frac{I}{K} - \frac{s_w}{s_c - s_w} \frac{Y}{K}. \qquad (6.12)$$

In order to obtain the rate of profit on the left-hand side of this equation it is necessary to add P_w/K to both sides of equation (6.12). In his initial presentation of this model, Pasinetti assumed that the rate of interest earned by workers on this saving is equal to the rate of profit. "In a long-run equilibrium model, the obvious hypothesis to make is that of a rate of interest equal to the rate of profit" [1962, p. 109].[11] This, plus the assumption that in "dynamic equilibrium" [p. 109], the ratio (K_w/K) of the total capital accounted for by workers' savings, is equal to the ratio (S_w/S) of current workers' saving to total current saving, give rise to a simple expression for the rate of profit when the appropriate substitutions are made in this term and in equation (6.12).

$$\frac{P}{K} = \frac{1}{s_c} \frac{I}{K}. \qquad (6.13)$$

provided that $I - s_w Y \neq 0$.

The conclusion, expressed in equation (6.13), that the equilibrium rate of profit depends only, given the rate of accumulation, on the propensity to save of capitalists, is dependent on very special equilibrium assumptions. Not only is the particular short period for which the equation is developed characterized by long-period equilibrium, the economy has been in such a situation, with unchanged propensities to save and rate of accumulation, for an indefinitely long interval of time in order to have K_w/K equal to S_w/S.[12]

In his consideration of why equation (6.13) holds in his model even when the propensity to save of workers is positive, Pasinetti points out that in what he terms "long-run exponential growth" [1962, p. 110], the ratio of profits received by any category of individuals in a particular short period (that falls in that special "long-run" situation) to its saving in that period, must be equal to this same ratio for any other category individuals. If there is a category of individuals whose only source of income is profits (for example, Pasinetti's "capitalists") then the saving this group would have made if it had the profit income received by any other group must be equal to the latter's *total* saving. From the equality between P_w/S_w and P_c/S_c, we obtain

$$\frac{P_w}{s_w(W + P_w)} = \frac{P_c}{s_c P_c} \tag{6.14}$$

which can be expressed as $s_w(W + P_w) = s_c P_w$.

It is this consequence of Pasinetti's steady-state assumptions that leads to the disappearance, from the equation for the rate of profit, of the propensity to save of those who have both profit and nonprofit incomes. Pasinetti's formulation also requires, unlike Kaldor's which attaches propensities to save to categories of income, a group whose only source of income is profits, a group that no matter how small will have its saving propensity determine the rate of profit in a "long-run exponential growth" situation. These special steady-state properties of Pasinetti's model are so strong that the conclusion that the basic rate of profit in the system depends only on the rate of accumulation and the propensity to save of capitalists, holds even if workers receive a rate of interest on their savings that is less than the rate of profit. Pasinetti returned to this question in a later paper [Pasinetti, 1974, pp. 121–146].

In a steady-state full employment equilibrium the rate of accumulation is equal to the natural rate of growth (G_n), and this equality can alternately be written using the ratio of saving to the value of capital. Thus

$$\frac{S}{K} = G_n$$

but in any short period that falls in the interval of "long-run exponential growth" —

$$\frac{S}{K} = \frac{S_c}{K_c} = \frac{S_w}{K_w}, \text{ and thus } \frac{S_c}{K_c} = \frac{s_c P_c}{K_c} = G_n, \text{ or}$$

$$\frac{P_c}{K_c} = \frac{1}{s_c} G_n. \tag{6.15}$$

The rate of profit received by capitalists depends only on the natural rate of growth of the economy and its propensity to save. The overall rate of profit in the economy then depends on the relationship between this rate of profit for capitalists and the rate of interest received by workers.

This analysis, of course, only provides the rate of profit that would exist in a situation of long-run exponential growth. In order to obtain the distribution of income between wages and profits in such a situation it is necessary to add information about the conditions of production. Given the rate of profit, the greater the capital/output ratio, the greater the profit share in total income, while the larger the output per unit of labor, given the capital/output ratio and the rate of profit, the larger the real-wage rate.

Pasinetti's model and the way in which he manipulates it are very elegant, but the level of abstraction of an analysis whose conclusions are dependent on unchanging conditions for an interval of time whose length approaches infinity is extremely high. In considering the implications of his conclusions, Pasinetti states that they:

> ...shed new light on the old classical idea of a relation between the savings of that group of individuals who are in the position to carry on the process of production and the process of capital accumulation. This idea has always persisted in economic literature but in a vague and muddled form. Economists have never been able to bring it out clearly. In particular they have always thought — and the post-Keynesian theories...seemed to confirm — that the relation between capitalists' savings and capital accumulation depended on particularly simplifying and drastic assumptions about negligible savings by the workers. The novelty of the present analysis has been to show that the relation is valid independently of any of those assumptions. It is valid whatever the saving behaviour of the workers may be [Pasinetti, 1962, p. 113].

This claim for the analysis does not pay sufficient attention to the very special assumptions needed to obtain these conclusions. The assumptions used by classical economists were based on features of the economies of their time, and the normal values that were the centers of their analyses did not require extreme steady-state properties. In the short-period, or even long-period, equilibrium situations examined in post-Keynesian theories, the value for the propensity to save of workers can affect profits and the rate of profits. It is the long-run exponential growth, or steady-state assumption, that makes that propensity irrelevant, an assumption that turns this analysis into a highly abstract logical exercise. This assess-ment of Pasinetti's analysis is not inconsistent with the view that Pasinetti expresses later in his paper about the interpretative value of his model. "I should look...at the previous analysis simply and more generally as a logical framework to answer interesting questions about what *ought* to happen if full employment is to be kept over time, more than as a behavioral theory expressing what actually happens" [1962, p. 119].[13]

The "Inflation Barrier"

There is in the post-Keynesian models an inverse relation, given the propensities to save and technical conditions of production, between the real-wage rate and the rate of accumulation at a point in time. (This inverse relation need not hold over time as the productivity changes experienced by an economy with a higher rate of accumulation make it eventually possible to achieve both a higher rate of accumulation and a higher real-wage rate.) In the short-period context of Kalecki's and Keynes' theories and, under competitive conditions in product markets, this appears as the inverse relation between the level of employment and the real-wage rate, referred to above. This inverse relation would help fuel trade union pressures for higher money-wage rates as employment increases, pressures that would become stronger in any case, as a result of falling unemployment and tightened labor markets. Robinson thus pointed out a potential flaw in full employment policies in a 1937 essay on full employment [Robinson, 1937, pp. 3–39]. The sharp increases in prices that would accompany movements toward full employment, as money wages increased, could result in the imposition of strong credit restraints by monetary authorities concerned about inflation, restraints that keep investment below the level consistent with full employment. Almost 20 years later Robinson coined the term "inflation barrier" to indicate that there "is a limit to the level to which real-wage rates can fall without setting up a pressure to raise money-wage rates. But a rise in money-wage rates increases money expenditure, so that the vicious spiral of money wages chasing prices sets in. There is then a head-on conflict between the desire of entrepreneurs to invest and the refusal of the system to accept the level of real wages which the investment entails; something must give way. Either the system explodes in a hyper-inflation, or some check operates to curtail investment" [Robinson, 1956, p. 48].[14]

This inverse relation extends to a comparison of equilibrium growth situations, with the rate of accumulation being substituted for the level of investment. Given the same techniques of production and degrees of thriftiness, the economy with a higher rate of accumulation has a lower real-wage rate. The operation of the inflation barrier can lead to what Kahn has called a "Bastard Golden Age" [Kahn, 1959, p. 200]. This is a state that is characterized by a constant rate of growth, but the rate of accumulation is insufficient to result in full employment. As Robinson writes, if "when organized labor has the power to oppose any fall in the real-wage rate," then "[I]nflationary pressure, bringing financial checks into operation, may arise when there is no scarcity of labor — indeed a great mass of non-employment — if the real-wage rate refuses to be depressed below a particular level" [Robinson, 1962, p. 58].

Recognition in post-Keynesian models of the possibility of running into an inflation barrier is a step toward recognition of the institutional and political constraints that could prevent the full-employment growth situations for which the Kaldor and Pasinetti approaches were developed. Unless the pressure to increase money-wage rates as the inflation barrier is approached leads to an increase in the degree of thriftiness (e.g., a reduction in rentier consumption), the constraints on the rate of accumulation that they trigger would adversely affect real-wage rates in future periods. The consequent slowdown in the rate of accumulation would have a negative impact on the rate of technical progress, since it is related to accumulation, as well as on the amount of productive capacity available.

Investment and the Profit Margin

The post-Keynesian theories of distribution presented in the preceding sections allow investment expenditures to have an indirect effect on profit margins as a result of their impact on effective demand. This effect appears in the initial version of Kalecki's model, where competitive market conditions for commodities are assumed, because larger investment expenditures lead to higher prices relative to wage costs and to higher output and employment, as the operation of less efficient plants and standby equipment become profitable. In Kaldor's model there is also an increase in profit margins, as higher investment leads to a higher profit share in the given output that is fixed by the assumption of full employment of labor and the available productive capacity. Even in Kalecki's later versions of his theory of distribution, where the manufacturing sector is characterized by oligopoly with fixed markups, the profit share of the economy's total output would increase with higher investment and output because of the increases in the prices of raw materials relative to wage costs. An increase in the profit share of the manufacturing sector's output would also occur, even with fixed markups, given the presence of overhead wages and salaries.

There have been attempts to make a direct connection between investment and the values for the fixed markups in oligopolistic industries [Eichner, 1973, 1976; Wood, 1975; Harcourt and Kenyon, 1976]. Retained earnings are a very important source of finance for investment in manufacturing industries, and the values of the markups set by firms are seen as being a function of the amount of investment that is to be financed. The larger this amount, other things being given, the larger the markup. Pricing, as well as investment, plans are considered to be long-term in nature, with the former supporting the latter. For example, Eichner [1976, p. 55] writes "that the pricing decision cannot be divorced from the industry's investment planning," and he uses the term "corporate levy" to represent "the amount of funds available to the megacorp from internal sources to finance investment expenditures" [p. 61]. In any given short period context the firm's gross profits, which overlap to some extent with this corporate levy,[15] will be a residual, but this levy enters the price leader's (the megacorp's) pricing formula as a planned amount, an amount that is tied to the cost of planned investment. This investment is related to the expected rate of growth in demand for the firm's output, a rate that Wood [1975, pp. 113–114] takes to be similar to Harrod's warranted rate of growth. This is consistent with Harcourt and Kenyon [1976, p. 454] who see decisions on investment plans being based on "the relation between the trend in actual rates of capacity utilization, and some desired rate of plant utilization, given its expectations about the future growth of market demand and the expected profitability of various alternative investment projects." Given these decisions, the price leader "then chooses a mark-up that will produce the required level of retained profits with which to finance the desired investment expenditure..." [p. 454].

It is useful to contrast the above approach with that taken by Kalecki, even though he also emphasized the importance of retained earnings in the financing of investment. "One of the important factors of investment decisions is the accumulation of firms' capital out of current profits" [Kalecki, 1971, p. 109]. For Kalecki it is past and current profits that help make possible future investment expenditures, while the price policies of oligopolistic firms are designed with a view to maximizing profits over time, even though "[I]n view of the uncertainties faced in the process of price fixing it will not be assumed that the firm attempts to maximize its profits in any precise sort of manner" [Kalecki, 1954, p. 12]. Its prices are set, as we saw in the section concerned with his theory of distribution, on the basis of unit prime costs, given the average price in the industry, and the degree of monopoly protecting the firm from competition. In any particular short-period situation the total value of investment decisions for the economy "is just so much as will equate the marginal risk to the gap between the prospective rate of profit and the rate of interest..." [Kalecki, 1937, p. 85]. The profits from carrying out past investment decisions in the succeeding short period will increase the wealth of firms, and "hence, the marginal risk would be less than the gap between [the] prospective rate of profit and the rate of interest" [p. 85] resulting in new investment decisions.

The contrast between Kalecki's approach to price-setting in oligopolistic industries, and that taken by the others discussed in this section, shows that the admitted importance of retained earnings as a source of finance for investment in manufacturing industries, does not necessarily lead to a pricing rule tied to planned investment. As Joan Robinson noted, in commenting briefly on Eichner [1976] and Wood [1975], "[S]uch theories can never be quite convincing for motivation in business is multi-dimensional and cannot be squeezed into a simple formula; moreover in modern conditions a market does not exist independently of the commodities which innovating firms choose to offer for sale. The question of the formation of profit margins still needs more investigation" [Robinson, 1980, p. 189].

Conclusion

Kalecki's theory of the determination of profits is an integral part of his analysis of cyclical behavior in capitalist economies. With the publication of Keynes' *General Theory*, it quickly became clear to Kalecki that his analytical framework could replicate Keynes' short-period equilibrium results in a very straightforward manner.[16] Kalecki's theory of distribution, since it contains the independence of investment from saving, and the inverse relation between the real-wage rate and the level of employment, along with the difference between the propensity to save out of wages and profits that is also in Keynes' model,[17] can be taken to be the theory of distribution that is implicit in the latter. This theory of distribution operates at the level of abstraction of the Kalecki and Keynes theories of employment, with a situation of full employment "being a limiting point of the possible positions of equilibrium" [Keynes, 1936, p. 3]. There is scope within the context of this theory to consider the possible effects of attempts by workers to improve their economic position by pressing for larger money-wage rates, and to examine some of the obstacles such attempts might face as prices, which are related to wage costs, are forced up when these attempts are successful. In Kalecki's general model of an open economy with workers' saving, the "class struggle" which is reflected in changing money wages and prices, could affect not only income shares by altering markups in manufacturing industries but also the level of profits because of their effects on the trade balance, the government deficit, and workers' saving.

The theories of income distribution put forth by Kaldor and Pasinetti deal only with the special case of full employment, and thus these theories are, from the perspective of Kalecki's and Keynes' visions of the realities of capitalist economies, themselves in the nature of a special case. Pasinetti's results are even more special than Kaldor's, since they are concerned not only with a situation of full employment but one that is part of long-run exponential growth, that has been proceeding at a constant rate for an interval of time whose length is tending to infinity. The derivation above of the results of Kaldor and Pasinetti, as well as those of Kalecki, makes clear that they all relate, as they must, to a particular short-period situation, since output is produced and income is distributed in such a situation. Kalecki's analysis deals with intervals of time longer than the short period by linking a string of adjacent short periods, with all of them sharing the same general characteristics. In particular, there would be no reason to expect full employment or that plant would be operated at desired rates, with output being sold at prices that provide for "normal" rates of profit. The long intervals of time dealt with by Pasinetti, in contrast, all have these special characteristics. A reason for the examination of these special cases by a post-Keynesian analyst is to allow for a comparison of results on distribution in such cases, with those obtained in neo-classical theory, a theory that concentrates on situations with these special characteristics.

Notes

1. Kaldor used the term "Keynesian" for this approach to distribution even though "Keynes...was never interested in the problem of distribution as such" [Kaldor, 1955–56, p. 227], on the grounds that one "may nevertheless christen a particular theory of distribution as 'Keynesian' if it can be shown to be an application of the specifically Keynesian apparatus of thought and if evidence can be adduced that at some stage in the development of his ideas, Keynes came near to formulating such a theory" [p. 227]. This "evidence" he finds in Keynes' reference in the *Treatise on Money* [Keynes, 1930, p. 139] to profits as a "widow's cruse," where "Keynes regards entrepreneurial incomes as being the resultant of their expenditure decisions, rather than the other way round" [Kaldor, 1955–56, p. 227n]. In the case of Kalecki it is not necessary to read into his analytical approach a possible application to the theory of distribution, because it was an integral part of his analysis.

2. Part of this treatment of prices, and the statement of the essential role of increases in bank credit in making it possible for firms to increase investment, found in Kalecki [1935a] were added to the English translation of part of the 1933 study [Kalecki, 1966, p. 1] that appears as chapter 1 in Kalecki [1971].

3. It is this case that appears in the English translation of part of the 1933 study, with a "rise of prices," relative to money wages accompanying an "increase in aggregate production" [Kalecki, 1971, p. 13]. This inverse relation between the level of employment and the real-wage rate, under short-period conditions, is also found in Keynes [1936, p. 17]. Their theories of employment are not dependent on the existence of competitive conditions in product markets [Keynes 1939],and Kalecki assumed in his later writings that markets for manufactured goods are oligopolistic.

4. In Asimakopulos [1983] quarterly values for a Kalecki-type profits equation are presented for the U.S. economy for the period 1950-1983. This equation differs from Kalecki's in using gross retained earnings as the profits term, with the determinants being gross investment, the government budget deficit, the international surplus, and the negative of personal saving. Since it deals with an actual economy in an actual period of time, there is no assumption that this period is characterized by short-period equilibrium.

5. In arriving at a value for the wage share in value added, Kalecki makes use of "the ratio of proceeds to prime costs," a ratio whose value "is determined...by the degree of monopoly" [1954, p. 28]. The wages that comprise the numerator of this wage share are only those that are part of prime costs, while the wages that belong to overhead costs are left out of the analysis. In his 1968 paper on trend and the business cycle, Kalecki referred to this share, correctly, as "the relative share of labor prime costs in the national income" [Kalecki, 1971, p. 168].

6. The possible triggering of credit restraints is also a feature of Joan Robinson's "inflation barrier" discussed below.

7. In connection with this theory of distribution Kaldor refers to Kalecki [1942], to which "I owe a great deal of stimulus" [Kaldor, 1955-56, p. 228n].

8. The short-period equilibrium for firms that appears in Keynes [1936] does not imply that there is full utilization of productive capacity. Firms would produce more, at higher marginal costs, if effective demand were greater.

9. Harrod does not make use of a capital/output ratio in his dynamic analysis, rather it is the ratio of the value of net investment in a short period to the increase in output over that period which appears in his equation for the warranted rate of growth. In response to Robinson's [1970] use of the stock of capital to present his analysis, Harrod [1970, p. 739] stated that "[I]n my book [Harrod, 1948] to which she refers, I deliberately avoided the use of this concept. It does not occur in my fundamental equation."

10. Pasinetti [1962, p. 106] implies that this logical slip is to be found in Kaldor's theory, but Kaldor, as we saw above, did not introduce saving propensities for capitalists and workers. For him s_w was the propensity to save out of wages and *not* the propensity to save of workers, while s_p was the propensity to save out of profits. He defined these propensities by first writing "S_w and S_p for aggregate savings out of Wages and Profits," and then "assuming simple proportional savings functions $S_w = s_w W$ and $S_p = s_p P$" [Kaldor, 1955-56, p. 229]. He reiterated his position with respect to the propensity to save out of profits in a later paper: "I have always regarded the high savings propensity out of profits as something which attaches to the nature of business income, and not to the wealth (or other peculiarities) of the individuals who own property" [Kaldor, 1966, p. 310].

11. This assumption is certainly not "obvious" for a model in the "Cambridge" tradition, because the risks faced by individual enterprises are not absent even in long-run equilibrium for the economy as a whole. For example, Kahn in his analysis of some possible growth situations, writes of Robinson's "Golden Age," a state of equilibrium growth with full employment: "The risks of enterprise must be allowed. The fact that in a Golden Age capitalists' expectations are realised *in the broad* does not exclude the risks involved in the vagaries of technical processes and of consumers' behavior. For these reasons the risk-free rate of interest would even in a Golden Age lie below the rate of profit..." [Kahn, 1959, p. 201; italics in original].

12. Given any arbitrary starting point, this equality will only hold, given unchanged propensities to save, as the length of the time interval tends to infinity.

13. The analysis, and its provocative result, can also be viewed as having a role in the continuing controversy about the possible role of marginal products of factors of production in explaining factor shares, as can be seen from Meade [1963], Samuelson and Modigliani [1966], and Pasinetti [1964, 1966].

14. This feature also appears in Kaldor's theory of distribution presented above. His theory only holds for a certain range of values for the variables and, in particular, "the real wage cannot fall below a certain subsistence minimum" [Kaldor, 1955–56, pp. 232–233].

15. "On the one hand the corporate levy excludes...that portion of the megacorp's accounting profits that are paid out to the equity debt holders in the form of dividends. On the other hand, it encompasses, unlike the conventional notion of profits, both depreciation allowances and any expenditures on research and development, advertising and the like" [Eichner, 1976, p. 61].

16. "The theory of profits presented here is closely allied to Mr. Keynes' theory of saving and investment. It has been, however, developed independently of Mr. Keynes in [Kalecki, 1935a, 1935b]" [Kalecki, 1942, p. 260n].

17. Keynes did not make use of any such assumption in deriving his theory of effective demand, but he noted in discussing the possible effect on short-period equilibrium employment of a reduction in money-wage rates that this "transfer from wage-earners to other factors is likely to diminish the [economy's] propensity to consume" [Keynes, 1936, p. 262].

References

Asimakopulos, A. (1975). A Kaleckian theory of income distribution. *Canadian Journal of Economics* 8 (August): 313–333.

—————. (1983). A Kaleckian profits equation and the United States economy 1950–82. *Metroeconomica* 35 (Feb.-June): 1–27.

Eichner, A.S. (1973). A theory of the determination of the mark-up under oligopoly. *Economic Journal* 83 (Dec.): 1184–1200.

—————. (1976). *The Megacorp and Oligopoly, Micro Foundations of Macro Dynamics*. Cambridge: Cambridge University Press.

Harcourt, G.C., and Kenyon, P. (1976). Pricing and the investment decision. *Kyklos* 29 (Fasc. 3): 449–477.

Harrod, R.F. (1939). An essay in dynamic theory. *Economic Journal* 49 (March): 14–33.

—————. (1948). *Towards a Dynamic Economics*. London: Macmillan.

—————. (1970). Harrod after twenty-one years: a comment. *Economic Journal* 80 (Sept.): 737–741.

Kahn, Richard. (1959). Exercises in the analysis of growth. *Oxford Economic Papers* 11 (June): 143–156. Reprinted in Kahn (1972), pp. 192–207, and all page references in the text are to this reprinting.

—————. (1972). *Selected Essays on Employment and Growth*. Cambridge: Cambridge University Press.

Kaldor, Nicholas. (1955–56). Alternative theories of distribution. *Review of Eco-*

nomic Studies 23 (2): 83-100. Reprinted in Kaldor (1960), pp. 209-236, and all page references in the text are to this reprinting.

————. (1960). *Essays on Value and Distribution.* London: Duckworth & Co. Ltd.

————. (1966). Marginal productivity and the macroeconomic theories of distribution. *Review of Economic Studies* 33 (Oct.): 309-319.

Kalecki, Michal. (1935a). Essai d'une théorie de mouvement cyclique des affaires. *Revue d' économie politique* 49 (mars/avril): 285-305.

————. (1935b). A macrodynamic theory of business cycles. *Econometrica* 3 (July): 327-344.

————. (1937). A theory of the business cycle. *Review of Economic Studies* 4 (Feb.): 77-97.

————. (1939). *Essays in the Theory of Economic Fluctuations.* London: Allen and Unwin.

————. (1942). A theory of profits. *Economic Journal* 52 (June-Sept.): 258-267.

————. (1954). *Theory of Economic Dynamics.* London: Allen and Unwin.

————. (1966). *Studies in the Theory of Business Cycles: 1933-1939.* Oxford: Basil Blackwell.

————. (1971). *Selected Essays on the Dynamics of the Capitalist Economy: 1933-1970.* Cambridge: Cambridge University Press.

Keynes, J.M. (1930). *A Treatise on Money,* Vol. I. London: Macmillan.

————. (1936). *The General Theory of Employment, Interest and Money.* London: Macmillan.

————. (1939). Relative movements of real wages and output. *Economic Journal* 49 (March): 34-51.

Meade, J.E. (1963). The rate of profit in a growing economy. *Economic Journal* (Sept.): 665-674.

Pasinetti, Luigi. (1962). Rate of profit and income distribution in relation to the rate of economic growth. *Review of Economic Studies* 29 (Oct.): 267-279. Reprinted in Pasinetti (1974), pp. 103-120, and all references in the text are to this reprinting.

————. (1964). Professor Meade's rate of profit in a growing economy. *Economic Journal* (June): 488-489.

————. (1966). New results in an old framework: comment on Samuelson and Modigliani. *Review of Economic Studies* (Oct.): 303-306.

————. (1974). *Growth and Income Distribution: Essays in Economic Theory.* Cambridge: Cambridge University Press.

Robinson, Joan. (1937). *Essays in the Theory of Employment.* London: Macmillan.

————. (1956). *The Accumulation of Capital.* London: Macmillan.

————. (1962). *Essays in the Theory of Economic Growth.* London: Macmillan.

————. (1970). Harrod after twenty-one years. *Economic Journal* 80 (Sept.): 731–737.

————. (1980). *Collected Economic Papers*, Vol. V. Oxford: Basil Blackwell.

Samuelson, Paul, and Modigliani, Franco. (1966). The Pasinetti paradox in neoclassical and more general models. *Review of Economic Studies* 33 (Oct.): 269–301.

Wood, Adrian. (1975). *A Theory of Profits*. Cambridge: Cambridge University Press.

7 THE NEO-RICARDIAN
APPROACH AND THE
DISTRIBUTION OF INCOME
Alessandro Roncaglia

This chapter is concerned with the impact of Piero Sraffa's contributions to economic theory on the analysis of income distribution. We will proceed by first examining Sraffa's critique of the traditional marginalist approach. We will then consider the classical approach based on the notion of the surplus that Sraffa wants to use to replace the marginalist one. Within this classical tradition, the problem of income distribution can be tackled by considering the real wage rate as determined by sociohistorical forces of custom and habit. Alternatively, there is the possibility of concentrating attention on the forces determining the rate of profits, while considering the real wage rate as a residual distributive variable. Along this line, we will examine, first, Pasinetti's "technological-normative" conception of a "natural rate of profits"; then, the idea

Thanks (without implication) are due to Tom Asimakopulos, Jan Kregel, Heinz Kurz, Carlo Panico, Luigi Pasinetti, Fabio Petri, Giorgio Rodano, Annalisa Rosselli, Ian Steedman, and Mario Tonveronachi for reading and commenting on a previous draft of this chapter.

that the rate of profits is determined by the interest rate, which in turn is determined by monetary forces.

The final section is devoted to considering, though in very general terms, another line of analysis of income distribution. This line of research, which in our opinion promises to be the most fruitful, consists in assuming as given (by past history) the values taken by the distributive variables at a given moment in time and, then, in analyzing the factors affecting their changes over time. Specifically, we should consider both the factors affecting the movements of money wage rates and those affecting the movements of the markup of money prices over money wage rates; this should allow us to consider, among other things, the impact of monetary and financial elements on income distribution. It is, however, necessary to stress that this line of analysis is open only if we accept a specific methodology related to Sraffa's analytical contribution, based on the *separability* of the analysis of different economic issues, and on the possibility of recourse to different analytical levels for dealing with the different issues.

The Sraffian Critique of the Marginalist Approach

As is well known, Sraffa's writings provide the background for a radical shift in the "research programme" of economic science: away from the dominant marginalist approach, toward the so-called surplus approach rooted in the classical tradition. (For a discussion of the nature of, and the reasons for, this shift, see Roncaglia, 1978.) In short, and with drastic simplifications, we can summarize the long and complex debate, which is, at least in part, still under way, as follows.

The critiques stemming from Sraffa's 1960 book, *Production of Commodities by Means of Commodities*, concern the theoretical foundations of the traditional marginalist conception of the economy. According to this conception, society is endowed with given amounts of basic productive resources (which can be reduced to the triad: labor, capital, and land). Competitive markets combine these productive resources in proportions which ensure their full utilization. According to traditional theory the market mechanisms determine equilibrium prices which ensure equality between supply and demand for each and every good, including the productive resources. Specifically, in the case of labor, the equilibrium wage rate ensures full employment.

Sraffa's critique centers on the traditional notion of capital as a scarce factor of production, and on the related notion of the interest rate as the

price for the use of this scarce factor of production (price in the traditional marginalist meaning of index of scarcity for the commodity being
considered). Sraffa's analysis points to the fact that the term "capital"
does not refer to a specific commodity, but to the value of a set of
different commodities utilized as means of production and themselves
produced by means of production. The value of capital can thus change,
either because of changes in the proportions of the various commodities
used as means of production, or because of changes in their prices. Sraffa
shows that a change in the interest rate (in Sraffa's own terms, in the rate
of profits), barring some very special exceptions, provokes changes in the
relative prices of the various commodities, and thus produces changes in
the value of capital, which can move in the same or in the opposite
direction of the rate of interest.

According to traditional theories, a fall in real wage rates caused by
unemployment should provoke a shift from the use of "capital" to the use
of labor; yet the "capital theory debates" of the 1960s based on Sraffa's
works showed that exactly the opposite can happen. It is possible, for
instance, that a lower wage rate (and consequently a higher profit rate),
produces an increase in the "quantity of capital" utilized in the economy
(the physical quantities of the various means of production remaining
unchanged). Even more importantly, it is also possible that a fall in the
real wage rate affects the relative prices of the various means of production in such a way that the utilization of production techniques employing
more machines (i.e., more "capital" in a physical sense) and less labor
becomes more profitable. This is the exact opposite of what should
happen according to traditional marginalist theories, which predict that
an increase in the price of any commodity should provoke a fall in the
demand for it. (For a bibliography of these debates, see Roncaglia, 1978.)

Thus, the Sraffian critique of the notion of capital as a scarce factor of
production turns out to be, at one and the same time, a critique of the
traditional marginalist theories of distribution and employment, whereby
equilibrium values for the distributive variables were determined by
market forces insuring equalization between supply of, and demand for,
"factors of production." Specifically, the critique affects the theoretical
foundations of the traditional market mechanisms insuring an automatic
tendency to full employment, namely the downward pressure on the
capital-labor ratio of a fall in real wages induced by unemployment. (A
similar critique applies to the idea that market mechanisms insure an
automatic tendency to some "natural rate of unemployment.")

Phenomena such as the possibility of multiple equilibria were already
recognized by some authors within the marginalist tradition, but their

relevance and their implications were not fully appreciated until after Sraffa's contribution and the debates in capital theory of the '60s. More recently, modern general equilibrium theory has admitted the possibility of multiple equilibria, and the possibility of underemployment equilibria, or of unstable equilibria. Yet, statements referring to "the" Walrasian full employment equilibrium were common in the neo-classical synthesis, where unemployment is considered as a short-run disequilibrium phenomenon, due to lags and rigidities in the working of market forces, and still abound in the monetarist literature, or in the rational expectations models of the new classical macroeconomics. (On this, see Roncaglia and Tonveronachi, 1985.) From this perspective, general equilibrium theorists criticizing monetarism and new classical macroeconomics (such as Hahn, 1982a), are in fact joining forces with the critical tradition stemming from Sraffa's analysis — though they deeply differ in their proposals for a reconstruction of economic analysis.

The Sraffian Reconstruction of the Classical Approach

Before considering how the distributive issue can be approached from a Sraffian standpoint, it is necessary to understand that Sraffa's analytical criticisms of traditional marginalist theories, recalled in the previous section, are founded in a more deeply rooted counterposition of the classical to the marginalist "vision" of the economy.

Following Sraffa [1960, p. 93], this counterposition can be characterized as "the striking contrast" between the classical "picture of the system of production and consumption as a circular process," and the marginalist "view...of a one-way avenue that leads from 'Factors of production' to 'Consumption goods.'" Here Sraffa hints at a difference in the basic conception of the economy, which is reflected in a basic difference concerning the choice of the data and the variables to be explained in the area of value theory, which is commonly regarded as the foundation for other aspects of economic analysis.

On one side, marginalist economists search for equilibrium prices and quantities — including the "prices" of the "factors of production," i.e., the equilibrium values for distributive variables — stemming from the confrontation of initial resource endowments (the supply side) and economic agents' preferences (the demand side).

On the other side, classical economists center their analyses around the notion of the surplus, defined as the portion of the product available once the initial stocks of means of production and the necessary means of subsistence for the workers employed had been reconstituted. (When workers participate in the partition of the surplus, i.e., when the wage rate is higher than the subsistence minimum, the notion of "necessary means of subsistence" loses its relevance, so that the whole wage can be considered as part of the surplus; see Roncaglia, 1974). In a market economy characterized by division of labor, at the end of the productive process each of the different sectors of the economy has to rebuild its own stocks of means of production in order to be able to start up a new cycle of production, and it does so by selling its own products to the other sectors and by acquiring from them its own means of production. Furthermore, the unity of a capitalist economic system is ensured by the freedom of movement of capital in the search of the most remunerative employment; classical economists translate this idea into the analytical hypothesis of the equality of the rates of profit in the various sectors.

When the system produces a surplus, the relative prices of the various commodities must be able to guarantee the "potential reproduction" of the economic system; that is, they must make it possible for each sector to replenish the capital advanced, at the same time supplying the necessary incentive to pursue productive activity in that sector (through, precisely, a uniform rate of profits in all sectors). Since the commodities are at the same time products and means of production, it is not possible to determine the price of an individual commodity independently of the others: given the interrelations between the various sectors of production, it is essential to consider the system as a whole. In addition, relative prices depend on the profit rate, and hence on the distribution of the surplus between the different classes of society. Rents can be taken care of through the theory of differential rent: what remains of the surplus is then allotted to profits and wages. One of the two distributive variables — wage rate or rate of profits — must then be determined exogenously to the system depicting market exchanges, while the other is determined endogenously, as pertaining to the residual part of the surplus, simultaneously with relative prices. Hence we arrive at Sraffa's system of equations:

$$Ap \, (1 + r) + lw = Bp$$

where A is the input matrix, B the output matrix, p the column vector of prices, l the column vector of labor inputs, r the rate of profits, w the wage rate (where wages are paid at the end of the production period). With the number of processes and the number of commodities equal to n, we have n equations and $n + 2$ unknowns (n prices and 2 distributive variables). When the system produces a surplus, there are economically meaningful

— i.e., nonnegative — solutions for the n variables remaining once a unit of measure for prices has been chosen (e.g., putting $p_n = 1$) and once an exogenous value has been attributed to one of the two distributive variables. This can be done by setting a specific value for w, which must be nonnegative and not higher than W, the maximum wage rate corresponding to zero profits; or, conversely, setting r exogenously, at a value which again must be nonnegative and not higher than R, the maximum rate of profits corresponding to zero wages. When the exogenously given distributive variable changes, the whole set of solutions for the endogenous variables (the $n - 1$ relative prices and the residual distributive variable) changes as well. In particular, we can write

$$f(r, w) = 0$$

a functional relationship connecting the wage rate and the rate of profits. For $0 \leq w \leq W$ this relationship, which is called *the wage-profit curve*, can be represented as a curve lying in the positive quadrant of a $w - r$ Cartesian space.

Thus Sraffa, following the classical approach, determines in his 1960 book (to which we refer the reader for a fuller treatment) the analytical relationship between income distribution and "natural" prices, expressing the conditions of "potential reproducibility" of the production process, on the basis of a given technology corresponding to a given set of activity levels.

The need to recall the difference between the marginalist approach which Sraffa criticizes, and the classical approach to which Sraffa returns, stems from frequent misinterpretations of the intentions of Sraffa's book. Sraffa's analysis in his 1960 book is framed in such a way as to be both *formally* consistent with marginalist general equilibrium analysis, and *conceptually* consistent with the classical approach. This apparent ambiguity is connected to the twin purposes of Sraffa's contribution: to provide both an internal criticism of the traditional marginalist theories of value and distribution based on the notion of "capital" as a "factor of production," and a solution to the problem of the relationship connecting relative prices and income distribution, which classical economists had been unable to solve. This apparent ambiguity, however, is clearly resolved in the Preface and in Appendix D of Sraffa's 1960 book: only if we *introduce* some additional elements — such as the assumption of constant returns to scale and the assumption of equality between endowments and demand of "factors of production" — *into* Sraffa's formal analysis, can we consider it as a special case of marginalist general equilibrium analysis (see e.g., Hahn, 1982b). Searching for an "equilibrium" point on the wage-profit frontier, on the basis of "supply and demand forces," even if they do not refer to a factor of production capital (but, e.g., to intertemporal preferences), goes directly against Sraffa's stated objective, of starting a reconstruction of the classical approach.

In fact, classical economists do not consider the simultaneous determination of relative prices, relative activity levels, and income distribution as an analytical necessity. Furthermore, in dealing with each of these problems in turn, classical economists leave aside the forces of supply and demand, which in their opinion are only active outside of "normal" situations. Thus, following the classical tradition, Sraffa views the study of the forces affecting income distribution as a specific problem, distinct from that concerning the forces affecting technology and technical change, or from the study of the relationship between relative prices and distributive variables. The latter is the specific problem analyzed by Sraffa in his 1960 book, a problem that is central to all theories of value and distribution. (Garegnani [1984] considers this problem to be "the core" of economic analysis.)

Class Conflict and the Wage Rate as the Exogenous Variable

How can we proceed, then, in tackling the problem of income distribution within the conceptual and methodological framework of the classical approach? As we have seen above, Sraffa's 1960 analysis of the relationship between prices and income distribution leaves one of the two distributive variables — wage rate or rate of profits — to be fixed exogenously. The other variable is then determined through the wage-profit curve connected to the structure of the economy at a given point in time, i.e., to the prevailing technology and to prevailing activity levels. This means that we may turn, alternatively, to the wage rate or to the rate of profits as the distributive variable for which an explanation must be sought outside of the Sraffian core.

In fact, the most immediate interpretation of the wage-profit curve depicted in Sraffa's 1960 analysis refers to the class conflict between workers and capitalists, which is commonly considered to play a central role in capitalist societies. With single-product industries the wage-profit curve is a monotonically decreasing relationship (although this relationship does not necessarily hold in the case of joint production). Furthermore, if the wage is measured in terms of the standard commodity (a unit of measure proposed by Sraffa in his 1960 book, which is a composite commodity corresponding to the net product of a system in which "the various commodities are represented among its aggregate means of production *in the same proportions* as they are among its products" [Sraffa, 1960, p. 19]), the wage-profit curve turns out to be a *linear* decreasing relationship. Thus it seemed natural, to Sraffa's first interpreters (such as Meek, 1961), to read into the standard commodity a tool for bringing to the fore the antagonistic relationship between profits and wages, namely between capitalists and workers, purified from all distortions connected to price movements. Some authors [Meek, 1961; Medio, 1972; Eatwell, 1975] in fact suggested that the standard commodity can be used for restating the Marxian notion of exploitation, according to which profits originate from the fact that workers are obliged to perform "surplus labor."

However, this interpretation of Sraffa's analysis does not provide new support for the Marxian theory of exploitation: wages, even when they are assumed to be at the subsistence level, are neither paid nor consumed in terms of the standard commodity [Roncaglia, 1978, pp. 77–79], and outside the very specific case of a standard system, all kinds of complications may arise in the relationship between rate of profits and rate of exploitation, such as the former being positive while the latter is negative, or the former increasing while the latter decreases [Steedman, 1977].

The interpretations of Sraffa's contribution discussed above can only be accepted as simply suggesting that class conflict is a key factor affecting income distribution. Thus we are led to analyze the elements affecting the bargaining power of the contending classes.

This approach to income distribution is common to classical economists, such as Adam Smith (see, e.g., Book I chapter 8 of the *Wealth of Nations*). In general, because of the dominant power attributed to capitalists (Smith), or because of acceptance of the Malthusian population mechanism (Ricardo), classical economists considered the natural wage rate in real terms to correspond to workers' subsistence level. This notion should not be interpreted in a strict biological sense: Torrens clarifies the point in the following passage.

Alterations . . . in the minimum of wages cannot be suddenly effected. So far as this minimum depends upon climate, it is unchangeable; and even so far as it is determined by the habits of living, and the established scale of comfort, it can be effected only by those circumstances of prosperity or decay and by those moral causes of instruction and civilization, which are ever gradual in their operation. The minimum of wages, therefore, though it varies under different climates, and with the different stages of national improvement, may in any given time and place, be regarded as very nearly stationary [Torrens, 1834, pp. 12–13; for a discussion of the classical notion of subsistence, see Roncaglia, 1974].

It would thus be possible to "close" Sraffa's model by assuming an exogenously given wage rate, corresponding to the value of a specific basket of commodities determined by "the habits and customs of the people," as Ricardo [1951, p. 96] puts it; and maintaining that systematic and persistent forces (such as the difference in bargaining power of the contending classes, or the Malthusian law of population recalled above) push wage rates toward this (historically determined) natural level.

This theory of distribution, dominant among classical economists, meets with two difficulties when referred to contemporary economic conditions. First, under modern conditions of constantly changing levels of personal income and of continuous revolutions in life-styles, it would be difficult to define a natural wage rate on the basis of workers' subsistence requirements — even when they are interpreted in a "historically relative" meaning, as referring to the "habits and customs of the people." Second, under modern conditions the classical mechanisms pushing wage rates to their natural level are no longer operative. The Malthusian population mechanism, even assuming that it was operative two centuries ago (which is doubtful: see Roncaglia, 1974), can nowadays be easily turned upside down: with the spread of birth control techniques, higher wage rates are more likely to produce lower, rather than higher, growth rates of population. As for the Smithian idea of a complete unbalance of bargaining power, the rise of trade unionism and of political democracy provides working classes with a noninsignificant bargaining power. (See Sylos Labini [1982, pp. 196–202] on the changes in the "wage equation" due to changes in the relative bargaining power of workers and entrepreneurs.)

It should also be recalled that — as stressed, e.g., by Nuti [1970] and Dobb [1973] — bargaining over money wages by itself does not determine real wages (see later discussion). In other words, the real wage is not the direct outcome of the bargaining process. Thus, even if in wage bargaining workers were to refer to objectives specified in terms of real wage rates, this fact, while affecting the rate of change of money wages, will not by itself directly determine real wages — unless we were to attribute to workers a full control not only over the bargaining process, but on general economic evolution as well. Often real wage objectives are but an ex-ante evaluation, on the side of the workers, of the circumstances influencing income distribution in a specific situation. Explaining real wage objectives thus presupposes an already existing theory of income distribution, rather than providing the basis for it.

We may conclude that under contemporary conditions we cannot refer to a "subsistence" level as a "center of gravitation" for current wage rates. Some alternative explanation of distribution is therefore required.

The "Technological-Normative" Approach to Income Distribution

In a brief remark on the issue of income distribution, Sraffa himself [1960, p. 33] suggests that "the rate of profits, as a ratio, has a significance which is independent of any prices, and can well be 'given' before the prices are fixed." However, there are different ways in which the rate of profits can be considered as the exogenous variable. One of them, developed by Pasinetti [1981, especially chapter 7] will be considered in this section.

Pasinetti's 1981 analysis may be considered a final stage of the so-called post-Keynesian approach. This approach is characterized by the idea that distributive variables are influenced by the process of accumulation. The "Kaldor-Pasinetti theorem" says that, given the saving propensities of workers and capitalists, any given rate of capital accumulation (which, under the hypothesis of a constant capital-output ratio, corresponds to the rate of growth of national income) implies a given rate of profits. This (monotonically increasing) relationship is interpreted by, for example, Eichner [1976], Wood [1975], Harcourt and Kenyon [1976], as reflecting the pricing process in a capitalist society, whereby prices are fixed in such a way as to provide firms with the finance required by the desired level of investments. In a more general way Joan Robinson refers to the Keynesian causal chain that starts with entrepreneurs' "animal spirits" (i.e., long-run expectations on the future course of the economy) which determine investments and, as a consequence, income distribution.

This theory meets with two difficulties, one at the macro and the other at the micro level. The first concerns the fact that in the general case where both workers and capitalists save, the level of investment may be used *either* in conjunction with an exogenously given level of national output for determining wage and profit shares, *or* in conjunction with an exogenously given income distribution for determining the level of national output. The assumption of full employment is thus a possible solution to this difficulty. The second difficulty concerns the micro version of the theorem: if each firm were to fix prices for its products on the basis of its needs for financing its growth, firms in sectors growing at a quicker pace would experience higher profit rates than firms in slowly growing sectors, and this would run counter to the role played by competition in equalizing profit rates throughout the economy.

The first element, namely the convenience to assume full employment, may explain why Pasinetti [1962] prefers to interpret the relationship between the growth rate and rate of profits as a *normative* relationship, i.e., as a formal requirement for the continuous prevalence of a state of full employment (a state which is not automatically insured by the market mechanisms of a capitalist society, but which might be produced by an active policy of aggregate demand management along Keynesian lines). Thus in his 1962 article Pasinetti prefers to refer to a planned economy, rather than to a capitalist one.

Later on, in the 1981 summingup of his analysis, Pasinetti develops the concept of a set of natural profit rates. According to Pasinetti [1981, pp. 127ff], these profit rates are produced "independently of the institutional set-up of society" from the "natural forces" of a growing economic system, namely "an evolving technology, a growing population and an evolving pattern of consumers' preferences." More precisely, the profit rates are determined by the "requirements for all these structural movements to take place in 'equilibrium' — by which is simply meant full employment and full capacity utilization." In other terms, in each (vertically integrated) sector the profit rate must be able to insure an amount of profits equal to the equilibrium value of investment, namely, the level of investment required for expanding production capacity at a rate equal to "the rate of growth of population" plus "the rate of increase of per capita demand for each consumption good" [Pasinetti, 1981, p. 130]. Thus productive capacity keeps pace with demand, at the sectoral level, while the employment of labor keeps pace with labor supply. Since profits are needed to finance investments, ". . . total profits emerge as a kind of prior claim to a share in the final national income, while total wages — by being (conceptually) determined after profits have been determined already — emerge as a kind of residual" [Pasinetti, 1981, p. 144].

The causal chain pointed out by Pasinetti is still the one originally characterizing the post-Keynesian approach — from growth to income distribution — where Joan Robinson's "animal spirits of the entrepreneurs" have been replaced by the above-mentioned "natural forces" affecting the growth and structural change of the economic system.

Two main elements must be stressed with respect to Pasinetti's "closure of the Sraffian system": the normative meaning attributed to the natural profit rates, and their implications when they are instead interpreted as positive, institutionally determined, economic variables.

First, it must be stressed that Pasinetti's natural profit rates are in fact a normative notion: i.e., the profit rates stemming, under certain assumptions, from the analytical requirement of continuous full employment and full (or normal) capacity utilization which Pasinetti imposes on his model. The capital theory debates of the '60s referred to above, with Pasinetti's well-known contributions, undermined the idea of an autonomous tendency of market economies toward a full-employment position. Thus Pasinetti's well-specified notion of natural profit rates, explicitly connected to the full employment assumption, does not correspond to a natural value of the profit rate in the classical meaning of the term *natural*. For the classical economists (and, later, for the marginalist economists as well) the determination of the natural wage and profit rates was part of the explanation of the *actual* values of the distribution variables in actual capitalist economies. More precisely, classical economists meant by "natural" the theoretical value of the economic variable under examination ("natural prices," "natural wages," etc.), as determined by those selected as the main forces acting on that variable (such as subsistence requirements for the natural wage, or technology and distributive variables for the natural prices). According to classical economists, "market" values deviate from the corresponding natural levels because of a multiplicity of casual elements, i.e., random factors and factors affecting in a nonsystematic way the variable under examination.

Pasinetti himself [1981, p. 151] stresses that "in a capitalist economic system, a structure of 'natural' rates of profit would inevitably clash with a few basic institutional mechanisms," such as the fact that "capital funds are to be left free to move from one sector to another," inducing a tendency "towards the equalization of the rates of profit all over the economy." Thus Pasinetti is aware of the second difficulty mentioned at the beginning of this section, which implies that the set of natural profit rates will not in general be realized by market forces in a capitalist economy: as we saw, the idea that firms are free to set their prices in such a way to finance their investments is incompatible with the presence of competition, which characterizes capitalist systems. For the capitalist economy Pasinetti [1981, p. 152] is thus led to a statement similar to his 1962 solution, namely to an "equilibrium rate of profit" which "represents the rate of profit that must be realized in order to maintain full employment and full productive capacity utilization in the economic system, over time." This rate of profits depends on the capitalists' saving propensity, on the rate of population growth, and on the average rate of technical change. But again nothing is said about the existence of forces that automatically insure the attainment of such an "equilibrium" value in an actual market economy: we are still confronted with a normative notion, not with a positive explanation of income distribution in actual economic systems. (Let us note that a normative analysis is by itself insufficient to specify the direction of cause-and-effect relationships.)

This brings us to the second aspect of Pasinetti's analysis to be considered here, namely the positive meaning which can be attributed to Pasinetti's natural profit rates. Clearly, they correspond to the sectoral profit rates which would hold in a post-Keynesian economy, where entrepreneurs are able to fix prices in such a way as to exactly cover their financial needs (and where, moreover, these needs exactly correspond to a level of investment, insuring continuous full employment in a growing economy). Such an assumption is in fact hidden by Pasinetti's reference to the natural properties of an economic system as being "independent of the institutional setup of society." But there are good reasons for being skeptical about the existence of such natural properties. In fact, all elements in Pasinetti's analysis (e.g., the notion of prices, with the implicit assumption that the "law of one price" holds; the notions of wages, profits, economic sectors) point to the specific institutional setup of market economies. Outside of a market economy dominated by the division of labor, there would be no logical necessity for a "surplus value" to be attributed in a specific way to the firms operating in each sector, namely exactly in proportion to the growth requirements of that sector; indeed, the very notion of value would have to be attributed some very different meaning.

Of course, what has been said up to now does not deny the importance of Pasinetti's analysis; our purpose here is simply to stress that it does not — indeed, is explicitly not intended to — provide a solution to the problem of income distribution as here considered, and as generally considered by both classical and marginalist economists: i.e., the problem of explaining which factors affect income distribution in a capitalist economy, and their mode of operation.

The Monetary Rate of Interest and the Rate of Profits

The post-Keynesian causal link between the rate of growth and the rate of profits, discussed in the previous section, goes in an opposite direction to the classical tradition. According to classical economists, it is the size of the surplus accruing to capitalists, and hence the rate of profits, which determines the pace of capital accumulation and hence the rate of growth of the economy, and not the other way around. However, the development of a full-fledged structure of financial intermediaries in the capitalist economies may cast doubt on the relevance of the classical causal chain to contemporary conditions. Recourse to finance may provide entrepreneurs with command over resources in a way that does not automatically correspond to ownership deriving from past income, and hence influenced from past income distribution. This is especially true in a Keynesian world in which demand calls forth the creation of the required resources.

A Keynesian modification of the classical approach to income distribution is suggested by Sraffa's carefully phrased hint that the profit rate "is... susceptible of being determined from outside the system of production, in particular by the level of the money rates of interest" [Sraffa, 1960, p. 33].

Sraffa's suggestion has been referred to approvingly by a number of authors, such as Nuti [1970, p. 368], Dobb [1973, p. 271], and Garegnani [1979, p. 73]. These authors, however, do not develop a full-fledged analysis of the asserted causal link connecting the rate of profits to interest rates. According to Dobb [1973, p. 271; italics added] "...the latter would presumably be fixed, *in the main*, by the Central Bank, whether acting on its own initiative or as an instrument of governmental monetary policy"; but this, rather than *determining* the rate of profits, would only set "a *minimum* rate of profits."

Analogously, Garegnani [1979, p. 81] refers to "...Keynes' suggestion that the average level of interest on long-term loans will be determined by conventional factors, ultimately subject to the policy of the monetary authorities"; but then he adds nothing on the specification of the market forces which should translate an exogenously given interest rate into a specific profit rate. (In fact, in a number of papers — see, for example, Garegnani [1984, 1985] — he refers to both alternatives, stressing as well the possibility of considering the real wage rate as an exogenous variable.)

More recently, Pivetti [1985] and Panico [1980, 1984, 1985] provided two different attempts at more detailed analyses of the causal relationship between interest and profit rates.

Pivetti's reasoning can be summarized in four steps. First, the rate of interest is interpreted as a "monetary magnitude," determined in financial markets, especially by customs and institutions, and by monetary authorities' decisions. Second, reference is made to the classical notion of profits (P) as consisting of two magnitudes, interests (I) and profits of enterprise (PE). Third step: the Marxian idea (as interpreted by Pivetti) according to which profits of enterprise are an endogenous variable determined as the difference between profits and interest $(PE = P - I)$, is replaced by the idea that profits of enterprise are exogenously determined, corresponding — because of competition among capitalists — to an objective evaluation of the entrepreneur's "risk and trouble." Conclusion: profits become the endogenous variable, determined by adding up the two constituent parts, interest and profit of enterprise $(P = PE + I$, where PE and I are the exogenous variables).

This conclusion requires that "lasting changes in the rate of interest...are not...associated with opposite changes in the normal profit of enterprise" [Pivetti, 1985, p. 18] and affect the ratio of prices to money wages. However, the adjustment process which, according to Pivetti, ensures this result meets with two difficulties [see Steindl, 1985]: first, the long-term rate of interest is assumed to affect prices and not investment and levels of production; second, the adjustment process is set out in terms of the influence of the real interest rate over the rate of profits, while the money interest rate — the observable magnitude — is only deduced ex post, on the basis of a rate of inflation which is assumed (contrary to empirical evidence: see, for example, Sylos Labini [1984, ch. 7]) as equal to the exogenously given rate of increase in money wages.

Panico's analysis of the relationship between interest rate and rate of profits is open to the interplay of a number of factors — so much so that it cannot be considered in itself (nor is it intended to be) a definite, self-contained theory of income distribution. In fact, it can be considered as a specification with direct reference to the relation between rate of interest and profit rate of a line of research proposed in more general terms by Kregel [1976] referring to a compatibility with the Sraffian analysis of the Keynesian notion of effective demand and the role of monetary forces over the determination of real variables.

As presented in Panico [1985], his analysis is based on the juxtaposition of Sraffa's 1960 model and a Keynesian analysis of liquidity preference derived from chapter 17 of the *General Theory* (where Keynes utilizes the notion of "own interest rates," developed in Sraffa, 1932). With a drastic simplification, we might say that the connection between the rate of profits and the structure of interest rates is provided by the (mainly conventional and institutional) factors determining the liquidity premiums of "monetary" assets (such as bank deposits) in comparison to "real" assets (productive capacity). Assuming these conventional and institutional factors to remain relatively constant over time, Panico [1985,

p. 54] reaches the conclusion that "a rise in the interest rates tends to raise the rate of profit and prices, while a fall in the interest rates tends to lower the rate of profits and prices."

This conclusion (and the frequent calls for caution in the analysis leading to it) is phrased so as to exclude the idea of a stable functional relationship between interest rates and rate of profits. Hence the specification of the factors determining interest rates and liquidity premiums cannot be considered in itself (nor is it intended to be) sufficient for explaining income distribution between wages and profits at a moment in time, on the basis of an exogenously given interest rate. Moreover, Panico's model (as presented in Panico [1985, pp. 54–56]) is based on the assumption of given technology and activity levels, while as Panico himself recalls in a number of passages, changes in activity levels (and hence in technology) necessarily interact with other factors (e.g., institutional changes or events in the financial markets) in the determination of liquidity premiums of monetary assets in comparison to real ones. However, it should be noted that Panico (differently from Pivetti) does not intend to provide a "closure" of Sraffa's 1960 analysis through the determining influence of the interest rate over the profit rate. His papers rather try to provide a number of useful suggestions as to how monetary factors may affect income distribution: suggestions which can be taken into account in an approach to income distribution such as that discussed in the following section.

All this does not imply that we should reject Sraffa's hint on the influence of the interest rate on the rate of profits. This hint can be interpreted in a broader way, reading in it the following four specific points. First, by that sentence Sraffa puts on guard against a simplistic interpretation of the wage-profit counterposition as expressing a class conflict centered on the bargaining, on the side of trade unions and entrepreneurs' associations, of a *real* rather than a monetary wage: a point that Keynes had already stressed as well. Second, by pointing to the influence of the interest rate on the rate of profits, Sraffa indicates, implicitly, a preference for this hypothesis in comparison with the post-Keynesian causal link, going from the rate of growth to the rate of profits, while leaving open the opposite, classical line of causality according to which income distribution affects the pace of accumulation and of economic growth (even if not necessarily in a precise, functional way). Third, Sraffa's reference to the rate of interest does not exclude other factors: especially, as we shall see in the next section, if we abandon the idea that the interest rate determines the natural position of the system on the wage-profit frontier. Last but not least, Sraffa's reference to the interest rate points to the compatibility of his analysis in his 1960 book with the recognition of the influence of monetary factors over real variables, central in Keynes' analysis of output and employment.

Changes Over Time of Wages and Profits as the Major Problem of Income Distribution

The survey of "Sraffian" analyses of income distribution conducted above leaves us in an unsatisfactory situation. We first examined the destructive implications of Sraffa's analysis for the traditional marginalist approach to income distribution. Then we considered on the one side the assumption of the wage rate as the exogenously given variable, justified by reference to the notion of subsistence wage, or to the wage being determined by the relative bargaining power of social classes; and, on the other side, some attempts at assuming the rate of profits as exogenously given, being determined either by the natural characteristics of the economy, or by the rate of interest; and we found these explanations equally unsatisfactory for providing a theory of income distribution. Thus we seem to find ourselves in a closed corner, since both alternatives implicitly suggested by the analytical tool of the wage-profit frontier are to be discarded.

There is, however, a very interesting way of tackling this dilemma, suggested by many elements dispersed here and there in the previous discussion. The point is, quite simply, that we should abandon the idea that at each point in time there are equilibrium or natural values for the distributive variables. Thus we should not try to solve the problem of income distribution by looking for a point on the wage-profit frontier representing a natural or equilibrium solution for the economic system under consideration. The role of economic analysis with respect to income distribution is rather to deal with the factors affecting changes over time of wages and profits.

Clearly, this involves prior rejection of the marginalist approach, according to which the problem of income distribution is an intrinsic, inseparable part of the wider problem of determining the equilibrium position for the economy as a whole. As shown above, Sraffa's analysis directly rejects the idea that distributive variables should be determined through the equilibrium condition between supply of and demand for "factors of production."

In fact, as we saw earlier, the classical approach revived by Sraffa does not look for the determination of an equilibrium position of the economic system based on the forces of supply and demand stemming from the confrontation of initial resource endowments and economic agents' preferences. The classical-Sraffian approach rather follows the procedure of tackling separately the different economic issues, for each of them isolating the main forces at work. This procedure does not require the building up of a formalized model unifying the various economic issues; nor does it require the existence of a unitary approach to all problems (such as maximization or minimization under constraint within the marginalist approach, as suggested by Samuelson, 1947). Thus, the very notion of equilibrium acquires in the classical-Sraffian approach a different meaning from that common in the marginalist approach. (On this, see Roncaglia, 1978.)

The building up of a general model of the economy is often insisted on, as a necessary precondition for verifying formal consistency between the treatment of different problems within the same approach. But formal consistency cannot be verified when two different problems are analyzed at different "analytical levels"; and we must admit the possibility that the analytical levels most appropriate to the analysis of various problems are different from one another. The idea of different analytical levels is common in modern science; for instance, the interpretation of how symbols interact in the human mind is developed "at a different level of abstraction" from the interpretation of the interaction of neurons in the human brain [see Hofstadter, 1979]. There is, however, a wider notion of consistency, which refers to the basic conception of the working of an economic system. This kind of consistency is necessary, in order to consider the set of specific theories, about specific aspects of economic reality, as a (loosely) unified building of economic science; and this is one of the main security systems against possible abuses of the idea of different analytical levels.

All this should be sufficient for justifying the method of dealing with income distribution by analyzing the factors affecting the changes over time of wage rates and profit rates, rather than trying to locate equilibrium values for the distributive variables (a point on the wage-profit frontier) at a moment in time. Income distribution (as well as technology and activity levels) strongly depends on its past history; and this fact can be accorded due prominence by assuming income distribution at a point in time to be given, with the analysis then concentrating on the factors that can lead to changes in this distribution.

The strong dependence of income distribution at a point in time on its past history is shown, among other things, by the references to habits, conventions, and institutional factors that abound in the analyses of our problem. However, referring to habits, conventions, and institutional factors as given data explaining income distribution, on the basis of their *relative* constancy over time, really constitutes an evasion from our task. In fact, habits, conventions, and institutional factors do not determine *uniquely* wage and profit rates, so that their mode of operation, and the elements affecting them *in a systematic way*, must also be considered as part of the analytical problem — if not the *main* part. Among these elements are wage and profit rates themselves, whose changes will not leave habits, conventions, and institutions unaltered. There is a complex interrelation between social and economic factors that can only be dealt with in an approach that recognizes these dynamic interrelationships over time.

In doing this, we meet again many of the aspects which we have already considered as relevant in the previous sections, such as wage bargaining, the transmission of cost increases to prices (including not only labor and raw material costs but also interest costs), etc. Many of these aspects have already been the subject of specific inquiries: we may refer, for instance, to the articles collected in Sylos Labini [1974 and 1984, especially ch. 7].

Here, we can only sketch the logical steps of a possible analysis of income distribution, compatible with the classical approach as restated by Sraffa and with the method suggested above. This series of logical steps provides us with a coherent framework within which we can organize the different aspects of an analysis of the factors affecting income distribution.

1. Let us start from a given wage-profit frontier, and a given point on this frontier.

2. Now let us consider wage bargaining. It affects the level of money wages. The outcome of the wage bargaining process is mainly influenced by the following factors: unemployment, affecting the relative bargaining power of the counterparts; past and expected changes in the cost of living, affecting workers' claims; political elements, affecting trade unions' combativity.

3. Then changes in money wages are translated into changes in unit labor costs in money terms. This requires taking changes in labor productivity, which can be affected by investments and by the rate of change in activity levels (e.g., because of increase or decrease in overmanning) explicitly into account. (It should be stressed here that changes in labor productivity, i.e., in technology, imply movements of the wage-profit frontier.)

4. The fourth step consists of considering how changes in unit labor costs are translated into changes of product prices. Two groups of ele-

ments are relevant here: (1) changes in other elements of cost (such as raw material prices and the prices of imported means of production, influenced by the exchange rate; or changes in interest or other financial charges), and (2) changes in the markup (which, as Sylos Labini [1984, ch. 7] shows, is mainly affected by the strength of external competition; but which, as suggested by Panico [1984, 1985] is also influenced by financial events and the stance of the monetary authorities).

5. The new money wage rate, the new technology, and the new level of money prices may now be used to derive a new wage-profit curve and a new wage-profit point on this curve.

6. The final step consists in considering the "feedback" influence of income distribution on the factors taken into account in the preceding steps: e.g., on technological change and on activity levels (and thus on unemployment) or, more specifically, on the general state of expectations (which affect not only investment but also financial events).

This series of logical steps does not provide, in itself, an analysis of the actual process of transition from the initial to the final wage-profit point and wage-profit curve. It does provide, however, a convenient logical arrangement of the various elements affecting income distribution over time. Once these elements are organized in this way, it becomes possible to evaluate their relative relevance and to analyze separately each of them and the factors affecting it. Also, it becomes possible to provide analytically grounded answers to questions concerning income distribution: for example, the role of the government, which we will briefly consider. (Another possible example is the role of sociological and political factors, the relevance of which can be easily recognized within this approach to the analysis of income distribution.)

The government, willingly or not, affects income distribution by its action, as we can see by considering the stages recalled above. It directly affects the wage-bargaining process through the setting up of industrial relations institutions; it affects unemployment through fiscal and monetary policy; it affects technical change through industrial policy; it affects production costs through the fiscal system (e.g., social security charges) as well as through public utility prices (e.g., electricity, which is commonly a nationalized sector or a sector of publicly administered prices) and monetary policy affecting interest charges, and especially (in open economies such as Italy) through the exchange rate. The government also affects the transmission of changes in costs to product price changes through, e.g., the permissive or restrictive stance of monetary policy, and possibly through direct price regulation. Again, all the government's instruments of intervention recalled above affect the way in which wage and profit rates react, directly or indirectly, on their main determinants.

Of course, the logical framework sketched above needs filling in, by an analysis of each step, and the factors relevant in each of them. But at least in part this has already been done. (See, e.g., Sylos Labini [1974 and 1984]; in particular, his analysis of the factors affecting markup movements.) Also, it is our contention here that this is more fruitfully done if we explicitly locate our analysis within the setting of the classical-surplus approach. Such a setting should, in fact, fulfill three tasks in relation to the analysis of income distribution. First, it should help to reject spurious elements, derived from traditional marginalist theory, and which in fact are only consistent with the approach criticized above, relying on supply and demand forces. Second, it should help (through the connection with Sraffa's analysis of the relationship between technology, relative prices, and income distribution) to give "systematicity" to the analysis of income distribution, namely to connect in a coherent way a mass of preexisting analyses of specific aspects relevant to our purpose. Third, as it has been suggested at the beginning of this section, the conceptual consistency with a basic conception of the working of an economic system is a security system against possible abuses of the idea of "different analytical levels"; and the survey conducted in the previous pages leads us to conclude that this idea provides the best line of research for an analysis of income distribution within the framework of the classical approach revived by Sraffa — namely what is commonly, but somehow restrictively, called the neo-Ricardian approach.

References

Dobb, M. (1973). *Theories of Value and Distribution Since Adam Smith*. Cambridge: Cambridge University Press.

Eatwell, J. (1975). Mr. Sraffa's standard commodity and the rate of exploitation. *Quarterly Journal of Economics* 89: 543–555.

Eichner, A. (1976). *The Megacorp and Oligopoly*. Cambridge: Cambridge University Press.

Garegnani, P. (1979). Notes on consumption, investment and effective demand. II. *Cambridge Journal of Economics* 3: 63–82.

—————. (1984). Value and distribution in the classical economists and Marx. *Oxford Economic Papers* 36: 291–325.

—————. (1985). Sraffa: classical versus marginalist analysis. Mimeo.

Hahn, F. (1982a). *Money and Inflation*. Oxford: Blackwell.

—————. (1982b). The neo-Ricardians. *Cambridge Journal of Economics* 6: 353–374.

Harcourt, G.C., and Kenyon, P. (1976). Pricing and the investment decision. *Kyklos* 29: 449–477.

Hofstadter, D.R. (1979). *Godel, Escher, Bach.* New York: Basic Books.
Kregel, J. (1976). Sraffa et Keynes: le taux d' intéret et le taux de profit. *Cahiers d'économie politique* 3: 155–163.
Medio, A. (1972). Profits and surplus value: appearance and reality in capitalist production. In E.K. Hunt and J.G. Schwartz (eds.), *A Critique of Economic Theory.* Harmondsworth: Penguin, pp. 312–346.
Meek, R. (1961). Mr. Sraffa's rehabilitation of classical economics. *Scottish Journal of Political Economy* 8: 119–136.
Nuti, D.M. (1970). "Vulgar economy" in the theory of income distribution. *De Economist* 118: 363–369.
Panico, C. (1980). Marx's analysis of the relationship between the rate of interest and the rate of profits. *Cambridge Journal of Economics* 4: 363–378.
———. (1984). Interest and profit in the theories of value and distribution. Ph. D. dissertation, University of Cambridge. Mimeo.
———. (1985). Market forces and the relation between the rates of interest and profits. *Contributions to Political Economy* 4: 37–60.
Pasinetti, L. (1962). Rate of profit and income distribution in relation to the rate of economic growth. *Review of Economic Studies* 29: 267–279.
———. (1981). *Structural Change and Economic Growth.* Cambridge: Cambridge University Press.
Pivetti, M. (1985). On the monetary explanation of distribution. Mimeo.
Ricardo, D. (1951). *Principles of Political Economy and Taxation* (1817). In P. Sraffa (ed.), *Works and Correspondence,* Vol. I. Cambridge: Cambridge University Press.
Roncaglia, A. (1974). Labor-power, subsistence wage and the rate of wages. *Australian Economic Papers* 13: 133–143.
———. (1978). *Sraffa and the Theory of Prices.* New York: Wiley.
Roncaglia, A., and Tonveronachi, M. (1985). The pre-Keynesian roots of the neoclassical synthesis. *Cahiers d'économie politique,* 10: 51–65.
Samuelson, P. (1947). *Foundations of Economic Analysis.* Cambridge, MA: Harvard University Press.
Sraffa, P. (1932). Dr. Hayek on money and capital. *Economic Journal* 42: 42–53.
———. (1960). *Production of Commodities by Means of Commodities.* Cambridge: Cambridge University Press.
Steedman, I. (1977). *Marx after Sraffa.* London: New Left Books.
Steindl, J. (1985). Comment on Prof. Pivetti's paper. Mimeo.
Sylos Labini, P. (1974). *Trade Unions, Inflation and Productivity.* Lexington, MA: Lexington Books.
———. (1982). *Lezioni di economia,* vol. II. Roma: Edizioni dell'Ateneo.
———. (1984). *The Forces of Economic Growth and Decay.* Cambridge, MA: MIT Press.
Torrens, R. (1834). *On Wages and Combinations.* London: Longman.
Wood, A. (1975). *A Theory of Profits.* Cambridge: Cambridge University Press.

8 THE GENERAL EQUILIBRIUM THEORY OF DISTRIBUTION

Michael C. Howard

There are various forms of general equilibrium theory. Marxian, neo-classical, modern forms of Keynesianism and Sraffian economics may all be so classified since each exhibits a concern with the equilibrium states of whole economies, represented in a disaggregated form, rather than that of some sector. They differ in the way economies are conceptualised and the properties attributed to equilibrium states. This chapter is concerned with the neo-classical version, which is usually referred to as Walrasian theory, after its originator Leon Walras [1874]. Furthermore, attention is limited to the theory in the context of competition (where each agent is a *price taker*). Walrasian theorists have treated noncompetitive economies, but they have done so to a much lesser extent and the competitive version is far more advanced.

The quality that designates an economics as neo-classical is the derivation of agents' supplies and demands from particular types of maximization problems. It is assumed that each consumer's domain of choice, preferences, and assets, and each producer's technology, are exogenously given, as are the institutions allowing economic interaction to occur through voluntary contracts. On this basis, every consumer maximizes utility subject only to a budget constraint, and every producer maximizes profit constrained only by technology [see Samuelson, 1947]. A set of prices that makes their choices (i.e., their demands and supplies) compatible is a general equilibrium.

Initially Walrasian analysis was but one of several neo-classical approaches that emerged from the "marginal revolution" in the late nineteenth century [see Blaug, 1978]. Since then it has not only been increasingly refined but it has become the dominant form of neo-classical theorizing. Indeed, it can be argued that of all the original neo-classical formulations of price theory, the Walrasian alone remains theoretically coherent as a general theory, all the others requiring special assumptions to ensure their validity [see Howard, 1983]. However, within this theory, two subvarieties may be distinguished, that of Arrow-Debreu and temporary equilibrium analysis. They differ in their treatment of time — in how economic agents relate to the future. Neither is specifically oriented to the treatment of distributional problems, but as general theories of market prices their propositions can be applied to distributional phenomena. Nevertheless, since each is formulated on a high level of abstraction, their content is often not very definite or specific.

In the next section the Arrow-Debreu model is outlined; some of its distributional implications are considered in the following section. This is followed by a similar treatment of temporary equilibrium theory in section III. Finally, a number of limitations of both types of theory is considered.

I

The hallmark of the Arrow-Debreu version of Walrasian theory is its treatment of commodities from which follows, when combined with other assumptions, a particular treatment of markets. Commodities differ from one another quite obviously in their physical properties. The novelty of Arrow-Debreu is to consider them as different also according to their "date of availability." Thus, units of the same physically specified good are regarded as different commodities if they become available at different times. The rationale for doing so is straightforward. Both producers' profits and consumers' utility will be sensitive to the date of commodity use. In other words, consumers' preferences embody a "time preference," while producers' costs and revenues are dependent upon the dates that inputs are acquired and outputs are disposed of. Consequently, agents' demands and supplies for a particular physically specified commodity may vary depending upon its date of availability.

When this characteristic of commodities is combined with assumptions

TABLE 8-1.   Arrow-Debreu equilibrium

Physical specification	Date		
	1	$\cdots$	*T*
1	p_{11}	$\cdots$	p_{1T}
.	.		.
.	.		.
.	.		.
n	p_{n1}	$\cdots$	p_{nT}

made in the standard neo-classical treatment of consumption and production, an important result emerges. Consumers are typically assumed to have *complete* preferences. Faced with choices between different consumption bundles, they are *always* able to state the relations of preference (or indifference) they have between them. Analogously, for each set of prices, producers can completely rank input-output combinations according to profitability. Coupling these completeness properties with the definition of commodities in terms of date means that each agent will form demands and supplies over *all* goods, and will do so at a *single decision date*. So, in addition to spot markets (dealing in commodities for immediate delivery) there will exist a comprehensive set of forward markets (relating to commodities available in the future). If there are n physically specified commodities and T time periods, there will exist nT markets of which n will be spot markets and $n(T - 1)$ futures markets.[1]

An Arrow-Debreu equilibrium, or as it is sometimes called, an intertemporal equilibrium, will thus be a set of prices that brings all supplies and demands into balance (which clears all markets). It may be pictured as in table 8-1. Here, p_{ij} represents the price of the ith physically specified commodity at date j. Since all demands and supplies are formed in the present (date 1), the prices will be *present value* prices. They pertain to contracts made in the present and are paid or received in the present, despite the fact that $n(T - 1)$ of the commodities will not be delivered until some date in the future.

II

In such an equilibrium each type of labor, working under the same conditions, will be receiving the same rate of wages. The rate of return on any loan, or investment, covering the same time period will also be equalized. These results follow logically from the assumption that agents are maximizing in a state of general equilibrium. There is, however, no assurance that such distributional magnitudes will remain unchanged through time. The uniform rate of return between any two dates may, for example, exhibit all manner of variation between different pairs of dates. Similarly wage rates can fluctuate with the variation of demands and supplies over time. But all agents will know these respective patterns and be fully adjusted to them from the very first period when *all* choices are formed. There is no element of uncertainty. Each agent knows the full characteristics of those matters on which their decisions depend, and there is a comprehensive set of markets in which they can be carried out at the initial date. There is in consequence no activity of arbitrage or speculation, nor is there any need for the complex structure of financial institutions characteristic of actual capitalist economies. Of course, this is a highly fictitious picture of the world, but it is possible to argue that its qualities can be positively useful in understanding reality. Some examples of this will be provided in the following pages.

The causation structure of Arrow-Debreu theory is absolutely clearcut. Equilibrium prices and quantities are determined by the exogenously specified elements indicated in the opening section. Thus, workers' wages, capitalists' profits, landowners' rents, and rentiers' interest receipts all reflect the optimizations conducted by agents on the basis of a given allocation of assets and technology, in an institutional framework enforcing the rule of contract. This may be rephrased by stating that it is the rational choices of free individuals which account for the pattern of distribution, including the extremes of wealth and poverty, privilege and deprivation. Naturally, this latter formulation is particularly amenable for use in apologetics seeking to buttress the status quo.

However, the concern of Walrasian theorists has been predominantly analytic, and the ideological properties of their work are much more ambiguous. A major concern has been to find those conditions that ensure the existence of an equilibrium, and that also guarantee that any equilibrium is unique and stable [see Debreu, 1959; Arrow and Hahn, 1971]. The results have implications for neo-classical theory generally, since much of it may be viewed as dealing in models which are special cases of Arrow-Debreu, i.e., cases in which the assumptions made are particular examples of the more abstract assumptions used in Arrow-Debreu theory.[2] Moreover, these problems are of crucial importance.

We may illustrate this with reference to the existence question. This is concerned with the problem of determining what types of consumers' preferences, producers' technologies, and distribution of assets will al-

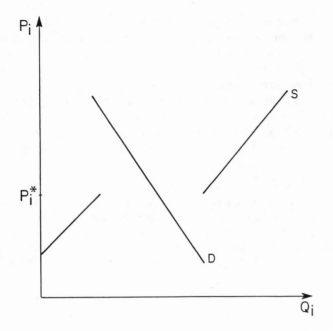

Figure 8–1. Example of Non-existence of Equilibrium.

ways imply that an equilibrium can occur. Conversely, the problem can be stated as that of finding what characteristics of the exogenous data threaten the possibility of there being a set of prices which will clear all markets simultaneously. Since economic theory is essentially equilibrium theory (i.e., its propositions pertain to the properties of equilibria) the significance of this question is difficult to devalue.

Many existence results have been proved. One is that a market clearing price vector is assured only if demands and supplies vary *continuously* with prices. Thus, in the partial equilibrium example illustrated in figure 8–1, the supply function is discontinuous at P_i^* and no equilibrium exists. Such "holes" are easily given an economic rationale. In this case, imagine producers falling into two homogenous groups such that at the price P_i^* all members of the least efficient group start producing simultaneously.

The chief significance of this result is negative. It indicates that the results of equilibrium theory need to be treated with some scepticism. And the analysis of uniqueness and stability reinforces this conclusion. Further restrictive assumptions are required to guarantee that if equilibrium exists it is unique and stable. Since comparative static propositions rest upon these properties,[3] even those who whole-heartedly adhere to a neo-classical *weltanschauung* may be unwilling to place much trust in the empirical application of such propositions. This necessarily applies to statements on distributional matters.

Even if one throws caution to the wind on the grounds of pragmatism (i.e., on the view that it is the predictions derived, not the assumptions on which they rest, which are important [see Friedman, 1953]), Arrow-Debreu theory is not particularly comforting. The reason is succinctly expressed by Arrow and Hahn.

> The main problem we set ourselves in this chapter [i.e. ch. 10] is an inquiry into the power of general equilibrium models in giving unambiguous predictions of how the equilibrium of the economy will be affected by a given parameter change....This problem must be intimately related to that of the uniqueness of equilibrium.... Even so, the kind of parameter changes for which predictions become possible is pretty limited [Arrow and Hahn, 1971, p. 245].

Once general equilibrium analysis moves away from binary changes, in which the market conditions of only two goods are directly affected by a parameter change,

> ...we must expect to have fairly precise quantitative information as to the relationship between goods before being able to make the kind of statement that was possible for binary changes [Arrow and Hahn, 1971, p. 254].

Consequently, the

> ...most notable conclusion of our investigations...appears to us to be that for very many interesting problems of comparing equilibria, the information provided by the foundations of the models, profit and utility maximization, are insufficient in giving us definite answers to our questions.... Now while such results as we were able to establish are useful and worth having, the main negative lesson is also useful, for it points to the dangers of partial analysis, in which it is often possible to get quite definite predictions of the consequences of a given parameter change [Arrow and Hahn, 1971, pp. 261–262].

The distribution theory inherent in Arrow-Debreu theory is thus highly limited. It certainly does not make bold and sweeping claims as to the "laws of motion" of a capitalist system analogous to that found in Marx's *Capital* [1867, 1885, 1894]. Some may use this to defend the theory, others to condemn it, but there can be no doubt that a large degree of indeterminacy is characteristic of abstract general equilibrium analysis.

Nevertheless, there are some definite conclusions on distributional matters. For example, the theory implies that in an equilibrium pure profits will be zero. The logic of this is contained in the remarks that opened this section, but it can be illustrated more fully as follows. As indicated at the end of section I, the prices of an Arrow-Debreu equilibrium are present value prices. These will define a set of interest rates operative between any two dates. (Although it is traditional to represent present value magnitudes as being derived from discounting procedures specified in terms of interest rates, the contrawise relation also holds; given a set of present value prices, a set of interest rates can be defined.) Thus, if in table 8–1 commodity 1 at date 1 represents the *numeraire*,[4] we can define the rate of interest prevailing between period t and $t + \alpha$ as

$$r^1_{t,t+\alpha} = \frac{p_{1,t} - p_{1,t+\alpha}}{p_{1,t+\alpha}}$$

This expresses the extra amount of commodity 1 that can be received on loans between t and $t + \alpha$ for every unit of commodity 1 lent at date t (or its equivalent in other commodities) for the duration of α.

It is now easy to show that in an intertemporal equilibrium no capital asset will receive a profit over and above the relevant rate of interest. In such an equilibrium, the returns to scale facing any producer must be constant or decreasing. (If they were increasing, the producer in question could not be maximizing profits.) Assume initially that they are constant throughout, as represented in figure 8–2.

For all sets of prices $p_2/p_1 >$ slope of Oa, like that represented by the iso-profit lines marked (1) and (2), the maximum profit which is possible is zero. In this case, the highest iso-profit line that can be reached is the one that passes through the origin. Therefore, the optimal choice is to produce nothing with no inputs. In the case where $p_2/p_1 <$ slope of Oa, such as that represented by the iso-profit lines (3) and (4), ever higher profits may be achieved with more production. Therefore, there is no maximal choice and such a set of prices cannot be an equilibrium one. Where the price set is such that p_2/p_1 equals the slope of Oa, all efficient input-output combinations are optimal and profits are zero.

In the case of decreasing returns it does appear that positive pure profits are possible. However, the appearance is illusory. Consider the case depicted in figure 8–3. If p_2/p_1 is equal to the slope of bc, Q^*_1 is produced using Q^*_2 as input, and a positive return above interest of Ob (measured in units of Q_1) results. However, such a return is not properly classified as a profit return. There is only one reason why production

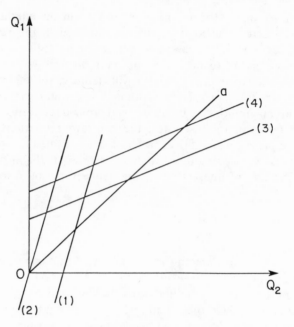

Figure 8–2. Constant Returns and Zero Profits.

conditions of the form represented in figure 8–3 can occur, namely that there is some input which cannot be increased. In the absence of such a constraint, no profit-maximizing producer will ever produce at a position where returns are decreasing. With all inputs variable, it would always be possible and more advantageous to duplicate production units and realize constant returns. Consequently, a production set such as that represented in figure 8–3 reflects the fixity of at least one input; and the return Ob that stems from this limitation is an *economic rent*,[5] not a pure profit in the usual sense of this term.

This is an important conclusion. It means that any observed profits over and above interest must derive from those phenomena from which Arrow-Debreu theory abstracts. In this sense, the work of Schumpeter and Knight receives some support from the analysis of intertemporal equilibrium. Schumpeter considered the (temporary) market power associated with innovating entrepreneurs to be the central matter, while Knight emphasised that the origin of pure profits lay in noninsurable uncertainties.[6] More generally, it illustrates the usefulness of "unrealis-

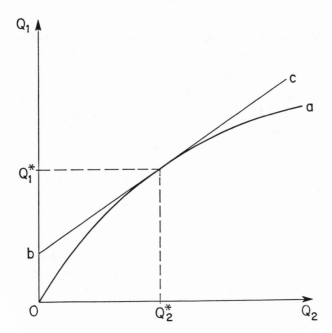

Figure 8–3. Decreasing Returns, Zero Profits and Economic Rent.

tic" models. By comparing their results with "reality," a clue is provided as to the cause of real-world phenomena. The construction of economic models that do not seek to mirror the empirical world may thereby be justified as a productive endeavor.

The theory of Arrow-Debreu may also be used to argue against the distribution theories emanating from the surplus tradition. Ricardo [1821], Marx [1894] and Sraffa [1960] all agree, albeit in different ways, that a necessary and sufficient condition for positive profit to occur is that the economy be capable of producing a surplus. (The term *profit* as used in these approaches would be classified as interest by neo-classicals, but we shall retain the nonneo-classical usage in this part of the exposition.) The rationale for this can be indicated by a simple example.

Consider a constant returns economy in which there is only one produced commodity which, together with labor, produces itself. The technology of this economy can be represented as

$$a + l \rightarrow 1$$

where a is the input of the produced commodity required to produce one unit of itself as output, and l is the labor input. A Sraffian economist would represent the equilibrium of such an economy as

$$ap_1 (1 + \pi) + lw = p_1 \tag{8.1}$$

where p_1 is the price of the produced commodity, π is the rate of profit, and w is the wage. Clearly the maximum rate of profit (the rate associated with zero wages) is

$$\pi \max = 1/a - 1.$$

This will be positive if, and only if, $a < 1$, i.e., where the economy can produce a surplus.

Arrow-Debreu highlights the questionable assumption on which this conclusion rests, and in doing so queries the connection of surplus to profitability. Notice that in equation (8.1) the same price (p_1) applies to the commodity as input as is applied to it as output. But the theory of dated commodities considered in section I challenges the appropriateness of this. And once the invariability of price with date is relaxed, it is impossible to derive any conclusion connecting profit to surplus. Instead of equation (8.1) we now have

$$ap_{11} (1 + \pi) + lw = p_{12}$$

where p_{11} is the price at the input date and p_{12} is the price at the time of output. The maximum rate of profit is now given by

$$\pi \max = 1/a \cdot p_{12}/p_{11} - 1$$

and nothing can be inferred as to the size of the maximum π from the magnitude of a alone. Theorists in the surplus tradition have provided no arguments as to why the considerations lying behind the Arrow-Debreu theory of dated commodities are without force. Consequently, they have provided nothing which could be used to parry this criticism.

III

As treated above, Arrow-Debreu theory deals with a world of certainty, and its conclusion that markets will be comprehensive is patently at variance with reality. These two matters are connected and have led Walrasian theorists to formulate an alternative theory of "temporary equilibrium." Actual consumers are likely to be particularly uncertain as to those commodities which will be available in the future, what their preferences will be, and the exact value of their assets. Similarly, producers will be especially uncertain as to future technological conditions. The effect of this is that futures markets will be incomplete and trading will take place sequentially. Consequently an Arrow-Debreu equilibrium is impossible; any equilibrium will be temporary.[7]

Hicks [1939] conceptualizes the matter as follows. There are a number of periods, and at the beginning of each, spot markets exist together with a limited number of futures markets covering those commodities which can be traded on a forward basis. Since futures markets are not comprehensive, agents have to estimate some future prices in order to carry out optimal current transactions. On the basis of these expectations, agents trade in those commodities for which markets exist. Equilibrium is a situation where there is a consistency of agents' plans involving commodities on those markets, i.e., it involves only a balance of supplies and demands on the operating markets. The contracts which have been made govern agents' behavior during the rest of the period. At the beginning of the next period markets "reopen" and new trading can occur. Depending upon what has happened in the first period, and upon the state of the markets in the second period, the expectations formed at the beginning of the first period may turn out to be correct or incorrect in varying degree. Therefore, expectations may be revised and market prices in the second period will reflect these new expectations. At the start of the third period, markets reopen again. The economy thus proceeds through a sequence of temporary equilibria.

A temporary equilibrium is therefore an equilibrium on a restricted set of markets and is dependent upon agents' price expectations. Consequently, it is very different from the notion of intertemporal equilibrium dealt with in section I. However, the problems of existence, uniqueness, and stability have their counterparts in the temporary equilibrium framework. For example, it can be shown that the conditions required to guarantee the existence of a temporary equilibrium are essentially the same as those that ensure the existence of intertemporal equilibrium. In particular, demands and supplies must vary continuously with market prices. Such matters are not our prime concern but they need to be remembered. They reinforce the point made in the preceding section, that all neo-classical equilibrium theory may be of limited applicability, and its results should be treated with caution.

Moreover, comparative static propositions depend crucially on what is assumed about how agents form their expectations. Since economists know little on this matter, temporary equilibrium theory is even more devoid of hard content than Arrow-Debreu. This has not escaped the critics:

[If we develop] an analysis where the outcome depends upon expectations the assumptions about which can be varied almost indefinitely...then theory becomes barren of definite results [Garegnani, 1973, p. 365].

As one would expect, this property manifests itself in the area of distribution. Indeed, many of the concepts traditionally used to pose distributional problems may not even be well defined in the general model of temporary equilibrium. Take, for example, the concepts of national income and profit. Both of these involve a valuation of capital goods, and this is dependent upon expectations about future prices. In a sequence of equilibria where these expectations are continually proved wrong, the valuation will be arbitrary and unstable. Thus the concepts of income and profit will not be clearcut. Consequently, rates of profit and shares in income will also be ill-defined.

How, then, do we set up the traditional problems of distribution analysis? Only by adopting rather drastic assumptions about agents' expectations and the nature of economies in which they are formed. More specifically, the closer agents' expectations are to being rational, the less economies are subject to structural change, and the smaller are random shocks, the closer will be a sequence of temporary equilibria to an Arrow-Debreu equilibrium where the problem of the previous paragraph evaporates.[8] Furthermore, in this case the distributional propositions of Arrow-Debreu theory would be shared by temporary equilibrium theory. In the light of the indefiniteness portrayed in the preceding section, this is perhaps not much of a conclusion. However, it does give some additional content to the distribution theory associated with temporary equilibrium, and at least the traditional distribution problems can be posed.

IV

In recent years the type of theory discussed in this chapter has been the focus of intense criticism, especially from the perspectives of Keynesian and Sraffian theories. Much of it reflects only a confusion as to the nature of Walrasian analysis, but some of the considerations brought to light have real force.

Beginning in the early 1960s, Keynesian economists have reshaped their theory into forms which are directly comparable to that of Walrasian theory. In doing so they have uncovered a significant defect. The analysis of the preceding sections assumes agents formulate their demands and supplies on the belief that they can trade whatever quantities they desire as long as they provide equivalents in exchange. Consequently, consumers are assumed to maximize utility constrained only by a budget which is dependent upon their asset holdings and prices, while firms are assumed to maximize profits subject only to a technological constraint. And it is from these maximizations that demands and supplies are derived.

The limitation of this Walrasian conceptualization can be explained by considering a set of prices in which Walrasian demands and supplies are inconsistent. Obviously in this case not all demands and supplies can be realized simultaneously, and some of those agents on the long side of markets will be rationed if trades actually occur at these prices. In these circumstances it is not unreasonable to hypothesize that agents will develop expectations as to the probability of rationing in the future. If these probabilities are nonzero, this will affect other demands and supplies. For example, a consumer who is quantity-rationed in the sale of labor and expects this to continue at future dates will not necessarily change his or her willingness to supply labor from that specified by Walrasian theory, but is likely to reduce demand for currently available consumption goods. A firm which is quantity-rationed in the sale of its output and expects this to continue at future dates will not necessarily change its willingness to supply output from that indicated by Walrasian theory, but is likely to reduce demand for currently available labor. Agents' supplies and demands will not, therefore, be correctly specified by Walrasian theory, and the outcome of their equilibration may involve significant deviations from market clearance [see Clower, 1965; Malinvaud, 1977; Negishi, 1979; and Hahn, 1984].

Since this criticism bears upon the foundation of Walrasian theory, its distributional implications cannot remain unscathed. For example, involuntary unemployment insofar as it affects the distribution of income and wealth in Walrasian theory, does so only as a disequilibrium phenomenon. But, on the basis of the Keynesian criticism, its stature is now raised to that of a property that can characterize equilibria. Given the thought patterns of economists, it is thereby made less easy to write off the distributional impact of unemployment as transitory, and more difficult to defend a market determined distribution of income and wealth.

The claims of the Sraffian-based critics, sometimes referred to as neo-Ricardians, seek to go well beyond all this. They question the coherence and relevance of all supply-and-demand theory and although their focus has been primarily on neo-classical analysis, their position suggest a no more favorable disposition to the kind of Keynesianism just outlined. In relation to non-Walrasian forms of neo-classical theory, the record of these critics is impressive. They have exposed logical flaws in both the Austrian version of neo-classicism and in the theory of capital productivity stemming from J.B. Clark. However, no equivalent success has been forthcoming in relation to the type of theory discussed in this chapter; no logical defect has been found in modern forms of Walrasian theory. Instead neo-Ricardians have charged that Walrasian equilibria are not genuine equilibria because in general, they will not be characterized by a uniform rate of profit as conceptualized in the equilibria of their own theory, and which they take as correctly reflecting the competitive mechanism of capitalist economies [see, for example, Garegnani, 1976].

In this they are partially correct, but the criticism is misplaced. It is true that a neo-Ricardian uniform rate of profit will occur in Walrasian equilibria only under special conditions. But Walrasian theory itself suggests that this is no defect because such a rate of profit will not characterize actual economies, or be a particularly useful construct in analyzing them. The neo-Ricardian uniform rate of profit is derived from models in which the set of prices applicable to outputs is the same as that applied to inputs. The Arrow-Debreu conception of commodities, of course, questions precisely this matter. And on this basis, as indicated in section II, Walrasian theory can launch a counterattack against the paradigm of its neo-Ricardian critics.

More substance is found in the critical perspective of Marxism, which also questions the appropriateness of treating individual choices as the foundation on which to construct an economics. Unlike the neo-Ricardians, however, Marxism provides a theory of action (the materialist conception of history) to sustain its critique, and one that commits it to no particular stand in relation to specific neo-classical results. On the Marxian view, for which there are tomes of supportive evidence, individual characteristics are formed by the system in which individuals act, so the fundamental determinants of economic phenomena are supra-individual. So, instead of seeing these phenomena as reflecting "choices," the emphasis lies in representing economic systems as self-reproducing structures in which individuals perform as functionaries. Via such a viewpoint, economic theory may totally bypass neo-classical maximizations and free itself from the indefiniteness that stems from them.

V

This lack of definite content has been repeatedly encountered in the preceding sections. It can, of course, be overcome to the degree that specific assumptions about the exogenous data, discussed in the opening section, are made. Obviously, the less abstract the assumptions are, the more concrete the propositions will be that can be derived. Thus, for example, it is possible by focusing on particular types of technology and preferences, and assuming very specific types of asset distributions, for Walrasian theory to develop "special case" conclusions that conform to those derived from neo-Keynesian and neo-Ricardian models [see, for example, Bliss, 1975; and Howard, 1979]. Or, through definitizing the exogenous data in alternative ways, it is perfectly feasible to generate very particular predictions about the effect of comparative static changes such as ones commonly found in elementary textbooks expressed in the medium of partial equilibrium analysis [see, for example, Malinvaud, 1972, pp. 125–130]. The problem for Walrasian theorists is that what is appropriate to assume cannot be determined a priori, and empirically grounded assumptions are insecure to the extent that the relevant characteristics are ephemeral. And one reason why the phenomena that neo-classical theory takes as exogenous may be such is because of the dynamics inherent in actual market economies which Walrasian theory takes as its object of study. Unlike traditional forms of economic life, a propensity for change has been incorporated into the very institutional structure of these economies.

Neo-classicism provides nothing by which this problem may be resolved; and, not surprisingly, the theory we have considered remains at a high level of abstraction. A necessary consequence is that its distributional content remains relatively sparse. This means, among other things, that Walrasian analysis cannot shed much light upon the distribution of income and wealth in any actual capitalist economy. Nevertheless, it is also true to say that, for those who take the neo-classical perspective at all seriously, it provides an invaluable standard by which clear thinking can be enhanced and alternative theories evaluated.

Notes

1. The terms *futures markets* and *forward markets* are used synonymously.

2. For example, the general equilibrium models of typical intermediate textbooks, usually framed in terms of Edgeworth boxes, may be so considered. They are simply formulations of Arrow-Debreu where the number of agents and commodities are limited to two, and where the time horizon, T, is one.

3. If, for any set of exogenously specified elements, equilibria are multiple, it is unclear which equilibria should be compared. If equilibria are unstable, comparative static propositions may be amiss in their predictions as to the direction of change following a parameter shift.

4. The numeraire is the unit in which prices are measured, or "money." In the Arrow-Debreu model there is no rationale for the existence of money in the sense of specialised

means of payment. Therefore, prices have to be measured in units of some commodity, and the reference to money designates only this function. The price of such a numeraire is obviously unity. In terms of itself, it has a price of 1.

5. At least since the time of Ricardo, the concept of economic rent has referred to returns over and above what is necessary to maintain the resource in question in its current use. Ricardo used the concept in relation to land, but neo-classicals have generalized it. The price of any resource factor whose returns are purely rental in nature is equal to the capitalized value of its rents. The rate of return to its owner is, therefore, equal to the relevant rate of interest.

6. See Schumpeter [1912] and Knight [1921]. An exposistion of these works is contained in chapter 13 of Howard [1983] where they are also subjected to a critical evaluation.

7. The Arrow-Debreu model can incorporate uncertainty through the device of defining commodities by "state of the world" characteristics; see Debreu [1959]. However, this does not detract from the importance of temporary equilibrium theory and the considerations dealt with in this section. It should also be noted that although forward markets are not comprehensive in any actual economy, some do operate. Therefore, a temporary equilibrium model can legitimately include some futures markets; the key factor is only that they are not complete and rational agents will thereby be forced to form expectations on which their current actions depend.

8. Rational expectations may be defined as a situation in which agents form their expectations in ways that conform to those that would be derived from analyzing the actual determining structure of the economy. The occurrence of random shocks will mean that expectations will not be perfectly accurate, but only correct "on the average." Stated alternatively, the expected frequency distribution of future market clearing prices held by agents will be the distribution actually encountered if the structure remains unchanged. There will be less of a dispersion in this distribution the less important random shocks are, and agents' expectations will approximate more closely those associated with perfect foresight. If the structure of the economy is subject to change, agents will have to find new rules by which expectations may be formed, and this will take time.

References

Arrow, K.J., and Hahn, F.H. (1971). *General Competitive Analysis*. Edinburgh: Oliver & Boyd.

Blaug, M. (1978). *Economic Theory in Retrospect*, 3rd edition. Cambridge: Cambridge University Press.

Bliss, C.J. (1975). *Capital Theory and the Distribution of Income*. Amsterdam: North-Holland.

Brown, M., Sato, K., and Zarembka, P. (eds.) (1976). *Essays in Modern Capital Theory*. Amsterdam: North-Holland.

Clower, R.W. (1965). The Keynesian counter-revolution: a theoretical appraisal. In F.H. Hahn and F. Brechling (eds.), *The Theory of Interest Rates*. London: Macmillan, pp. 103–125.

Debreu, G. (1959). *Theory of Value*. New Haven, CT: Yale University Press.

Friedman, M. (1953). *Essays in Positive Economics*. Chicago: University of Chicago Press.

Garegnani, P. (1973). Summary of the final discussion. In J.A. Mirrlees and N.H. Stern (eds.), *Models of Economic Growth*. London: Macmillan.
—————. (1976). On a change in the notion of equilibrium in recent work on value and distribution: a comment on Samuelson. In M. Brown, K. Sato, and P. Zarembka (eds.), *Essays in Modern Capital Theory*. Amsterdam: North-Holland, pp. 25–45.

Hahn, F.H. (1984). *Equilibrium and Macroeconomics*. Oxford: Blackwell.

Hahn, F.H., and Brechling, F. (eds.) (1965). *The Theory of Interest Rates*. London: Macmillan.

Hicks, J.R. (1939). *Value and Capital*. Oxford: Oxford University Press. (2nd edition, 1946).

Howard, M.C. (1979). *Modern Theories of Distribution*. London: MacMillan.

—————. (1983). *Profits in Economic Theory*. London: MacMillan.

Knight, F.H. (1921). *Risk, Uncertainty and Profit*. Boston: Houghton Mifflin.

Malinvaud, E. (1972). *Lectures on Micro Economic Theory*. Amsterdam: North-Holland.

—————. (1977). *The Theory of Unemployment Reconsidered*. Oxford: Blackwell.

Marx, K. (1867). *Capital*, Vol. I. London: Lawrence & Wishart (1970).

—————. (1885). *Capital*, Vol. II. London: Lawrence & Wishart (1970).

—————. (1894). *Capital*, Vol. III. London: Lawrence & Wishart (1972).

Mirrlees, J.A., and Stern, N.H. (eds.) (1973). *Models of Economic Growth*. London: Macmillan.

Negishi, T. (1979). *Microeconomic Foundations of Keynesian Macroeconomics*. Amsterdam: North-Holland.

Ricardo, D. (1821). *On the Principles of Political Economy and Taxation*, Vol. I of *The Works of David Ricardo*, P. Sraffa (ed.). Cambridge: Cambridge University Press (1951).

Samuelson, P.A. (1947). *Foundations of Economic Analysis*. Cambridge, MA: Harvard University Press.

Schumpeter, J.A. (1912) *The Theory of Economic Development*. Cambridge, MA: Harvard University Press.

Sraffa, P. (1960). *Production of Commodities by Means of Commodities: Prelude to a Critique of Economic Theory*. Cambridge: Cambridge University Press.

Walras, L. (1874). *Elements of Pure Economics*, edition definitive, 1926. Translated by W. Jaffe. London: Allen & Unwin (1954).

9 FACTOR SHARES IN CANADA, THE UNITED STATES, AND THE UNITED KINGDOM

Camilo Dagum

On income distribution, the history of economic thought recognizes two mainstreams of research. One stems from Ricardo [1817] and deals with the income distribution among factors of production, i.e., the functional distribution of income. It purports to account for the factor prices' formation, such as wage and profit rates, and the share that the corresponding factors of production (e.g., labor, capital, and land) have in national income.

The second mainstream of research stems from Pareto [1895, 1897] and is concerned with the distribution of income among a set of economic units, such as family, household, and individual, with or without disaggregating the set of individuals or family heads according to some socioeconomic attribute such as gender, race, education, age, or profession. It considers the income received by each economic unit regardless of the property claim of the factors of production, except when the income is disaggregated by sources (e.g., wages and salaries, self-employment in-

I am grateful to my student Marc Prud'homme for his computational assistance.

come, investment income, transfer payments, and others). It is called the size or personal income distribution and purports to explain the generation and the shape of the income distribution among microeconomic units, and its associated measure of income inequality.

Although the personal and the functional income distributions belong to the microeconomic and the macroeconomic domains of inquiry, respectively, there are important macroeconomic forces conditioning the personal income distribution (e.g., research and development programs, the institutional structures of education, taxes, and inheritance), and microeconomic forces conditioning the functional income distribution (e.g., the economic agents' modes of action and interaction concerning their decisions to consume, invest, accumulate, and upgrade their professional qualifications).

The primary purpose of this chapter is the analysis of data on the factor shares in national income of Canada, the United States, and the United Kingdom, which is the content of the third section. The second section discusses the different methods of partitioning the proprietors' income (farm and nonfarm income from self-employed and unincorporated enterprises) between labor and property income. The fourth section specifies a model of functional distribution of income and fits it to the time-series data for the United States' labor share and the labor share of a cross-section of 30 countries. The fifth section presents the conclusions.

The Unincorporated Sector and the Twofold Division of National Income

The functional income categories present the frequent contradiction, or at least a lack of correspondence between the theoretical concepts and their empirical counterparts. Economic theory reasons in terms of wages, profits, and rent as the income flows from the labor, capital, and land factors of production, whereas the national accounts systems use the categories of employee compensation, proprietors' farm income, proprietors' nonfarm income, rental income of persons, corporate profits, and net interest as components of the net national product at factor cost, i.e., prior to any secondary distribution of income such as transfer payments.

The employee compensation which also includes the employers' contributions for social insurance and to private pension, health and welfare funds, workers' compensation, directors' fees, corporate executives' salaries, and some other minor payments to the employees is taken as a proxy variable for labor income. The sum of rental income of persons, corporate profits, and net interest is a proxy variable for property income. However, they are short of representing the total labor and property incomes. Hence they do not yet exhaust the total income to be distributed because of the remaining category, the proprietors' income, which encompasses both labor and property income of the proprietors (employers and self-employed in unincorporated business or economic activities). Its relative importance as a percentage of national income, and in some countries and periods its absolute importance too, decreases (whereas the corporate sector increases) as a result of the degree of economic growth, industrialization, and modernization of national economic systems.

The size of the unincorporated sector and its percentage share in national income is strongly correlated with the importance of the agrarian sector in total economic activity, and with the structure of land tenure and exploitation. For instance, in the 1950s the national income of Mexico could roughly be equally imputed to employee compensation, property income, and proprietors' income [Banco de Mexico, 1969]. Since then, the proprietors' income share steadily decreased in favor of the other two income categories as a consequence of the rapid process of economic growth and modernization (the average rate of growth was over 6% from the decade of the 1930s to the decade of the 1970s) which encompassed a trend toward the corporate mode of production.

The growing share of labor and corporate incomes in the distribution of the net national output is a common trend in contemporary economic systems. In the United Kingdom, characterized by a small territory, high population density and being the cradle of the industrial revolution, the decline of the proprietors' share and a fortiori the farm proprietors' share in national income started much earlier in time. This decreasing trend in the farm proprietors' share in total income is observed in national income accounts estimates for the United Kingdom from 1860, the year at which data are first available. With different time lags, similar patterns of behavior are observed in the United States and Canada.

In the classical twofold division of national income between labor and capital (property) incomes, given that the national income accounts present as a separate category the proprietors' income, we have to find an appropriate criterion to impute the latter between the two main categories of factor income, i.e., labor and property income.

Several authors such as Johnson [1954], Sultan [1954], Phelps Brown and Hart [1952], Phillips [1960], and Kravis [1959] proposed alternative hypotheses to account for the labor and property parts of the proprietors' income. Lebergott [1964] made a critical assessment of some of these hypotheses and of their corresponding labor and property estimates.

The main hypotheses entertained in the literature consider either an imputation criterion to distribute the proprietors' income between labor and property, or establish a procedure to directly estimate the labor and property shares in national income. We consider the following approaches:

(1) imputation criteria — asset basis, labor basis, proportionate basis, and economywide basis; and (2) wage-income or pay-parity ratio.

Imputation Criteria

Asset Basis. The *asset basis* approach to the proprietors' income division between labor and property imputes to property income the average rate of return of this productive resource in the corporate sector and the balance is imputed to labor. Following the asset basis approach applied by Johnson [1948], Kravis and Lebergott [1968] estimate the factor shares for the United States. To impute the property share, they distinguish the following types of assets: farm real property, farm nonreal property, and tangible assets of nonfarm unincorporated businesses. To each one of them, the estimated market rate of return for a similar type of property in the U.S. economy was applied. In the approach followed by these authors [p. 138], "...for farm real property, rents were estimated on the basis of rents on rented farm land; for farm nonreal property, the interest rates on farm mortgages were taken as the rate of return; and for [nonfarm] unincorporated businesses the rate of return was taken to be the same as that for manufacturing corporations." The return to proprietors' labor is the residual component of their net income.

Labor Basis. The *labor basis* approach reverses the procedure of the asset basis mode of imputation. Instead of estimating the property share of the proprietors' income, the labor share is estimated and the property share is obtained as a residual component.

To estimate the labor remuneration of the proprietors it is assumed that the annual labor income of a proprietor is equal to the annual earnings of a hired worker in the same industrial sector and with similar skills. The authors' rationale for this procedure is the observed wide interindustrial differences in annual earnings and labor qualifications. However, in their estimates, Kravis and Lebergott considered only two "industries," farm and nonfarm, and for each one of them the average labor income is estimated.

Proportionate Basis. The asset and labor bases of estimation have serious shortcomings, including their implicit assumptions to be discussed below, which are revealed by the observed quantitative differences obtained by the application of these alternative methods of imputation in the twofold division of national income, i.e., labor and property incomes. With the purpose of "overcoming" their limitations, an eclectic method of imputation was proposed. Kravis and Lebergott [1968, p. 138] labeled this the *proportionate basis.* In this approach, the labor component of the proprietors' income is estimated following the labor basis, and the property component is obtained applying the asset basis. Finally, the two imputations are adjusted proportionately so that their sum is equal to the actual proprietors' income. In their actual estimates, Kravis and Lebergott assume that the property returns of proprietors bear the same ratio to the sum of rent, interest, and corporate profits, as proprietors' assets bear to all other tangible assets. Thus if we have estimates of the proprietors' assets K_u and all other tangible assets K_c, and also the property return R_{cp} (rent, interest, and corporate profits) given by the national income accounts, then the property return R_{up} of proprietors is determined according to the proportionate basis, with R_{up} equal to the ratio $R_{cp}K_u/K_c$. *Mutatis mutandis*, a similar approach to estimate the labor return of proprietors would run into the unmanageable problem of estimating the human capital embodied in the proprietors and nonproprietorial members of the labor force unless we feel satisfied with their corresponding man-hour estimates.

Economywide Basis. The *economywide basis* approach makes the simple assumption that the proprietors' income in each year is distributed between labor and property income in the same proportion observed for these shares in the rest of the economy. This is an unwarranted homogeneity assumption across economic sectors. Its use results in limiting the analysis of factor shares to those sectors where these factor incomes can be estimated directly.

As an illustration of the four imputation criteria, table 9–1 presents their application to the U.S. national income for the period 1900–1963. The entries in table 9–1 are averages of percentage shares by decades as given by Haley [1968] and Kravis and Lebergott [1968]. The former estimates the property share applying the four imputation criteria (columns 2 to 5), and the latter apply only the first three criteria (columns 6 to 8). Column 1 presents the property share before the imputation of the estimated proprietors' property income, i.e., the sum of rent, interest, and corporate profits.

Table 9-1 reveals large discrepancies among estimates based on the alternative imputation criteria used by Haley and by Kravis and Lebergott. Large discrepancies are also observed between estimates by authors using the same imputation criterion. These discrepancies might be caused in the first place by the inaccuracy of the implicit economic assumptions supporting the imputation criteria, which will be discussed after we present the wage-income ratio criterion. The simplified statistical assumptions such as the disaggregation of the economy into two "industries," farm and nonfarm, are also a source of systematic estimation errors.

Wage-Income or Pay-Parity Ratio

The *pay-parity ratio* [Sultan, 1954; Phillips, 1960] or *wage-income ratio* [Phelps Brown and Browne, 1968] approach is not exactly a method of imputing the proprietors' income between labor and property. Rather, it is a useful framework to analyze the time path of total employee compensation and total property income, which include the estimated parts of the proprietors' labor and property incomes, respectively, and to assess the existence of distributional shifts between these two factor shares.

Let N_w be the number of wage and salary earners and N be the total number of individuals in employment, i.e., the sum of wage and salary earners N_w and nonwage and nonsalary earners N_c. Also let w or W/N_w be the employee compensation per unit of wage and salary earners, and y or Y/N the income per unit of employment. The wage-income or pay-parity ratio is by definition

$$w/y = (W/Y)(N/N_w).$$

The secular decreasing trend of N/N_w that results from the growing share in output and employment of the corporate sector would determine a decreasing value of the wage-income ratio if it is not offset by an increase in the employee compensation-national income ratio W/Y. On the other hand, if W/Y rises proportionately more than the decrease of N/N_w, a distributional shift from property to labor income has taken place. Equivalently, given a constant value of $y = Y/N$, the value of $w = W/N_w$ will increase if an increment in W is not matched by a proportional increase in the number of wage and salary earners N_w.

The pay-parity or wage-income ratio does not require a controversial *a priori* imputation assumption to distribute the proprietors' income between labor and property income. However, as Covick [1983, p. 393] observed, "...the adoption of the pay-parity ratio approach is equivalent

TABLE 9–1. Property share in the U.S. national income (averages of percentage shares for individual years in overlapping decades, 1900–1963)

| Period | Interest, rent, and corporate profits (1) | Total property share, various concepts | | | | | | |
| | | Haley [1968] | | | | Kravis & Lebergott [1968] | | |
		Asset basis (2)	Labor basis (3)	Proportionate basis (4)	Economywide basis (5)	Asset basis (6)	Labor basis (7)	Proportionate basis (8)
1900–09	21.4	36.8	23.0	30.6	28.0	30.6	32.2	32.1
1905–14	21.8	38.0	24.4	30.7	28.3	31.2	32.8	32.9
1910–19	22.6	38.0	30.6	31.9	29.8	32.6	35.8	34.8
1915–24	21.8	34.6	23.9	29.8	27.6	31.0	32.4	31.8
1920–29	22.0	32.3	21.9	28.4	28.6	29.2	28.5	28.8
1925–34	21.1	27.9	17.2	26.8	25.1	26.6	26.4	25.3
1930–39	18.1	23.9	12.7	23.4	21.3	22.9	19.8	21.4
1929–38	17.8	23.5	11.2	23.2	21.1	22.6	19.8	22.0
1934–43	18.4	24.3	17.0	24.2	22.0	23.6	23.5	22.9
1939–48	18.3	25.8	21.5	24.3	22.1	23.5	25.6	24.0
1944–53	18.1	24.7	21.5	23.8	21.6	23.1	24.7	23.6
1949–58	19.0	26.0	21.9	23.8	22.0	23.0	22.7	23.2
1954–63	18.3		19.9	22.4	20.7		20.6	21.8

Sources: Columns 1 to 5, Haley [1968, p. 24].
Columns 6 to 8, Kravis and Lebergott [1968, p. 134].

to the *implicit* adoption of a labor basis imputation of the income of employers and selfemployed into labor and property components." In fact, according to the labor basis approach, the proprietors receive a labor compensation equal to the average income of wage and salary earners, i.e., $w = W/N_w$. Therefore, total labor income (TLI) is

$$TLI = W + (N - N_w)W/N_w = WN/N_w.$$

Dividing this equation by Y we have

$$TLI/Y = (W/Y)(N/N_w) = w/y,$$

the wage-income ratio.

The different results obtained by application of the four methods of imputing the proprietors' income between the labor and property components, whereby table 9–1 is a case in point, recognize the existence of economic processes significantly different from those implied by the simplified assumptions supporting each method of imputation. The labor and asset bases approaches make the implicit assumption of a perfectly competitive economy, in which the wage and property rates of return are equalized in the labor and capital markets, respectively. Hence, they ignore the existence of labor unions, and monopolistic and oligopolistic market structures, and their corresponding impact on the functional distribution of income. They also ignore the impact of the business cycle. In periods of high unemployment, there is a larger percentage of workers self-employed earning less than the average of those employed in the corporate and public sectors.

A pure economic rationale stemming from a highly simplified assumption of a perfectly competitive economy has the unavoidable implication that the decision to be either a wage or salary earner or self-employed is an opportunity-cost decision problem. Expectations of rates of return for self-employment higher than the market rates of return on both the labor and capital productive factors will determine the decision to quit employment as a wage or salary earner and start as a self-employed entrepreneur. Hence, given the often misleading use of the symmetric property in mainstream economic thought, we might conclude that when the opportunity cost favors the wage or salary earners, the self-employed entrepreneurs would liquidate their businesses to become employees in the corporate and government sectors.

There are also socioeconomic forces influencing the choice between self-employment and being a wage or salary earner such as social status, independence, ownership control, provision of employment opportunities to family members, and the opportunity of making an advantageous use of tax stimuli and loopholes.

Haley [1968] made a critical assessment of both the asset and labor bases methods of imputation that deserves further investigation. He stated [p. 26] that "... entrepreneurial [proprietors'] income does not run at a high enough level to provide *both* a return to entrepreneurial labor equal to employed labor's average compensation and a return to entrepreneurial investment equal to the rate of return on other property." Thus neither of these bases for separating out an imputed property share from entrepreneurial income carries much conviction. *A fortiori* we should extend this conclusion to the other methods of imputation, and the results presented in table 9–1 corroborate this conclusion.

An appropriate basis for imputation would require a survey of the proprietors' sector, disaggregating it by type of activity and, for each one of them, making an evaluation of the labor and property input of the proprietors.

The Functional Distribution of Income in Canada, the United States, and the United Kingdom

The time-series data of the functional distribution of income in Canada, the United States, and the United Kingdom are now discussed. Each case study is analyzed according to its corresponding national accounts system that provides the total income estimates and its distribution by categories of incomes. For this reason, we analyze the distribution of national income in Canada and the United States, and that of the gross national product (GNP) in the United Kingdom. The United Kingdom national accounts also publishes the capital consumption estimates and the net national product at factor cost.

Canada

The historical statistics volume and the annual publication of the national income and expenditure accounts of Statistics Canada provide the annual data from 1926 of the national income at factor cost and the GNP distributed by category of income and expenditures.

For the quatriennium of 1926–1929 and quinquennial periods thereafter until 1984, table 9–2 presents the percentage shares of the following components of national income:

1. Employee compensation, which includes wages, salaries, supplementary labor income, and military pay and allowance (column 1);

2. Corporate profits before taxes (column 3);

TABLE 9–2. Factor shares in national income at factor cost: Canada 1926–1984 (percentage shares for periods shown)

Periods	Employee compensation (1)	Property income Total (2)	Property income Corporate profits (3)	Property income Interest (4)	Property income Inventory valuation adjustment (5)	Proprietors' income Total (6)	Proprietors' income Farm proprietors (7)	Proprietors' income Nonfarm (including rent) (8)	Net national income (9)
1926–29	55.0	15.0	12.1	2.6	0.3	30.0	11.6	18.4	100
1930–34	68.4	11.7	6.1	2.7	2.9	19.9	4.8	15.1	100
1935–39	63.0	15.3	13.8	2.2	−0.7	21.7	7.4	14.3	100
1940–44	62.6	16.1	15.2	2.3	−1.4	21.3	9.5	11.8	100
1945–49	62.3	14.7	15.3	2.0	−2.6	23.0	9.9	13.1	100
1950–54	62.8	17.5	15.6	2.8	−0.9	19.7	8.0	11.1	100
1955–59	66.5	17.7	14.5	3.7	−0.5	15.8	4.2	11.6	100
1960–64	68.3	17.9	13.9	4.3	−0.3	13.8	3.6	10.2	100
1965–69	70.5	18.0	14.0	4.7	−0.7	11.5	2.8	8.7	100
1970–74	71.7	18.4	14.6	5.8	−2.0	9.9	2.6	7.3	100
1975–79	72.9	20.0	14.4	8.1	−2.5	7.1	2.1	5.0	100
1980–84	70.7	22.1	12.5	11.2	−1.6	7.2	1.2	6.0	100

Sources: Statistiques Historiques du Canada, 2e édition, Statistics Canada, 1983.
National Income and Expenditure Accounts, Statistics Canada, Catalogue 13–201, Annual Publication.

3. Interest and miscellaneous investment income, which includes profits (net of losses) of government business enterprises, and interest and miscellaneous investment income of government (column 4);

4. Inventory valuation adjustment (column 5);

5. Farm proprietors' income (column 7); it is the accrued farm income estimate of farm operators from farm production;

6. Net income of nonfarm unincorporated business including net income of independent professional practitioners and imputed net rent of owner-occupied dwellings (column 8);

7. Property income as the addition of corporate profits, interest, and inventory valuation adjustment (column 2); and

8. Proprietors' income as the addition of the employers' and self-employees' income from farm and nonfarm unincorporated enterprises (column 6)

The imputation to the three main categories of income, i.e., employee compensation (column 1), property income (column 2), and proprietors' income (column 6), exhaust the national income at factor cost.

It follows from column 1 of table 9–2, that the employee compensation presents a systematic upward trend passing from 55% in the 1926–1929 period to over 70% in the last four periods.

The percentage jump in employee compensation during the great depression is substantial. During the period 1926–1929 this share was, on the average, 55% of national income, and it jumped to an average of 68.4% during the great depression period of 1930–1934. It peaked at 77.1% in the worst depression year of 1933 (column 2 in table 9–4), and fell to an average of 63% in the 1935–1939 period, remaining at about this level until the 1950–1954 period. A steady upward trend in this share is then observed for three consecutive quinquennia, i.e., until the 1965–1969 period, when the employee compensation share in national income reached an average value of 70.5%. It rose slightly in the following two periods, but then settled at an average value of 70.7% in the 1980–1984 period.

An annual analysis of the labor (employee compensation) share in national income would show a clear countercyclical behavior of this category of income, thus corroborating a similar phenomenon observed in other countries.

The share of corporate profits moves procyclically, and this value was sharply reduced in the great depression period of 1930–1934, when it averaged 6.1%. In all the other intervals its value fell within the range of 12% and 16%.

The interest share [column 4 in table 9–2] was relatively stable during

TABLE 9-3.   Canadian business cycles, 1951-1984

Recessions	Expansions
1951:2-1951:4	1952:1-1953:2
1953:2-1954:2	1954:3-1956:4
1957:1-1958:1	1958:2-1960:1
1960:2-1961:1	1961:2-1969:4
1970:1-1970:2	1970:3-1974:1
1974:2-1975:1	1975:2-1979:3
1979:4-1980:2	1980:3-1981:2
1981:3-1982:4	1983:1-

the first half of our period, but it then showed a systematic increase, with a strong acceleration in the last decade. These high values in the last few years reflect the very high interest rates resulting from high inflationary pressures, world economic uncertainty, international speculation and capital mobility, and the growing importance of the financial system in economic activity.

After World War II, the total property share (excluding the unincorporated sector) stabilized at about 18%, and after the "oil crisis," started a sustained increase, which can almost exclusively be attributed to the rapid increase of the interest share in national income.

As a percentage of national income, the income of the unincorporated sector declined very fast. The farm income (column 7) showed by far the fastest decrease. In the last quinquennium, it represented barely 10% of its value in the predepression period of 1926-1929, whereas the nonfarm unincorporated sector (column 8) declined to one-third of its predepression period value. This is consistent with the sustained upward trend of the corporate sector share in total output, employment, and income during the process of economic growth and modernization in contemporary economies. In the last two periods (1976-1984), the total share of the unincorporated (farm and nonfarm) sector fell to about 25% of its value in the predepression period.

The recession and expansion periods of the Canadian economy, for the 1951-1984 period as published by Statistics Canada (1985), are presented in table 9-3.

Table 9-4 presents data for factor shares in the years corresponding to the recession troughs and expansion peaks for the 1950-1984 period plus the troughs of the great depression, i.e., 1933. It adds further information

TABLE 9–4. Business cycle peaks and troughs, and factor shares: Canada 1950–1984

	Recession troughs				Expansion peaks		
Year (1)	Labor share (2)	Property share (3)	Proprietors' share (4)	Year (5)	Labor share (6)	Property share (7)	Proprietors' share (8)
1933[1]	77.1	4.6	18.3	1950[1]	62.9	15.2	21.9
1951	62.6	15.0	22.4	1952	62.0	17.3	20.7
1954	67.3	15.6	17.1	1956	66.3	16.8	16.9
1957	69.1	15.6	15.3	1959	68.9	15.9	15.2
1960	69.9	15.5	14.6	1969	72.6	16.4	11.0
1970	74.1	15.5	10.4	1973	71.7	18.1	10.2
1974	71.4	19.2	9.4	1979	72.6	20.8	6.6
1980	72.4	21.3	6.3	1981	74.8	18.9	6.3
1982	77.0	16.1	6.9	1984[2]	68.3	23.6	8.1

Sources: Current Economic Analysis, Statistics Canada, Vol. 5(1), 1985.
Statistiques Historiques du Canada, 2e édition, Statistics Canada, 1983.
National Income and Expenditure Accounts, Statistics Canada, Catalogue 13–201, Annual Publication.

1. Added by the present author.
2. It is an expansion but not a peak year.

to that provided by table 9–2 and confirms the countercyclical behavior of the labor share and the procyclical behavior of the property share. The procyclical behavior of the proprietors' share is obscured by its rapid decreasing trend.

The United States

For the United States there exists a rich source of factor shares estimates going back to 1870. Budd [1960] covers the period 1850–1910.

Studies on the functional distribution of income prior to the great depression of the 1930s rely on estimates by King, Martin, Gale Johnson, and Kuznets. Lebergott [1964] made a thorough review and assessment of these estimates.

The U.S. factor-shares data for the period 1870–1984 are examined here. The sources are the *Historical Statistics of the United States* published by the U.S. Bureau of the Census, and the *Survey of Current Business*, a monthly publication of the U.S. Department of Commerce (Office of Business Economics), which provides the official measurement of the flow of product, income, and expenditure in the U.S. economy. A comprehensive summary of these and other socioeconomic statistics are included in the annual publication of the *Economic Report of the President*.

Table 9–5 presents the percentage shares in national income by decades for the 1870–1949 period, and afterward by quinquennium. The national income is partitioned into the following three main categories of income: (1) employee compensation (labor), (2) proprietors' income (unincorporated farm and nonfarm enterprises), and (3) property income (interest, rent, and corporate profits).

During the final three decades of the last century, the labor share in national income was stable, at about 50% (column 1 in table 9–5). Since the first decade of the present century it started a sustained growth marked by countercyclical fluctuations. (The value for this share at the beginning of this century was almost the same as the corresponding value in Canada for the period 1926–1929.) A significant jump in its value took place during the great depression, that was only partly mitigated by the effects of the expansion of economic activity in the late 1930s and early 1940s. There was an increasing trend in the postwar period, with the value for the labor share reaching 74.3% in the 1980–1984 interval.

The property share (column 2) presents a mild decreasing trend from about 24% in the 1870–1890 period to about 18% in the decade of the

TABLE 9–5.   Labor, property, and proprietors' income at factor cost: United
States, 1870–1984 (percentage shares for periods shown)

| | U.S. factor shares | | |
| | Labor | Property | Proprietors |
Period	(1)	(2)	(3)
1870 and 1880	50.0	23.6	26.4
1880 " 1890	52.5	24.5	23.0
1890 " 1900	50.4	22.3	27.3
1900–09	55.0	21.4	23.6
1905–14	55.2	21.9	22.9
1910–19	53.2	22.6	24.2
1915–24	57.2	21.8	21.0
1920–29	60.5	21.9	17.6
1925–34	63.0	21.2	15.8
1930–39	66.7	17.0	16.3
1935–44	64.7	18.4	16.9
1940–49	65.4	17.1	17.5
1950–54	67.0	17.9	15.1
1955–59	68.6	18.2	13.2
1960–64	69.3	18.9	11.8
1965–69	70.3	19.2	10.5
1970–74	73.4	16.6	10.0
1975–79	72.9	17.6	9.5
1980–84	74.3	18.2	7.5

Sources: Historical Statistics of the United States, U.S. Bureau of the Census, 1960 (up to
    1925–1934).
    Survey of Current Business, Office of Business Economics, U.S. Department of
    Commerce, Monthly Publication (from 1930–1939). Figures computed by author.

1950s, a value that remained relatively stable during the remainder of the
period.

The proprietors' income share (column 3) declined systematically from
a peak estimate of 27.3% in the final decade of the last century to 7.5%
in the 1980–1984 period. This decline reflects the sharp drop in the farm
proprietors' share of income and output in total economic activity.

For the period 1900–1984, table 9–6 presents more detailed information on both property and proprietors' shares. The property share is

TABLE 9-6. U.S. property and proprietors' shares at factor cost, 1900–1984 (percentage shares for periods shown)

	Property share				Proprietors' share		
Period	Total (1)	Rent (2)	Corporate profits (3)	Net interest (4)	Total (5)	Farm (6)	Nonfarm (7)
1900–09	21.4	9.1	6.8	5.5	23.6	n.a.	n.a.
1905–14	21.9	9.1	6.9	5.8	22.9	n.a.	n.a.
1910–19	22.6	7.7	9.7	5.2	24.2	n.a.	n.a.
1915–24	21.8	7.6	8.9	5.3	21.0	n.a.	n.a.
1920–29	21.9	7.6	8.2	6.2	17.6	n.a.	n.a.
1925–34	21.2	6.6	6.4	8.1	15.8	n.a.	n.a.
1930–39	17.0	4.3	5.8	6.9	16.3	6.6	9.7
1935–44	18.4	3.2	11.9	3.3	16.9	6.8	10.1
1940–49	17.1	3.0	12.5	1.6	17.5	7.0	10.5
1950–54	17.9	3.4	13.1	1.4	15.1	4.9	10.2
1955–59	18.2	3.6	12.4	2.2	13.2	3.1	10.1
1960–64	18.9	3.5	12.3	3.1	11.8	2.4	9.4
1965–69	19.2	2.7	12.5	4.0	10.5	2.0	8.5
1970–74	16.6	1.7	9.5	5.4	10.0	2.2	7.8
1975–79	17.6	0.6	10.2	6.8	9.5	1.5	8.0
1980–84	18.2	0.4	7.8	10.0	7.5	1.0	6.5

Sources: *Historical Statistics of the United States*, U.S. Bureau of the Census, 1960 (up to 1925–1934), series F44–48.
Survey of Current Business, Office of Business Economics, U.S. Department of Commerce, Monthly Publication (from 1930–1939). Figures computed by author.

disaggregated in its three main categories of income, i.e., rent, corporate profits, and net interest, and from the 1930–1939 period, the proprietors' share is disaggregated in farm and nonfarm income.

The U.S. rent share (column 2 in table 9–6) shows a steady decline from an average of 9.1 in 1900–1909 to 0.4% in the 1980–1984 period. It presents a procyclical behavior. During the great depression (1930–1939) it fell to 4.3% from an average of 7.6% during the 1920–1929 period.

The share of corporate profits before taxes (column 3) presents strong procyclical fluctuations. It increased from an average of 6.8% in the first decade of this century to a peak of 13.1% during the Korean War. The subsequent decline was mild, with values about 12%, until the oil crisis in the 1970s, and the recession in 1981–1982, when high interest rates contributed to push down the average corporate share in 1980–1984 to 7.8%.

It can be observed that the net interest share (column 4) presents two long cycles during the 1900–1984 period. After a stable pattern of behavior during the first quarter of this century, it started a rapid increase for about 15 years, until the end of the fourth decade, when it observed a rapid decrease from a peak of 8.1% in the 1925–1934 period to 1.4% in the 1950–1954 period, the minimum interest share in the recorded history of the U.S. economy. Then it started a sustained increase, reaching the maximum of 10% in the 1980–1984 period, at a time of high real interest rates in very unstable and speculative international financial markets.

Although farm and nonfarm incomes of employers and self-employed are only published since 1929, the volume *Historical Statistics of the United States* [pp. 141–142] presents the gross private product of farm and nonfarm since the 1869–1878 period. It shows a clear decreasing trend of the farm–nonfarm gross private product ratio from 60% in the 1869–1878 period to less than 4% in the decade of the 1970s. A similar trend for the farm income share in national income since 1869–1878 can be inferred. In table 9–6, column 6 presents the farm share since the 1930–1939 period. With the exception of the World War II years (when the increase in agricultural prices overcompensated the decline in its output share and determined a mild income share increase), farm share in national income presented a sustained and rapid fall from about 7% in the 1930–1959 period to 1% in the 1980–1984 period.

The nonfarm proprietors' share (column 7) presented a stable behavior during the 1930–1949 period and afterward started a mild decreasing trend. It fell to 6.5% in the 1980–1984 period, a decline of 1.5 percentage points with respect to the previous period, which also reflects the impact of the severe 1981–1982 recession.

An analysis of the annual data for the net national product by category of income would confirm the countercyclical labor share and the procyclical property share behavior, particularly that of the corporate profits. Table 9–7 presents, quarterly dated, an identification of the U.S. recession and expansion periods from 1953 to the present, according to the National Bureau of Economic Research.

Table 9–8 presents data on shares for the years of the U.S. business cycles peaks and troughs for the 1953–1984 period to which we add share data for the 1983 great recession trough and the 1952 peak corresponding

TABLE 9–7.   U.S. bureau cycles, 1953–1984

Recessions	Expansions
1953:3–1954:2	1954:3–1957:3
1957:4–1958:2	1958:3–1960:2
1960:3–1961:1	1961:2–1969:4
1970:1–1970:4	1971:1–1973:4
1974:1–1975:1	1975:2–1980:1
1980:2–1980:3	1980:4–1981:3
1981:4–1982:4	1983:1–

TABLE 9–8.   U.S. business cycle peaks and troughs, and labor and corporate profits shares, 1952–1984

	Recessions troughs			Expansions peaks	
Year (1)	Labor share (2)	Corporate profits share (3)	Year (4)	Labor share (5)	Corporate profits share (6)
1933[1]	75.1	−3.8	1952[1]	67.3	12.9
1953	68.6	12.3	1957	69.2	12.9
1958	69.3	10.7	1959	68.7	12.6
1960	69.8	11.6	1969	72.5	11.0
1970	74.3	9.0	1973	72.4	10.1
1974	74.1	8.5	1979	72.8	9.8
1980	74.4	8.0	1981	73.9	7.7
1982	75.7	6.0	1984[2]	73.1	9.0

Source: Survey of Current Business, Office of Business Economics, U.S. Department of
       Commerce, Monthly Publication.

1. Added by the present author.
2. It is an expansion but not a peak year.

to the expansion prior to the 1953:3–1954:2 recession. The figures in columns 2 and 5 make clear the countercyclical behavior of the labor share, while the figures in columns 3 and 6 shows the procyclical behavior of corporate profits.

The United Kingdom

Table 9–9 presents the average percentages of the United Kingdom factor shares in gross national product for periods of 4, 5, or 10 years from 1860 to 1984. For the period 1860–1959 we reproduce the factor shares estimates given in Feinstein [1968, table 1, pp. 116–117]. From 1960–1964 to 1980–1984, the data in table 9–9 are calculated from information in the *National Income and Expenditure*, an annual publication of the U.K. Central Statistical Office.

The United Kingdom factor shares followed a pattern similar to that of the corresponding income categories in the United States and Canada, although the extent of the changes during the great depression and World Wars I and II were different. In the period 1860 to 1914, the labor share (column 1 in table 9–9) presented a very mild increasing trend, passing from an average value of 45.2% in the 1860–1869 period to 47.3% in the 1910–1914 period. There was a substantial increase over the next 10 years, reaching an average value of 58.5% in the 1921–1924 period. This level was maintained until World War II, with an increase to an average of 65.3% shown for the 1946–1949 period. Thereafter the labor share increased, slowly peaking to an average value of 68.8% in 1975–1979 and then falling to 66.6% in 1980–1984.

Among the components of gross property share, corporate trading profits (column 4) fluctuated between 12.5% and 18% without showing any pattern of either increasing or decreasing trend. Rent (column 5) shows a clear and sustained decreasing trend from an average of 14.8% in 1860–1869 to 3.9% in 1950–1954, mildly increasing afterward, reaching 6.9% in 1980–1984.

Both corporate trading profits and rent show procyclical behavior and are closely determined by the structural evolution and constraints of the British economy, whereas the third component of gross property income, i.e., net property income from abroad (column 6) encompasses the rise and fall of the United Kingdom as a world economic power. It increased from 3% in 1860–1869 to a peak of 8.4% before World War I, steadily declining afterward and reaching its minimum of only 0.6% in 1975–

TABLE 9–9. United Kingdom factor shares in gross national product at factor cost, 1860–1984 (percentage shares for period shown)

Period	Employee compensation (1)	Proprietors' income Farm (2)	Proprietors' income Nonfarm (3)	Gross property income Corporate trading profits (4)	Gross property income Rent (5)	Gross property income Net property income from abroad (6)	Gross property income Total (7)	Gross domestic Product (8)	Gross national Product (9)	Capital consumption (10)	Net national product (11)
1860–79	45.2	6.4	30.6		14.8	3.0	n.a.	97.0	100	5.9	94.1
1870–79	45.2	4.5	32.1		13.7	4.5	n.a.	95.5	100	5.7	94.3
1880–89	46.2	2.7	31.4		13.9	5.8	n.a.	94.2	100	5.3	94.7
1890–99	48.0	2.4	30.8		12.5	6.2	n.a.	93.8	100	4.7	95.3
1900–09	47.7	2.3	31.3		12.1	6.6	n.a.	93.4	100	5.2	94.8
1910–14	47.3	2.5	13.7	17.1	11.0	8.4	36.5	91.6	100	5.3	94.7
1921–24	58.5	2.1	15.1	13.0	6.8	4.5	24.3	95.5	100	7.3	92.7
1925–29	58.1	1.3	14.8	12.5	7.5	5.8	25.8	94.2	100	6.7	93.3
1930–34	59.3	1.6	13.4	12.5	9.0	4.2	25.7	95.8	100	7.0	93.0
1935–38	58.9	1.6	11.6	15.0	8.8	4.1	27.9	95.9	100	7.1	92.9
1946–49	65.3	2.9	9.4	16.8	4.0	1.7	22.5	98.3	100	8.8	91.2
1950–54	65.3	2.8	7.8	18.0	3.9	2.1	24.0	97.9	100	8.9	91.1
1955–59	67.0	2.3	6.9	18.0	4.5	1.3	23.8	98.7	100	9.0	91.0
1960–64	67.4		8.6	17.9	4.9	1.2	24.0	98.8	100	9.0	91.0
1965–69	67.3		9.3	16.7	5.5	1.1	23.3	98.9	100	9.9	90.1
1970–74	67.6		10.1	14.5	6.4	1.4	22.3	98.6	100	11.2	88.8
1975–79	68.8		9.3	14.7	6.6	0.6	21.9	99.4	100	13.2	86.8
1980–84	66.6		8.9	17.0	6.9	0.6	24.5	99.4	100	14.3	85.7

Sources: C.H. Feinstein [1968], up to 1955–1959.
U.K. National Income and Expenditure, Central Statistical Office, for the 1960–64 period, and U.K. National Accounts, Central

1984. In 1980 it recorded a negative value for the first time in the historical interval covered.

A Factor Share Model and Its Applications

Given that the factor shares are nonnegative and bounded within the unit interval, they can be meaningfully modeled by saturation curves. Among such curves we specify, for the i th factor of production, a four-parameter version of the logistic model [Dagum, 1972, 1973] which is defined for parameters a, b, c, and p by

$$\mu_i(y) = a + b(1 + py^{-c})^{-1}, \; y > 0$$

$$(a, c, p) > 0, \; b \text{ real,}$$

where y represents the labor productivity and $\mu_i(.)$ is the factor share.

The observed characteristics of regularity and permanence of the labor share in national income in actual economic processes point to a clear increasing trend of it as a function of the economic growth and technological structures of national economies. A proxy indicator that represents these economic forces is the man-hour or man-year productivity y. Hence, for the labor share $\mu_1(y)$ say, we have $b > 0$ and the derivative and asymptotic constraints

$$d\mu_1(y)/dy > 0, \; \lim_{y \to 0} \mu_1(y) = a, \; \lim_{y \to \infty} \mu_1(y) = a + b < 1.$$

Therefore, the range of the labor share is from a to $(a + b)$.

The same model has the power to fit and describe the other factor shares trends.

For factor shares with decreasing trends such as the proprietors' income share, we have $b < 0$ and $\mu(y)$ decreases from an upper limit a to an asymptotic lower and positive limit $(a + b)$.

For factor shares that might be represented by a constant trend, the parameter b is set at zero so $\mu(y)$ is a for all y.

The four-parameter logistic model thus has sufficient flexibility to fit factor shares having either increasing, decreasing, or constant trends.

This particular curve was fitted to time series data for the United States' labor share and also to the labor shares found in a cross-section of 30 countries. In both cases the nonlinear least-squares method of estimation was applied.

In particular, the logistic model was fitted to data for the United States' labor share during the period 1870–1984, where y represents the index (base 100 in 1967) of total private output per man-hour (Kendrick's estimates, NBER), giving the following result:

$$\mu_1(y) = 6.65 + 79.34 \ (1 + 6.54y^{-0.75})^{-1}, \ R^2 = 0.95.$$

Hence the estimated percentage range of the U.S. labor share is from 6.65 to 85.99.

The residual terms, i.e., the difference between the observed and fitted data, are predominantly positive during recession periods and negative during expansion periods, which agree with the labor share countercyclical behavior. Besides, the high value of R^2 adds further support to the power of the logistic model to describe this factor share trend.

The fitted model of the labor share of a sample of 30 countries[1] with data corresponding to the 1963–1970 period, where y represents the per capita GNP in constant 1969 prices in dollar equivalents (because of the lack of labor productivity data), is given by the following result:

$$\mu_1(y) = 6.69 + 81.29 \ (1 + 17.86y^{-0.44})^{-1}, \ R^2 = 0.89.$$

We can further fit this mathematical representation to each factor share and then test the hypothesis that the sum of the fitted data is equal to 1 (or 100 when working with percentage shares). Alternatively, we can fit all but one factor share and estimate the excluded one by substracting the sum of the fitted shares from one.

Conclusion

Although distinguished economists such as Keynes, Schumpeter, and Joan Robinson advanced the hypothesis of a constant labor share, empirical studies did not substantiate it either before or after distributing the proprietors' income between labor and property. Tables 9–1, 9–2, 9–5, 9–6, and 9–9 confirm this conclusion for the three cases studied.

Either before or after imputing the estimated proprietors' labor income to the labor factor of production, the labor share shows an increasing trend, the proprietors' share a decreasing one, and the property share presents a mild decreasing trend.

There are also cyclical changes in the labor and property shares. The former presents a countercyclical and the latter a procyclical behavior. This is mainly a consequence of the greater stability of many types of wage incomes in the face of cyclical fluctuations in output. An exhaustive explanation of this phenomenon would demand not only economic but also sociological and political analyses, i.e., a truly interdisciplinary approach. At the very foundation of this wider approach we would identify the dominant social philosophy in each country and the relative economic dependence in an international competitive environment as important elements in determining degree of countercyclical sensitiveness of the labor share.

The sharp historical decline of the proprietors' share relative to the corporate share in the total national output of Canada, the United States, and the United Kingdom is the result of the growing importance of the corporate sector of the economy due to the process of economic growth and technological change, and the growth of the public sector during the great depression and World War II.

In the twofold partition of national income, several types of explanations have been advanced to account for the increase in the labor share and the corresponding decrease in the property share. Following Kravis and Lebergott [1968, p. 139], they "...may be classified into three categories, according to the nature of the key variables selected: structural, factor-oriented, and aggregative."

The structural approach considers shifts in the relative importance of different industries in the process of economic growth, changes in the bargaining power of unionized labor and the monopolistic power of the employers, and the distribution and concentration of firm sizes. This is a sound research approach but is still in a preliminary state of development. It offers good potential for a cogent explanation of the determinants and variations of the relative shares of labor and property incomes.

The factor-oriented and the aggregative explanations are supported by conventional economic analyses and cannot offer a sound basis to account for the factor shares dynamics. The factor-oriented explanation uses the property-wage income ratio, the value of capital (price times quantity) divided by the payment to labor. The latter is shown as a product of a wage rate and man-hours or man-years of employment. In modern economic systems, measures of man-hours or man-years cannot serve as an appropriate base to analyze the distribution of income between labor and property, because they often ignore the human capital elements of labor. Lacking accurate measurement of human and physical capital, time series estimates of capital-labor relative prices as, for example, in Kravis [1959, table 10], make no sense at all.

The lack of correspondence between the theoretical and the empirical factor incomes categories makes it difficult to assess the validity of alternative theories of income distribution. This difficulty is compounded for those theories built upon an explicit relationship between social classes and ownership of productive factors such as the Marxian, because in contemporary economic systems there is a spectrum rather than a dichotomic polarization of social classes. Besides, very often economic units draw income from more than one factor of production. The trend and cyclical behavior of the three cases studied are representative of the observed time path in many national economies. They have to be explained by any theory that purports to account for the dynamics of both factor prices and factor shares.

Note

1. The 30 countries in the sample ordered by increasing values of per capita GNP at constant prices (dollar equivalents) are: Malawi, Korea, Paraguay, Colombia, Malaysia, Peru, Costa Rica, Chile, Uruguay, Spain, Venezuela, Ireland, Italy, Japan, Israel, Austria, New Zealand, Finland, Netherland, Belgium, Australia, Norway, France, Luxembourg, Germany (F.R.), Denmark, Switzerland, Canada, Sweden, and the United States.

References

Banco de Mexico. (1969). *Cuentas Nacionales y Acervos de Capital, 1950–1967.* Document of the Department of Economic Research, Banco de Mexico.

Budd, E.C. (1960). Factor shares, 1850–1910. *Studies in Income and Wealth.* Princeton: Princeton University Press, 365–406.

Covick, O. (1983). Relative wage shares in Australia. In K. Hancock, Y. Sano, B. Chapman, and P. Fayle, (eds.), *Japanese and Australian Labor Markets: A Comparative Study.* Canberra: Australian-Japan Research Centre, pp. 372–417.

Dagum, C. (1972). A stochastic model of the functional distribution of income. *International Economics and Development, Volume in Honor of Raul Prebisch.* L. di Marco (ed.). New York: Academic Press, pp. 245–265.

————. (1973). Un modèle non linéaire de répartition fonctionnelle du revenu. *Economie Appliquée* 26: 843–876.

Feinstein, C.H. (1968). Changes in the distribution of the national income in the United Kingdom since 1860. In J. Marchal and B. Ducros, (eds.), *The Distribution of National Income.* London: Macmillan, pp. 115–139.

Haley, B.F. (1968). Changes in the distribution of income in the United States. In J. Marchal and B. Ducros (eds.), *The Distribution of National Income.* London: Macmillan, pp. 3–29.

Johnson, D.G. (1948). Allocation of agricultural income. *Journal of Farm Economics* 30: 724–729.

————. (1954). The functional distribution of income in the United States, 1850–1952. *Review of Economics and Statistics* 36: 175–182.

Kravis, I.B. (1959). Relative income shares in fact and theory. *American Economic Review* 49 (5): 917–949.

Kravis, I.B., and S. Lebergott. (1968). Income distribution. *International Encyclopedia of the Social Sciences*. Vol. 7. London: Macmillan, pp. 132–154.

Lebergott, S. (1964). Factor shares in the long term: some theoretical and statistical aspects. *Studies in Income and Wealth*. Princeton: Princeton University Press, pp. 53–86.

Marchal, J., and B. Ducros (eds.). (1968). *The Distribution of National Income*. London: Macmillan.

Pareto, V. (1895). La legge della domanda. *Giornale degli Economisti*. Gennaio, pp. 59–68.

————. (1897). *Cours d'économie politique*. New edition by G.H. Bousquet and G. Busino (1964). Genève: Librairie Droz.

Phelps Brown, E.H., and Browne, M. (1968). *A Century of Pay*. London: Macmillan.

Phelps Brown, E.H., and Hart, P.E. (1952). The share of wages in national income. *Economic Journal* 62: 253–277.

Phillips, J.D. (1960). Labor's share and wage-parity. *Review of Economics and Statistics* 42(2): 164–174.

Ricardo, D. (1817). *Principles of Political Economy*, New edition by Piero Sraffa: *Works and Correspondence of David Ricardo*. Cambridge: Cambridge University Press (1951).

Statistics Canada. (1985). *Current Economic Analysis*, 5(1), Catalogue 13–004E.

Sultan, P.E. (1954). Unionism and wage-income ratios, 1929–1951. *Review of Economics and Statistics* 36(1): 67–73.

10 ECONOMIC DEVELOPMENT AND INCOME DISTRIBUTION

Robin Rowley

The Presidential Address of Kuznets [1955] to the American Economic Association in 1954 initiated a stream of research on the secular evolution of income distribution with particular interest aroused by a simple empirical law or hypothesis. Although economists have a long-standing tradition of searching for regularities in the functional distribution of income and in life-cycle features of poverty incidence, Kuznets shifted attention to long-run features of the size distribution of income across stable economic units rather than functional groups. In a series of papers, for example [1955, 1963, 1973], he developed awareness of a simple U-shaped pattern in some data for size distribution and sought to clarify both the determining processes underlying this pattern and the data deficiencies that constrain attempts to clarify such processes.

As other economists took up Kuznets' themes, the existence of a U-shaped pattern persisted as a primary focus of attention, but it was surrounded by an increasing number of other concerns. Not least among these additions were:

1. The explication of growth processes (affecting migration, major structural transformations, the world allocation of economic activities, social relations of production, ownership, social classes and colonialization, and the stability of governments;

2. The generalizability of past growth experiences of today's richer countries to potential growth in other countries;

3. The choice of suitable indices of size distribution, their manipulation into meaningful components, and means of separating secular trends from cyclical phenomena;

4. The applicability of both structural and exploratory statistical models to data for developing countries; and

5. The political consequences of changes in inequality.

The treatment of such concerns within the context of the U-hypothesis draws on a host of other theoretical developments such as surplus-labor models due to Lewis, Fei, and Ranis, dual-economy models, and migration models due to Harris and Todaro. [See, for example, Robinson, 1976]. Comprehensive surveys of technical issues affecting measures of distribution are provided by Cowell [1977], Kakwani [1980], and Sen [1973], while summaries of potential processes in development and of empirical evidence for many countries are available in Bigsten [1983], Fields [1980], Lecaillon and associates [1984], and Adelman and Morris [1973].

In the sections that follow, a modest attempt is made to describe some of Kuznets' treatment of the potential relationship between size distribution and development, to indicate five basic methods that have been used to explore this relationship, and to take up three interesting aspects of this field of research. The chapter closes with a final comment appraising past efforts.

Kuznets' Pattern of Development

With "perhaps 5 per cent empirical information and 95 per cent speculation, some of it possibly tainted by wishful thinking," Kuznets [1955, p. 26] conjectured a widening of inequality in secular income during the early phases of economic growth when the transition from the preindustrial to the industrial civilization was most rapid, stabilization of inequality for a while, and then some later narrowing. This long swing of inequality in secular income became, in subsequent reexpressions, the U-hypothesis, and was variously described as a law, a stylized fact, and a stable empirical association. With most qualifications dropped, the U-hypothesis is the assertion that, during development, the distribution (generally of recorded income) will initially become more unequal and only later will become more equal.

The definition of secular income and the choice of units over which distribution is to be determined are difficult elements in this long swing. Kuznets gave five rules for specification, all of which contain seeds for controversy. First, recipient units should be based on family-expenditure units with appropriate scaling for size to enhance their comparability, rather than on income. Kuznets opted for data expressed in per-capita terms, but his specification permits use of equivalent scales based on average consumption patterns in relation to age and other characteristics of the recipient units. The choice of unit is clearly crucial if comparisons are to be made across countries with varying habitational arrangements due to extended families and attitudes to kinship.

The second rule for specification is that distribution should be determined over all units in a country rather than over a subpopulation of the units determined by level of income. This completeness requirement seems to preclude focus on poverty alone. The next rule advocates segregation of units "to avoid complicating the picture by including incomes not associated with full-time, full-fledged participation" by main income earners in economic activity. Thus omissions are considered appropriate for such earners in "learning" or retired stages of individual life cycles. (In many respects, such omissions foreshadow later attempts to redefine indices of unemployment and prices omitting exogenously caused inflation components or adjusting for structural changes in the labor force.)

The fourth rule indicates that income should be defined as that received by individuals and would include income in kind but exclude capital gains. In practice, outside developed countries, researchers have enjoyed little flexibility in the choice of definition for income. Data are generally so limited that researchers take what they can obtain! The final rule requires recipient units to be grouped according to secular income, free from cyclical and other transient disturbances. To achieve this, one would need to average income over a long period within each stable recipient unit. Since longitudinal data at the individual level are rarely available even in advanced countries such as the United States, Britain, and Canada, this requirement is never met. Some governments occasionally reveal summary indices for income distribution using income over longer than annual intervals, but these are difficult to identify with secular influences alone. This is considered briefly in a later section when the problem of "income mobility" is discussed.

Kuznets himself advocates reliance on averages over "say a generation of about 25 years" with separation between resident and migrant units of recipient groups. (These groups are defined according to persistence and nonpersistence within ordinal rankings of income throughout the averaging period. They will also be reconsidered in the later section.) He indicates a strong position [1955, p. 2] which is seldom made clear in discussions of the U-hypothesis: "Without such a long period of reference and the resulting separation between 'resident' and 'migrant' units at different relative income levels, the very distinction between 'low' and 'high' income classes loses its meaning, particularly in a study of long-term changes in shares and in inequalities in the distribution."

Given such strictures, it is surprising that the long-swing conjecture would generate much interest. To explain this, we must note determining forces identified by Kuznets and, also, his practical suggestions which permitted use of available statistics despite their inadequacies relative to the five rules of specification. We should note, too, the political dimension for the U-hypothesis demands attention either to be refuted or to be a comforting influence if perceived inequality increases at some stage in the process of development. In the latter situation, concern obviously shifts to methods of accelerating movement along the U-curve.

Forces acting to increase the inequality of the size distribution include: (1) the concentration of savings in the hands of higher income units; (2) the pronounced structural adjustment away from agriculture and involving both industrialization and urbanization; (3) changes in the scale of productive units; (4) shifts from personal enterprise to impersonal organization of economic firms; (5) changes in the occupational status of some labor and the "specialization" of some work; and (6) governmental subsidies to industry.

Clearly this list is incomplete. It contains enough significant entries to generate interest in elaborating the impact of the interacting forces and, also, enough gaps to stimulate expansion of the list. (Bigsten [1983], Fields [1980], and Lecaillon and associates [1984] provide further detail on such additions.) Countervailing influences can also be identified for, in the U-hypothesis, the predominance of these factors disappears. Concentration of savings, for example, can be affected by legislative actions, inflation, legal restrictions on yields for property income, constraints on interest rates protecting the market for government bonds, and outright confiscation. Further, it is also easy to envision shifts within the developing industrial structure (due to technological changes, the end of decline for agriculture, and modified labor conditions) that would enhance the functional share of labor in total product and reorder income distribution. A subsequent lowering of income inequality requires the countervailing influences to overcome the initial forces or for the impact of these forces to be modified in the process of development.

Kuznets' starting point was the economic growth experienced in "advanced" or older developed countries, for which better data were available three decades ago. His long-swing conjecture is historical, qualitative, and limited. The subsequent reexpression as the U-hypothesis, with widespread applicability to both advanced and developing countries, is not a straightforward adjustment. By 1973, the limited spread of economic growth to developing countries and further reflection on the economic plight of such countries reinforced awareness of the *historical* nature of development and the pressure of international influences on income distribution, inadequately recognized in Kuznets [1955, 1963]. Kuznets [1973, p. 255] recognized the "growth position of the less developed countries today is significantly different in many respects, from that of the presently developed countries on the eve of their entry into modern economic growth." In particular, developing countries are more backward, followers rather than leaders, prone to higher rates of natural increase, and have access to a limited stock of technological innovations.

Even if the historical nature of development were less relevant, the *qualitative* nature of the long-swing ought not to be ignored. All countries may experience a U-shaped pattern of development without their sharing a common quantitative pattern. The presumption of a common path for development to be followed by all countries, apart from minor displacements, is a major restriction that is unnecessary outside cross-sectional regression models. (This is taken up in the section below.) Finally, because the long swing is defined in terms of aggregate indices or income quantiles and because active forces determining development are typically represented by aggregate data or broad categorizations, the predictive value of the U-hypothesis is *limited*. It serves as a coordinating principle for research on income distribution in the process of development rather than as a quantitative hypothesis.

Five Methods of Investigation

The U-hypothesis and the mechanisms associated with it have been explored in a variety of different ways. To illustrate some of these, five methods of investigation are briefly described below. All involve mathematical representations but are otherwise distinctive. Taken together, they provide a clear picture of current practices by economists who use the U-hypothesis and related notions to explore development or to guide the directions in which the mathematical and statistical tools for exploration are being amended.

Stylized Facts

Income distribution can be characterized by graphs (such as the Lorenz curve), indices of concentration or inequality (such as the Gini coefficient and other choices described in Cowell [1977], Kakwani [1980], and Sen [1973], probability-type density functions with few parameters, and quantile tabulations. Changes in income distribution in relation to economic development must be associated with comparisons across such characterizations and linked to specific indicators of the state of development, such as per-capita national product. The associational relationships found in this context are often termed "stylized facts" since they have no clear connection with causality. Evidence of this type is summarized in Bigsten [1983], Fields [1980], and Lecaillon and associates [1984], while other surveys, often concentrating on evidence from cross-sectional analyses, are available from Adelman and Morris [1973], Braulke [1983], Chenery [1960], Chenery and Taylor [1968], Chenery and Syrquin [1975], Cline [1972, 1975], Cromwell [1977], Oshima [1962, 1970], and Paukert [1973]. In order to illustrate a typical approach, the contribution of Ahluwalia [1976] is an appropriate choice. It reveals how data for a diverse collection of countries are combined in a regression model, which is linear in its parameters. The framework permits the least-squares principle to be invoked and estimates obtained for these parameters. It also encourages the use of terms such as *testing* and *statistical significance*.

The dependent variables for the regression model are income shares for particular quantiles. (In other studies, the Gini coefficient or an alternative index of inequality is used instead.) Explanatory variables include per capita GNP and its squared values to represent the secular trend for the U-hypothesis. Short-term influences are identified with the inclusion of the rate of growth of GNP over some interval. Factors associated with the various elements in growth processes are then linked to explanatory variables based on available measures of literacy rates, school enrollment, rates of population increase, the share of agriculture in GNP, and a host of similar summary statistics. In this respect, Ahluwalia is influenced by Adelman and Morris [1973] and Chenery and Syrquin [1975], with empirical fits being interpreted as "at best descriptions of 'average' cross-country behavior; leaving ample room for inter-country differences." Clearly analyses of this type are far removed from the format used by Kuznets.

Inferences in this approach are based on comparisons of estimated parameters for different quantile groups and on apparent statistical significance. This reveals the principal weakness of the model, for the inferences are only as good as the estimates on which they are based. There are evident deficiencies whether the model is considered structural or exploratory. It is difficult to believe that the parameters of such equations are stable across countries while the structural perspective is further weakened by the failure to provide a clear statement of properties assumed for explanatory variables and equation errors. The latter cannot be normally distributed and are probably neither free from autocorrelation nor homoscedastic. This invalidates reliance on apparent statistical significance for calculated standard errors of estimates and t-statistics are based on incorrect formulae. Nor are these calculations valid from an exploratory perspective, for they are then affected by pretest biases. Overall, the picture is a dismal one and cannot be resolved by moving to more sophisticated methods of estimation (such as the SUR procedure of Theil and Zellner). Stylized facts are, therefore, curious statistical artifacts.

Components of Change

The problem of imposing a common statistical framework with strong probability restrictions on data for different countries does not arise in the second method of investigation to which we now turn. Instead attention is focused on measures of inequality for individual countries. Sen [1973, pp. 24–46] provides a list of such measures, while Fields [1980, pp. 98–124] indicates how they can be associated with decomposition procedures, the essential feature of the second method. Any given index G is arranged as the sum of components $(G_1, G_2, \ldots, G_n)$ with weights $(w_1, w_2, \ldots, w_n)$ and a residual R:

$$G = w_1 G_1 + w_2 G_2 + \cdots + w_n G_n + R.$$

If the components are meaningful, a formula of this type can be used to explore determinants of inequality, including those identified with the processes affecting the U-hypothesis. Appropriate references for the mathematics of decomposition and the application of decomposition formulae to development issues are provided by the following: Bourguignon [1979]; Fei, Ranis, and Kuo [1978]; Fields [1979a, 1979b]; Fields and Fei [1978]; Pyatt [1976]; Pyatt, Chen, and Fei [1980]; Rao [1969]; Shorrocks [1982, 1983]; and Theil [1979]. These are foreshadowed by Kuznets' treatment [1955, p. 7] of a simple model with two components distinguishing urban populations from rural ones. In nonformal discussion, he reveals how the intersectoral differences in per-capita income, intrasectoral distributions, and sector weights might affect inequality as urbanization occurs.

Four classification schemes dominate actual choices of components in decomposition formulae. These are (1) spatial, as when the "convergence" of regional income is being explored; (2) by economic sector for urban-rural comparisons; (3) by type of income with separate components for earnings, investment income, revenue from land holdings and transfers, for example; and (4) by the significant socioeconomic characteristics of recipient units such as the size of these units, the age and sex of their designated head, levels of educational achievement, and the numbers of earners and dependent children. Each classification determines the number of components with G_i representing a measure of inequality within a category. Provided the residual R is small and the components are sufficiently distinct, the formula involving components can be used to express how factors underlying them might contribute to overall inequality. Further, to the extent that some components are relatively large or small, the formula permits derivation of qualitative inferences associated with structural transformations, for example, the shift from rural to urban location or the growth in the number of dependent children.

A list of desirable decomposition properties is provided by Fields [1979a, 1980]. He indicates that the output from decomposition procedures should permit: (1) decomposition of overall inequality into intrafactor and interfactor components; (2) measurement of the gross and marginal contributions of each factor to total inequality; (3) testing of the statistical significance of main, marginal, and interaction effects of factors; and (4) estimation of income-level impacts. Clearly ease of interpretation should be added to the list. Fields [1979a, p. 448] argues that the analysis of variance decomposition is preferable to Atkinson, Gini, and Theil alternatives by reference to these and other properties. "All in all, analysis of variance procedures based on the logarithms of income have the most desirable properties with no offsetting limitations. The use of ANOVA procedures in future research on the determinants of LDC inequality appears warranted." This view is not generally accepted. Most researchers seem to prefer to continue using particular indices of inequality with which they have experience. Instead of moving toward the use of ANOVA decompositions, many prefer to modify other indices with standardizations (rather like using base-weighted indices in other areas), the reordering of recipient units in the calculation of the components (for example, deriving a quasi-Gini measure for the distribution of earners after the recipient units have been arranged in order of increasing total income), and other adjustments. My appraisal of these efforts is that they have, in skillful hands, enhanced our ability to describe the processes linking income inequality and economic development, but the final choice among alternative decompositions and indices must await further experience. Indeed we may eventually conclude that a final choice is unnecessary. Using more than one decomposition procedure may remind us of their potential flaws and may yield evidence on the robustness of inferences derived from them.

The Kuznets Process

As Kuznets made clear, the U-shape of income distribution during economic development is not implied either by specific patterns discerned in data or by theoretical manipulations. It is, in essence, speculative. Although consideration of the impact of potential mechanisms in the process of change encourages us to think in terms of phases which reveal widening or narrowing of income inequality, there is nothing inevitable in the shape of overall outcomes. The regression method involved in the derivation of stylized facts and the decomposition of aggregate measures into components are always based on the use of summary statistics, simplified expressions of basic mechanisms, and a host of instrumental assumptions. Thus inferences drawn from the pursuit of these two methods may be sensitive to the choice of index, estimation technique, adjustment of data, criterion for decomposition, abstractions for mechanisms, and other elements. Robinson [1976] provides an excellent example of the ease with which a researcher can move from simple manipulation of a single index of inequality and a few empirical observations to wider generalizations including the U-hypothesis. The danger is one of arguing from a specific model to a general statement without adequate qualification. Similar complaints can be lodged against interpretation of cross-sectional stylized facts, as by Ahluwalia [1976], for this stresses quantile data or aggregate indices of inequality rather than the complete picture of inequality.

Anand and Kanbur [1984, 1985] take up some of the issues indicated by appraisals of empirical and mathematical studies using quantiles and aggregate indices. By focusing only on population shifts, they explore (1) under what conditions the U-hypothesis for alternative indices emerges as a necessary implication of such shifts; (2) the feasibility of working with cumulative distribution functions for income rather than a single index; (3) relative degrees of confidence in the occurrence of the phases of widening and narrowing inequality; and (4) different turning points and functional forms associated with the U-hypothesis by alternative choices of indices. Clearly this effort is limited since it ignores significant influences outside the shift of population to modern (urban, industrial, advanced) activities from traditional (rural, agricultural, backward) ones. They term this shift "the Kuznets process."

Kuznets' treatment of population movements contains a numerical example which assumes that, during the course of development, population moves from a low-mean, low-inequality sector to a high-mean, high-inequality sector with both sectoral means and levels of inequality remaining fixed despite the migration. Clearly this latter restriction needs to be relaxed. Anand and Kanbur [1984] reveal how alternative assumptions regarding the intertemporal movement of, for example, the ratio of sectoral means, will affect the functional form and turning point for the U-hypothesis with the Theil index of inequality. Among other important findings, they assert (1) if two sectoral distributions do not satisfy a dominance relation, we cannot make general statements about the behavior of income distribution during economic development; (2) for all commonly used measures of inequality, there is an ambiguity in the behavior of inequality at the end of the development process (which is consistent with comments in Adelman and Morris [1973] and Ahluwalia [1976]); (3) each index has its own turning-point condition and its own functional form; and (4) models of migration must deal with problems of heterogeneity and selectivity among subpopulations and, especially, migrants for such individual features may have major impact on overall inequality.

This method of using cumulative distributions and multiple comparisons across instrumental assumptions and across alternative indices seems very promising especially if it can be developed further to include graphical and other empirical guides. Its novelty precludes fuller appraisal.

Historical Perspective

In contrast to the narrow focus of the formal methods indicated in the previous two sections, there are opportunities in some developed countries (the United States and Britain) to explore wider perspectives due to the availability of collated sets of longitudinal data with adequate content. Since the original statement of the long swing in income distribution was, as indicated above, historical and qualitative in form, there is clearly scope for exploring the evolution of U.S. and British economies with the U-hypothesis acting as a coordinating principle. Kuznets [1977] and Williamson [1977, 1985] provide suitable illustrations of descriptive and analytical uses of these historical data. The cliometric method permits a wide variety of techniques, formal and nonformal, to be brought to bear. Their principal characteristic is one of historical specificity which limits their generalizability to past developments rather than to the plight of currently poor developing countries but which need not diminish their value in other respects. For example, Kuznets' discussion [1977] of the "making-up" character of economic growth with the important distinction between late starters and early starters; Williamson's consideration [1977] of volatile periods of changing income distribution, relative prices and output mix; and Williamson's framework [1985] for assessing whether British capitalism bred inequality are all major contributions to our understanding of economic development, past and present. The historical perspective can often help us begin to assess large issues that are quite outside the realm of stylized facts, component analysis, and the limited range of comparisons made by Anand and Kanbur.

These large issues involve major demographic trends (sectoral mobility, waves of immigration, and secular decline in the rate of natural increase for richer countries), wars, technological innovations, and competitive expansion toward colonization as stressed by Kuznets. To this list, Williamson [1977] adds certain elements of price behavior which have generally been associated with cyclical movements rather than with secular ones. By considering U.S. historical experience, he raises a series of interdependent questions identified with instability, disequilibria and heterogeneous price shifts; namely, (1) although nominal and real inequality indicators almost always move together, why is the differential impact of prices by class never as large as the nominal inequality movements; (2) why do periods of "stretching" in the pay structure and increasing nominal inequality in the size distribution always contain relative price changes which inflate the cost of living for the poor faster than for the rich; and (3) why does the opposite almost always occur for periods of leveling in the nominal size distribution?

The study by Williamson [1985] is the most ambitious of our three illustrations of the historical perspective. This seeks to describe British experience during a period of about 150 years ending with the outbreak of World War I. The Kuznets U-hypothesis and familiar assertions of historical stability in earnings by Bowley, Soltow, and others provides a suitable framework for discussion. In an earlier exploration of U.S. inequality, Williamson and Lindert [1980] found a "convincing explanation" of an apparent Kuznets curve but acknowledged the generalizability problem since "a sample of one did not necessarily make a successful theory." The Bowley-Soltow [1937, 1968] assertions of stability point to long-run developments unaffected by a considerable churning of levels of individual income (as is often found in post-fisc distributions for developed countries following cyclical changes and tax modifications) but are adversely affected by deficiencies in data. With respect to revised evidence, Williamson [1985] finds a Kuznets curve traced out for Britain over the century and a half after 1760. His evidence suggests (1) a modest leveling in incomes across the late nineteenth century with a universal egalitarian drift (the income share at the top fell, the share at the bottom rose, the relative pay of the unskilled improved, pauperism fell, and the earnings distribution narrowed); (2) a rise in inequality across the century following 1760 (with universal features, too) apart from an interruption during the French Wars; and (3) the possibility that the evolution of the distribution of earnings is not matched by that of the distribution of income.

Such findings are scarcely dramatic without more appreciation of the determining influences. The most satisfying aspect of Williamson's effort is found in his search for these determinants. He argues continuing with the above, (4) the leveling phase in the apparent U-curve is certainly not due to intraoccupational influences but rather to "the steady contraction of the wage structure, pay ratio convergence, and the decline in skill premia"; (5) at other times, the growth of inequality is driven by relative scarcity of skills and by variations in the premia that these skills command through time; (6) Kuznets' employment-mix effect (associated with the shift to occupations requiring higher skills) is confirmed as a major force adversely affecting the inequality of earnings; and (7) the phase of increasing inequality also reveals a rise in real wages. (This last finding contrasts with arguments raised in Adelman and Morris [1973] and Ahluwalia [1976], which consider the joint occurrence of more inequality and an absolute decline in mean incomes.) The primary novelty of the findings stems from their stress on elements of wage determination, the consequences of an industrialization bias, disequilibrating factor demand, and the accumulation of skills. Other elements arise in the explication of Williamson's model and exert a considerable stimulus for other researchers to follow his example and extend the cliometric method.

Voltaire provided the aphorism that history is a fable agreed upon. The historical perspective of Kuznets [1977] and Williamson [1977, 1985] is certainly not "agreed upon." As with the Anand and Kanbur approach to the Kuznets process, confidence in empirical findings may increase only with more familiarity. The promise of the cliometric method is still to be confirmed and will always be inhibited by shortages of appropriate data, the common reluctance to integrate formal models (mathematical and econometric) with more traditional approaches to history, and by difficulties in justifying essential abstractions from the rich complexity of real historical developments. However, even a partial failure of the method may yield valuable insight on the mechanisms underlying the U-curve or alternative regularities in distribution during economic development.

Computer Models

Many expressions of the U-hypothesis are deceptively simple. The relationship between income distribution and economic development depends critically on structural change within developing countries, and the significance of Kuznets' commentaries [1955, 1963] stems from his stress of such change. A particular political dimension is involved since the first phase of the Kuznets curve could be associated with a conflict between the growth of overall national income and an increase in the wealth of the poor. It is also affected by suggestions that policy actions to stimulate overall growth and those serving to reduce inequality are possibly incompatible. Empirical evidence (for example, Adelman and Morris [1973], Ahluwalia [1976], and Williamson [1985]) is mixed as to whether this initial phase is characterized by absolute decline in mean income for the poorer groups. Given this background, attention can be shifted from the simple U-hypothesis to the mechanisms underlying it. As Adelman and Morris [1973, p. 186] argue, "...economic structure, not level or rate of economic growth, is the basic determinant of patterns of income distribution," so exploration of structure is essential. Clearly, structural characteristics will differ across countries and across time so dependence on estimated parameters for aggregate equations is unwarranted. There is an evident need to move beyond these aggregate equations despite data deficiencies and other complications at microeconomic levels. This stimulates interest in computer-based models that are flexible and can use both real and hypothetical data.

Bigsten [1983, ch. 6] illustrates the application of computer models to development in the Philippines (Bachue), South Korea (Adelman and Robinson), and Brazil (Taylor and associates). Other accounts are given in Adelman [1975], Kelley and Williamson [1973, 1984], and Taylor and associates [1980]. These models can be recursive, or involve "dynamic" general equilibrium. They can be economywide [Taylor and associates, 1980] or can focus on particular processes such as industrialization and urbanization [Kelley and Williamson, 1984]. Their primary interest is in the explication of *interactions* among structural components, with experimental manipulation on eclectic grounds. Adelman [1975, p. 303], for example, suggests that the Adelman-Robinson model for South Korea "is capable of portraying a large variety of economic and institutional rules of the game" and permits variation in the degree of monopoly, the operating principles for credit markets, the clearing principles for labor and commodity markets, and the permissible degrees of disequilibria in individual markets. "The model combines Keynesian and Walrasian analysis (it can operate in either mode, depending on the labor market specification). It portrays a monetary economy (combining Schumpeter-Wicksell with Walras) open to foreign trade. It can be run in an equilibrium or in a disequilibrium mode."

Lysy and Taylor in [Taylor and associates, 1980] illustrate the simulative aspect of computer models for development and reveal the use of sensitivity experimentation and of multiple working hypotheses to clarify the impact of evolving structural change. The richness of sectoral detail that can be integrated in the model is clear from conclusions derived by them from their simulative experiments. These include suggestions that (1) reduced labor substitutability reduces aggregate supply, leading to inflation and to real income losses for proprietors, thus reducing inequality; (2) structural rigidities in the economy are unequalizing; (3) less flexible supply in labor-surplus sectors reduces real output and makes income distribution worse; (4) changes in the pattern of investment, even when the overall level of real investment remains the same, can lead to significant improvements in distribution; (5) redirecting transfers from rich households to poor leads to significant improvements in distribution with no deflation; (6) significant improvements will, however, result from shifts away from wage taxes to profit taxes; (7) devaluation increases domestic savings, leading to deflation and an improvement in distribution; (8) low-skill groups benefit much more from expansions in exports of agricultural goods and processed foods than do high-skill groups, while the opposite holds for the exports of modern technology and industrial goods; and (9) elimination of wage differentials across sectors leads to massive labor shifts from initially low-wage to high-wage industries which cause large increases in aggregate supply.

The items in this list are seductive for they overlook political constraints. Simulative experiments can assume radical transformations to initiate a stream of subsequent changes. Magnitudes of effects following more modest transformations suggest, however, that "...tinkering with tax rates, profit redistributions, and wage structures will not move the Brazilian economy very far toward egalitarianism," and the empirical findings "may provide some sort of guide for taking small equalizing steps, but they say very little indeed about the design of larger political and economic changes in Brazil."

Despite qualifications of this type, computer-based models stressing simulation rather than estimation will continue to expand. They provide the most flexible method of exploring potential consequences of structural transformations. Their advantages over other approaches (comprehensiveness, flexibility, and explicitness) are conditional on the availability of appropriate software capability, the familiarity of researchers with its use, and their skill in both modeling the sectoral interactions and the interpretation of simulated outcomes.

Three Aspects

The five broad methods of analysis provide ample means of exploring income distribution. There remain the problems of refining appropriate concepts, adding significant features of real changes, and widening the scope of models underlying all forms of analysis. To illustrate these problems, brief attention is given below to three issues. First, consideration is directed to income mobility whereby the heterogeneity of individual experience affects the relevance of overall adjustments in size distribution. Such mobility influenced Kuznets' discussion of the choice of recipient groups for the definition of distribution in long-run analyses. It is also found in most treatments of "churning" behavior, in which tax changes are seen as redistribution of post-fisc income within middle-income classes. The second issue to be considered is the widening of structural phenomena to include an international perspective involving dependency and nonstationary elements in economic development. Finally, we point to recent attempts to establish longitudinal families or households. These attempts are presently restricted to developed countries, where large data files have been merged and further consolidation explored.

Income Mobility

Suppose three individuals, denoted A, B, and C, have income $1, $2, and $3, respectively. Now consider two alternative situations. In one situation, the income levels change to $3, $1, and $2 while, in the second situation, these levels remain unchanged. In both situations, the size distribution is unaltered. However, discussions of income inequality may differ between them, for one situation may represent an ossified society with well-defined and distinct income groups while the other situation may represent a more fluid one with considerable scope for individual income mobility. The interpretation of change would also be quite different if the individuals are redefined as household or consumption units and if modified incomes stem from growth and contraction in the number of earners in these recipient units. It would also be affected if the relative size of the units is modified by marriage, migration, death, birth, and other demographic developments. Clearly the evolving size distribution of income is of little interest unless connected to an understanding of income mobility for individuals and of compositional changes in recipient units. The discussion of poverty, for example, has little substance unless some households remain poor through a long interval so that their poverty cannot be dismissed as transitory. Income inequality is also much less interesting if the relative "place" of units in the ordering of income is continually changing without constraint. Existence of considerable income mobility undermines the use of poverty lines to define the poor population, while differences in income mobility across groups of countries weaken comparisons focused on size distribution alone.

Kuznets' list of specifications, mentioned earlier, is clearly based on an awareness of the mobility aspect. His per-capita scaling (and its more sophisticated alternatives) are motivated by changes in size of recipient units (and, by extension, to different consumption patterns according to age and economies of size in purchasing behavior). Further, his stress on secular income and the attendant notions of generational intervals, resident and migrant groups is determined by a desire to reduce the impact of transitory changes in income comparisons. By assessing annual income as a proxy for secular income, Kuznets raises a further complication. He argues that as technology and economic performance rise to higher levels, incomes are less subject to transient disturbances. Thus the relationship between annual income and secular income is not independent of the state of development.

Initial reactions to transitory changes in income involved a suggestion that lengthening of the interval for observing the flow of income from one year to several years would reduce the impact of transitory elements. This view is now generally associated with Kuznets and Friedman, and it was developed (by reference to older concepts of life-cycle due to Rowntree and others) into currently popular notions of "permanent income" and "life-time income." These notions have been used in most developed countries to reexpress size distribution with modified income quantiles and to explore relationships between consumption, investment, and income of long-run character. These efforts are of limited value for they imply strong constraints on the nature of transitory changes in income. They are often undermined by the extent of individual changes when data on these from longitudinal sources are available.

Unfortunately awareness of the income mobility (for example, as revealed in the large U.S. files for linked annual income) is slight. Nevertheless a growing body of literature is beginning to reveal the leading edge of concern for "income dynamics," although contributors are primarily basing their work on data for developed countries. Appropriate examples are provided by Hart [1976a, 1976b], Horvath [1980], Klevmarken and Lybeck [1980], Lillard and Willis [1978], Morley [1981], Schiller [1977], Shorrocks [1978], and Steinberg [1978]. In a rare application to a developing country, Morley [1981] reveals the need to distinguish between the "poor" or the "rich" and "base-period poor or rich" for intertemporal assessments of income distribution in Brazil. His evidence suggests that (1) almost all the rise in the Gini coefficient results from the rise in intracohort inequality rather than from changes in the age-income profile as might be supposed from a superficial decomposition of this index; (2) statistics such as the share of income accruing to the poor, or the real income growth rate of the poor, are sensitive to growth in the income-earning population; and (3) significant upward mobility and rising inequality can and did occur together.

Evidence on mobility for Sweden, the United States, and Britain is summarized in Klevmarken and Lybeck [1980], which also contains accounts of some technical issues that arise in dealing with mobility. Looking forward, it seems that appropriate longitudinal data will never be available even for most developed countries so the exploration of mobility will again have to be based on simulative experiments and fragments of real evidence. The presence or absence of mobility, however, will inevitably come to dominate our thinking on income distribution.

The World Economy

While responses to income mobility must be preoccupied with the refinement of concepts and the complexities of modeling heterogeneous behavior, other problems in extending past treatment of the U-hypothesis contain markedly different concerns. Our second area of interest is the recognition of an international dimension in the analysis of income distribution during economic development. This extends from the widespread acknowledgment of dependency (with an international flow of income and division of labor as well as domestic impacts on the structure of wealth-holdings in developing countries) to the perception that past growth experience may not be replicated because of irreversible modifications partially associated with changes in the world economy. Since the field of dependency theory is so large, its ingredients cannot be adequately described here. (Best [1976], Nolan [1983], Rubinson [1976], and Rubinson and Quinlan [1977] only deal with a minor part of this field and need supplementing.)

If we accept the distinction between core nations and dependent or peripheral nations as meaningful, then it seems clear that the former reveal lower levels of income inequality than are found for the latter. This might be explained by reference to the U-hypothesis with core nations already high on the upswing of the second phase of this curve and peripheral nations either on the initial downswing or in the intermediate trough. On the other hand, differences in the extent of income inequality might be linked to the presence of dependency and, thus, to the structural characteristics of developing countries in contrast to those of developed ones. Dependency implies that a country's factor endowments may not be predetermined (or determined exogenously of developments in other geographic regions) for international migration, and the mobility of accumulated resources can have radical impacts. Further, income distribution in peripheral countries will depend on the international pattern of commodity specialization and on the emergence of a social class that mediates the fact of dependency. These and other features of asymmetric power relationships among countries are intimately involved with the processes of urbanization and industrialization in developing countries and, also, with the assimilation of technological advances, the shift from personal enterprise to impersonal organization of economic forms, the change in scale of productive units, and the modifications that occur in the occupational status of labor. Their relevance to income distribution is obvious.

Turning to the nonreplicable character of development, we can see modern economic growth as a distinct epoch [Kuznets, 1973] that is specific to the period since the close of the eighteenth century and to countries now considered developed. The structural transformations of these countries may then serve as a basis for assessing the feasibility of similar transformations for poorer countries today. To the extent that infeasibility arises, the view of economic growth as an epoch is confirmed. Kuznets [1973, pp. 255–256] identifies several grounds for pessimism concerning the replication of past growth. He points to (1) greater current backwardness (less developed countries have lower per-capita levels of product now than their past counterparts experienced in current developed countries prior to their industrialization); (2) follower status rather than leading status; (3) very high and persistent rates of natural increase in population; and (4) a much reduced stock of potential innovations. Such characteristics weaken the basis for simple empirical regularities linking income distribution and both past and current economic development. They strengthen the need to pursue approaches that contain more detailed explorations of distribution.

Longitudinal Families and Households

Experience with large-scale social experiments looking at guaranteed income programs, as well as health and housing in the United States has revealed the sensitivity of demographic behavior to price and income stimuli. Thus recipient units that underlie the size distribution of income in the United States are frequently unstable in their composition. Indeed this instability has led social scientists to explore "event histories" which record the timing and order of marital events including formation, births, marriage, and dissolution. If the size and other demographic characteristics of recipient units are endogenous (affected by prices and income), then many decompositions of aggregate indices of inequality based on demographic criteria are difficult to interpret. Similar considerations will also adversely affect other methods of analyzing income distribution. In 1983, the U.S. Census Bureau began collection of the Survey of Income and Program Participation (SIPP), with which it will seek to integrate information on economic life of individuals, health care, child care, housing, marital history, fertility, migration, and educational enrollment and financing. At about the same time, the treatment of families and households in economic theory was undergoing a significant modification. This was partially due to the effort of Becker and others to create a "new home economics" as well as the outcome of interdisciplinary collaboration associated with the social experiments. A final cause was the persistent success of the Panel Study of Income Dynamics maintained by the Institute for Social Research at the University of Michigan.

A major aspect of the potential use of SIPP data is the search for an adequate specification of the "longitudinal" family or household. Some features of this search are clarified in Duncan and Hill [1985] and McMillan and Herriot [1985], while its potential success is not inevitable. Earlier attempts to extend the life-cycle concept beyond Rowntree's simple taxonomy failed to yield a suitable framework for dealing with dynamic transitions between consecutive familial states. All that remains of them in economics is a collection of colorful phrases, such as the "empty nest," and some tentative linkages with a new discipline of family history studies.

Since the collection of consistent and comprehensive longitudinal data is costly and requires a heavy commitment of time, the U.S. program is unlikely to be repeated elsewhere. In particular, it is not feasible for developing countries where extended family and household arrangements are quite different from those found in the United States. The benefits to be derived from SIPP, therefore, are limited in scope outside the United States and are possibly constrained by both conceptual and practical difficulties in that country. Unfortunately the problem of unstable population units will continue unresolved.

Final Comment

The purpose of this brief survey is to clarify how relationships between the size distribution of income and economic development are being explored. An early reliance on cross-sectional regression models and very simple expressions of basic economic and demographic mechanisms has been largely supplanted by more sophisticated mathematical and econometric models, which stress sectoral interactions and additional complexities while shifting from a focus on estimation of a few "structural parameters" (or stylized facts) to the simulation of time paths of development for alternative hypothetical scenarios (or multiple working hypotheses). Kuznets' original list of dynamic forces affecting change has been widened to include intragroup elements as well as intergroup ones. It has also been extended to permit changes in relative mean incomes, prices, and international influences.

All five methods of analysis continue to be pursued, but computational improvements and greater facility with mathematical formulae have drastically changed the general content of research. Looking back over three decades of interest in the U-hypothesis, it is easy to find major contributions to our understanding of distribution and development from contemporary and historical perspectives. On the other hand, this effort has also enlarged both our appreciation of what more needs to be done and our willingness to tackle awkward issues. To eliminate any feelings of complacency, three particular aspects of this field are briefly discussed. They reveal substantial scope for further research beyond that indicated when the methods of analysis are illustrated.

References

Adelman, I. (1975). Development economics — a reassessment of goals. *American Economic Review* 65 (2): 302–310.

Adelman, I., and Morris, C.T. (1973). *Economic Growth and Social Equity in Developing Countries*. Stanford: Stanford University Press.

Ahluwalia, M.S. (1976). Income distribution and development: some stylized facts. *American Economic Review* 66 (2): 128–135.

Anand, S., and Kanbur, S.M.R. (1984). *The Kuznets Process and the Inequality-Development Relationship*, DP 249, Department of Economics, University of Essex.

————. (1985). Poverty under the Kuznets process. *Economic Journal. Supplement-1984 Conference Papers* 95: 42–50.

Best, M.H. (1976). Uneven development and dependent market economies. *American Economic Review* 66 (2): 136–141.

Bigsten, A. (1983). *Income Distribution and Development: Theory, Evidence and Policy*. London: Heinemann.

Bourguignon, F. (1979). Decomposable income inequality measures. *Econometrica* 47 (4): 901–920.

Bowley, A.L. (1937). *Wages and Income in the United Kingdom Since 1860*. Cambridge: Cambridge University Press.

Braulke, M. (1983). A note on Kuznets' U. *Review of Economics and Statistics* 65 (1): 135–139.

Chenery, H.B. (1960). Patterns of industrial growth. *American Economic Review*, 50 (September): 624–654.

Chenery, H.B., and Taylor L. (1968). Development patterns: among countries and over time. *Review of Economics and Statistics*, 50 (November): 391–416.

Chenery, H.B., and Syrquin, M. (1975). *Patterns of Development 1950–1970*. London: Oxford University Press for the World Bank.

Cline, W.R. (1972). *Potential Effects of Income Redistribution on Economic Growth, Latin American Cases*. New York: Praeger.

————. (1975). Distribution and development: a survey of the literature. *Journal of Development Economics* 1: 359–400.

Cowell, F.A. (1977). *Measuring Inequality*. Oxford: Philip Allen.

Cromwell, J. (1977). The size distribution of income: an international comparison. *Review of Income and Wealth*, Series 23, No. 3 (September): 291–308.

Duncan, G.J., and Hill, M.S. (1985). Conceptions of longitudinal households: fertile or futile? *Journal of Economic and Social Measurement* 13 (3/4): 361–375.

Fei, J.C.H., Ranis, G., and Kuo, S.W.Y. (1978). Growth and the family distribution of income by factor components. *Quarterly Journal of Economics* 92 (February): 17–53.

Fields, G.S. (1979a). Decomposing LDC inequality. *Oxford Economic Papers* 31 (3): 437–459.

————. (1979). Income inequality in urban Colombia: a decomposition analysis. *Review of Income and Wealth* 25: 327–341.

————. (1980). *Poverty, Inequality, and Development*. Cambridge: Cambridge University Press.

Fields, G.S., and Fei, J.C.H. (1978). On inequality comparisons. *Econometrica* 46 (March): 303–330.

Hart, P.E. (1976a). The comparative statics and dynamics of income distributions. *Journal of the Royal Statistical Society*, Series A, Vol. 139, Part 1: 108–125.

————. (1976b). The dynamics of earnings, 1963–1973. *Economic Journal* 86 (September): 551–565.

Horvath, F.W. (1980). Tracking individual earnings mobility with the current population survey. *Monthly Labor Review* 103 (May): 43–46.

Kakwani, N.C. (1980). *Income Inequality and Poverty*. Oxford: Oxford University Press for the World Bank.

Kelley, A.C., and Williamson, J.G. (1973). Modeling economic development and general equilibrium histories. *American Economic Review* 63 (2): 450–458.

————. (1984). *What Drives Third World City Growth?* Princeton, NJ: Princeton University Press.

Klevmarken, N.A., and Lybeck, J.A. (eds.). (1980). *The Statics and Dynamics of Income*. Clevedon: Tieto.

Kuznets, S. (1955). Economic growth and income inequality. *American Economic Review* 45 (2): 1–28.

————. (1963). Quantitative aspects of the economic growth of nations: VIII. Distribution of income by size. *Economic Development and Cultural Change*, Part 11, 11 (2): 1–80.

————. (1973). Modern economic growth: findings and reflections. *American Economic Review* 63 (3): 247–258.

————. (1977). Two centuries of economic growth: reflections on U.S. experience. *American Economic Review* 67 (1): 1–14.

Lecaillon, J., et al. (1984). *Income Distribution and Economic Development*. Geneva: International Labor Office.

Lillard, L.A., and Willis, R.J. (1978). Dynamic aspects of earnings mobility. *Econometrica* 46 (5): 985–1012.

McMillan, D.B., and Herriot, R. (1985). Toward a longitudinal definition of households. *Journal of Economic and Social Measurement* 13 (3/4): 349–360.

Morley, S.A. (1981). The effect of changes in the population on several measures of income distribution. *American Economic Review* 71 (3): 285–294.

Nolan, P.D. (1983). Status in the world system, income inequality, and economic growth. *American Journal of Sociology* 89 (2): 410–419.

Oshima, H.T. (1962). The international comparison of size distribution of family incomes with special reference to Asia. *Review of Economics and Statistics* 44 (November): 439–445.

————. (1970). Income inequality and economic growth: the postwar experiences of Asian countries. *Malayan Economic Review* 15: 7–41.

Paukert, F. (1973). Income distribution at different levels of development: a survey of evidence. *International Labor Review* 108 (August-September): 97–125.

Pyatt, G. (1976). On the interpretation and disaggregation of Gini coefficients. *Economic Journal* 86 (June).

Pyatt, G., Chen, C., and Fei, J.C.H. (1980). The distribution of income by factor components. *Quarterly Journal of Economics* 95: 451–474.

Rao, V.M. (1969). Two decompositions of concentration ratios. *Journal of the Royal Statistical Society* 132, Series A, Part 3: 418–425.

Robinson, S. (1976). A note on the U-hypothesis relating income inequality and economic development. *American Economic Review* 66 (3): 437–440.

Rubinson, R. (1976). The world-economy and the distribution of income within states: a cross-national study. *American Sociological Review* 41: 638–659.

Rubinson, R., and Quinlan, D. (1977). Democracy and social inequality: a re-analysis. *American Sociological Review* 42: 611–622.

Schiller, B.R. (1977). Relative earnings mobility in the United States. *American Economic Review* 67 (5): 926–941.

Sen, A. (1973). *On Economic Inequality*. New York: Norton.

Shorrocks, A.F. (1978). Income inequality and income mobility. *Journal of Economic Theory* 19: 376–393.

——————. (1982). Inequality decomposition by factor components. *Econometrica* 50: 193–211.

——————. (1983). The impact of income components on the distribution of family incomes. *Quarterly Journal of Economics* (May): 311–326.

Soltow, L. (1968). Long-run changes in British income inequality. *Economic History Review* 21 (1): 17–29.

Steinberg, E. (1978). The accounting period, earnings inequality, and intermittent workers. *1977 Proceedings of the Business and Economic Statistics Section, American Statistical Association*, Part 1. Washington, DC: ASA, pp. 216–221.

Taylor, L., et al. (1980). *Models of Growth and Distribution for Brazil*. London: Oxford University Press for the World Bank.

Theil, H. (1979). The measurement of inequality by components of income. *Economics Letters* 2: 197–199.

Williamson, J.G. (1977). 'Strategic' wage goods, prices, and inequality. *American Economic Review* 67 (2): 29–41.

——————. (1985). *Did British Capitalism Breed Inequality?* London: Allen and Unwin.

Williamson, J.G., and Lindert, P.H. (1980). *American Inequality: A Macroeconomic History*. New York: Academic Press.

Author Index

249

Subject Index

Aggregate production function, *see* Production function, aggregate
Aggregation, problems of, 87, 93
Analysis of variance decomposition, (ANOVA), 232
Analytical income categories, 9, 99–100
Arbitrage, 4, 18, 32, 184
Arrow-Debreu theory of general equilibrium, 4, 182–190, 195n
see also Walrasian general equilibrium

Bargaining power, 56, 63, 68–69, 71, 101, 166–167, 175, 177, 221
Bowley's Law, 87
Business cycle, Kalecki's theory of the, 11–12, 13n
Business power, 117–119

Capital accumulation, 6, 10–12, 51–52, 56–73, 112, 123, 146–151, 168, 174
Capital decumulation, 112
Capital intensity, *see* Capital/output ratio
Capital/labor ratio, 60, 92
Capital, measurement of, 80, 86, 92–93, 161
Capital/output ratio, 56–57, 60–64, 91–92, 144, 148, 154n
Capital-reversing, 93
Capital theory debates, 161–162, 170
Capitalists, as residuals conceptually, 33
Classical full employment, *see* Full employment, classical
Cliometric method, 235–236
Cobb-Douglas aggregate production function, 84–87, 94
see also Production function, aggregate

Collective bargaining, 97, 141
see also Wage bargaining
Constant elasticity of substitution, *see* Elasticity of substitution, constant
Constant returns to scale, 83, 92, 164
Corporate levy, 151, 155n

Degree of monopoly, 139–140, 151, 154n, 238
Derived demand, 77–78, 106, 108
Difference principle, 78
Disembodied technical progress, *see* Technical progress, disembodied

Economic rent, *see* Rent, economic
Elasticity of production, 85–87
Elasticity of substitution, 84–87, 90–91, 94–95
constant, 88
Embodied technical progress, *see* Technical progress, embodied
Exhaustion of product, 8, 81, 83, 121
Existence question, 184

Factor demand, 77, 94–99, 106–109
Factor-demand functions, 108
Factor supply, 77, 106, 126
Family-expenditure units, 227
see also Recipient units
Forward markets, *see* Futures markets
Full employment
of capital, 16, 29–30, 33, 38, 45n
classical, 18, 31
of labor, 6, 16, 19, 22, 45n, 134, 143, 149–150, 152, 160–161, 168–171

253